■ PEOPLES OF AFRICA ■

NATIONS OF AFRICA

THE DIAGRAM GROUP

☑

Facts On File, Inc.

Peoples of Africa: Nations of Africa

Copyright © 1997 by The Diagram Group

Diagram Visual Information Ltd

Editorial director:	Bridget Giles
Contributors:	Trevor Day, Theodore Rowland Entwistle, David Lambert, Keith Lye, Oliver Marshall, Christopher Priest
Editors:	Margaret Doyle, Moira Johnston, Ian Wood
Indexer:	David Harding
Art director/designer:	Philip Patenall
Artists:	Chris Allcott, Darren Bennett, Bob Garwood, Elsa Godfrey, Brian Hewson, Kyri Kyriacou, Janos Marffy, Kathy McDougall, Patrick Mulrey, Rob Shone, Graham Rosewarne, Peter Ross
Production director:	Richard Hummerstone
Production:	Mark Carry, Lee Lawrence, Ollie Madden, Philip Richardson, Dave Wilson
Research director:	Matt Smout
Researchers:	Pamela Kea, Chris Owens, Catherine Michard, Neil McKenna

With the assistance of:

Dr Elizabeth Dunstan, International African Institute, School of Oriental and African Studies, University of London

David Hall, African studies bibliographer at the School of Oriental and African Studies, University of London

Horniman Museum, London

Museum of Mankind library, British Museum

Survival International

WWF-UK

Facts On File Inc.
11 Penn Plaza
New York NY 10001

Library of Congress Cataloging-in-Publication Data

Nations of Africa / the Diagram Group.
    p.   cm. – (Peoples of Africa)
  Includes bibliographical references and index.
  ISBN 0-8160-3488-5 (alk. paper)
  1. Africa–Handbooks, manuals, etc. I. Diagram Group
  II. Series: Peoples of Africa (New York, N.Y.)
  DT2.68 1997
  960–dc20   96-38734

Facts On File books are available at special discounts when purchased in bulk quantities for businesses, associations, institutions, or sales promotions. Please call our Special Sales Department in New York at 212/967-8800 or 800/322-8755.

Cover design by Molly Heron

Printed in the United States of America

RRD DIAG 10 9 8 7 6 5 4 3 2 1

This book is printed on acid-free paper

Contents

Foreword

Nations of Africa, the sixth volume in the Facts On File *Peoples of Africa* series, focuses on the fifty-three nation states of the continent of Africa, from Algeria to Zimbabwe. When used in conjunction with the regional volumes, *Nations of Africa* provides an invaluable overview of the whole of contemporary Africa.
Inside this volume the reader will find:

- **The nations:** individual profiles of each African country arranged alphabetically. For each country, the capital city, currency, official name, major languages, and a description of the flag are all included. Further geographical, economic, social, and political overviews introduce the reader to life within each nation. The statistics given, such as population figures and per capita (for each person) income, are taken from reliable sources including 1996 United Nations and World Bank reports, which give the figures for 1994. Wherever possible, these sources provide the most recent population figures, but as many countries have not had a census for many years, the figures may be inexact.
- **Biographies:** over three hundred famous Africans are included in the biography section. A wide spectrum of notable men and women is covered, ranging from contemporary politicians, sports personalities, and artists to ancient kings and queens. The biographical entries are arranged alphabetically.
- **Further reading and combined index:** Following the nation profiles and biographies are a list of selected titles for people interested in reading more about the ethnic groups covered in the *Peoples of Africa* series, and a combined index for volumes one through to six of the whole series. As well as telling readers where information on the peoples covered can be found, the index allows the reader to access related information from different volumes.

The nations of Africa reflect a wide variety of climatic, geographic, and historical factors. Taken as a whole, *Nations of Africa* is intended to project a living portrait of the continent that, with the other volumes in the series, provides the reader with a memorable snapshot of Africa as a place of rich heritage, far-reaching influence, and ongoing cultural diversity. These nation profiles can be used by readers to supplement the information in volumes one through five, or they can simply be used on their own to access vital and interesting facts about African nations.

Nations of Africa

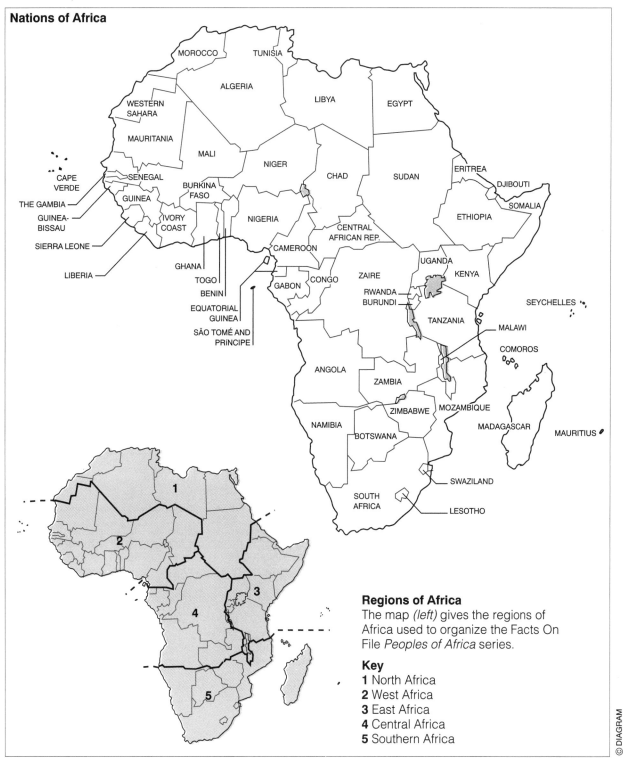

MOROCCO
TUNISIA
ALGERIA
LIBYA
EGYPT
WESTERN SAHARA
MAURITANIA
MALI
NIGER
CHAD
SUDAN
ERITREA
DJIBOUTI
SOMALIA
CAPE VERDE
SENEGAL
BURKINA FASO
THE GAMBIA
GUINEA
GUINEA-BISSAU
IVORY COAST
NIGERIA
CENTRAL AFRICAN REP.
ETHIOPIA
SIERRA LEONE
CAMEROON
UGANDA
KENYA
LIBERIA
GHANA
TOGO
BENIN
EQUATORIAL GUINEA
SÃO TOMÉ AND PRÍNCIPE
GABON
CONGO
ZAIRE
RWANDA
BURUNDI
TANZANIA
SEYCHELLES
MALAWI
COMOROS
ANGOLA
ZAMBIA
ZIMBABWE
MOZAMBIQUE
MADAGASCAR
MAURITIUS
NAMIBIA
BOTSWANA
SWAZILAND
SOUTH AFRICA
LESOTHO

Regions of Africa

The map *(left)* gives the regions of Africa used to organize the Facts On File *Peoples of Africa* series.

Key

1 North Africa
2 West Africa
3 East Africa
4 Central Africa
5 Southern Africa

© DIAGRAM

5

Algeria

Location: North Africa, facing the Mediterranean Sea **Neighbors:** Tunisia, Libya, Niger, Mali, Mauritania, Western Sahara, Morocco

Official name: People's Democratic Republic of Algeria
Divisions: Forty-eight provinces
Capital: Algiers
Largest cities: Algiers, Oran, Constantine, Annaba, Blida, Sétif, Sidi-bel-Abbès (in order of size)

Flag: The Algerian flag is green and white with a red star and crescent. Green is a traditional Islamic color and the red star and crescent, symbols of Islam, also appear on the country's green-and-white coat of arms

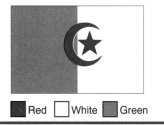

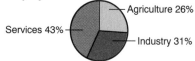
■ Red ☐ White ■ Green

National anthem: "We swear by the lightning that destroys"
Major languages: Arabic (official), Berber, French
Currency: Dinar = 100 centimes

1963 stamp marking promulgation of the Algerian constitution

GEOGRAPHY

With an area of 919,355 square miles (2,381,120 sq. km), Algeria is Africa's second largest country. It is nearly three times bigger than Texas in the United States (US).

Northern Algeria consists of the Tell, a region of coastal plains and hill country. Behind this region lie the Atlas Mountains, which extend across the country from Morocco to Tunisia. Plateaus in the Atlas range contain salt lakes, which periodically dry up. Algeria's chief rivers, including the Chelif, rise in the Atlas and flow north into the Mediterranean. Southern Algeria, which makes up about 80% of the country, consists of the Sahara Desert. Much of the Sahara is flat, but the Ahaggar Mountains in the south contain Algeria's highest peak, Mount Tahat, at 9,573 ft (2,918 m) high.

The Tell has hot, dry summers and mild, moist winters, but the rainfall decreases to the south. The Atlas range has forests of juniper, Aleppo pine, and cork oak. Temperatures in the Sahara often soar to 120 °F (49 °C) by day, but nights can be chilly. The Sahara contains little plant or animal life except at oases, which are fertile pockets.

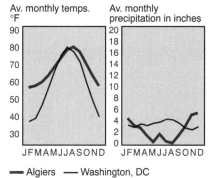

Av. monthly temps. °F

Av. monthly precipitation in inches

— Algiers — Washington, DC

ECONOMY

Chief farm products: barley, citrus fruits, cork, dairy products, dates, grapes, meat, olives, potatoes, wheat
Chief mineral resources: Oil and natural gas, iron ore
Chief industrial products: Cement, liquid natural gas, refined petroleum products, iron and steel, vehicles, textiles, processed food
Employment:

Agriculture 26%
Services 43%
Industry 31%

In the US, agriculture employs 3% of the work force, industry 25%, and services 72%
Exports: Oil and natural gas (97%)
Per capita income: $1,650 (as compared with $28,860 in the US)

PEOPLE
Population: 27,325,000 (about a tenth of the US population of 260,529,000)
Major ethnic groups: Arab, Berber, other including French
Religions: Islam (99.9%), Christianity (0.1%)

SOCIAL FACTS
● The average life expectancy at birth is 69 years, as compared with 76 years in the US
● Only 55% of the people live in urban areas, as compared with about 76% in the US
● 90% of Algerians live in the northern coastal region

● A million French settlers left Algeria after independence in 1962
● Muslim fundamentalists oppose westernization, and the government has attempted to curb French influences
● Most people in the cities wear Western dress and they are generally more westernized than rural people

KEY POINTS IN RECENT HISTORY
1954 War for independence from France begins, led by the Front de Libération Nationale (FLN)
1962 Independence day (July 3)
1963 Muhammad Ben Bella (an FLN leader) becomes president

1965 Military coup overthrows government; Houari Boumedienne becomes head of state
1978 Boumedienne dies
1991 Fundamentalist Front d'Islamic Salvation (FIS) wins first round of elections, the government cancels

second round; a state of emergency is then declared
1992 Military government is set up under President Muhammad Boudiaf, who is assassinated in July

*See **Peoples of North Africa** on the Arabs, Berbers, and Tuareg*

Angola

Location: Central Africa, facing the Atlantic Ocean
Neighbors: Zaire, Zambia, Namibia

Official name: Republic of Angola
Divisions: Eighteen provinces
Capital: Luanda
Largest cities: Luanda, Huambo, Benguela, Lobito, Lubango (in order of size)

Flag: The red and black flag contains an emblem, which includes a star to symbolize socialism; half of a gearwheel, to symbolize industry; and a machete, a large knife that is widely used in agriculture

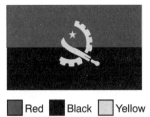

■ Red ■ Black □ Yellow

National anthem: "Oh Fatherland, never shall we forget"
Major languages: Portuguese (official), Umbundu, Kimbundu
Currency: Kwanza = 100 lei

1975 stamp marking Angola's independence

GEOGRAPHY

With an area of 481,354 square miles (1,246,702 sq. km), Angola is Africa's seventh largest country. It is about 1.8 times as large as Texas in the United States (US).

Most of the land forms part of the huge plateau that makes up Southern Africa. The interior is mainly between 2,000 and 4,000 ft (600–1,200 m) above sea level, but the highest point, Mount Moco, reaches 8,596 ft (2,620 m) in the west. Northeastern Angola forms part of the Congo (Zaire) River Basin. In the south, some rivers, including the Cubango and Cunene, flow into inland drainage basins rather than the sea.

Angola includes a small external enclave, Cabinda, that is cut off from the rest of the country by a strip of land 20 miles (32 km) wide belonging to Zaire. Cabinda contains most of Angola's oil reserves.

Angola has a tropical climate, but the altitude lowers temperatures in the interior. The coast is arid, but the rainfall increases to the east. Tropical savanna covers much of Angola, with open grassland in drier areas. Semidesert occurs on the coast, merging into the bleak Namib Desert in the south.

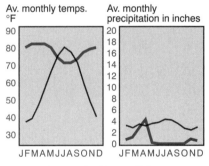

Av. monthly temps. °F

Av. monthly precipitation in inches

JFMAMJJASOND JFMAMJJASOND

— Luanda — Washington, DC

ECONOMY

Chief farm products: Bananas, cassava, coffee, corn, livestock, millet, palm oil, sugar cane
Chief mineral resources: Diamonds, oil, iron ore
Chief industrial products: Beverages, cement, chemicals, footwear, processed food, textiles
Employment:

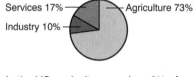

Services 17% — Agriculture 73%
Industry 10%

In the US, agriculture employs 3% of the work force, industry 25%, and services 72%
Exports: Oil (90%), diamonds
Per capita income: $726 (as compared with $25,860 in the US)

PEOPLE

Population: 10,442,000 (as compared with the US population of 260,529,000)
Major ethnic groups: Ovimbundu, Mbundu, Kongo, Luimbe-Nganguela
Religions: Christianity (90%), African religions (9.5%)

SOCIAL FACTS

● The average life expectancy at birth is 47 years, as compared with 76 years in the US
● Only 31% of the people live in urban areas, as compared with about 76% in the US
● Most Europeans left the country after

Angola became independent
● Angola takes its name from Ngola, the title of the early rulers of the country
● Angola, a former Portuguese territory, was a major source of slaves for Brazil
● Ethnic and political differences have caused civil war and marred progress since independence

KEY POINTS IN RECENT HISTORY

1961 Rebellions in Luanda and other parts of the country occur when supporters of the Movimento Popular de Libertaçâo de Angola (MPLA) demand independence from Portugal
1966 Southern rebels set up the Uniâo

Nacional para a Independência Total de Angola (UNITA) independence movement
1975 Civil war breaks out between rival groups in Angola, chiefly MPLA and UNITA; civil war continues after independence on November 11

1992 Parliamentary and presidential elections are won by the MPLA
1994 A peace agreement is signed
1995 United Nations forces arrive to supervise the peace process
1996 Angola joins the Community of Portuguese-speaking Countries

*See **Peoples of Central Africa** on the Chokwe, Kongo, Lunda, and Ovimbundu*

© DIAGRAM

Benin

Location: West Africa, facing the Gulf of Guinea
Neighbors: Togo, Burkina Faso, Niger, Nigeria

Official name: Republic of Benin
Divisions: Six provinces divided into eighty-four districts
Capital: Porto-Novo
Largest cities: Cotonou, Porto-Novo, Djougou, Abomey, Parakou (in order of size)

Flag: The three colors (a vertical strip of green in the hoist and yellow and red horizontal stripes) represent African unity. They are the colors used on the flag of Ethiopia, Africa's oldest independent nation

■ Red ☐ Yellow ■ Green

National anthem: "L'aube nouvelle" ("New dawn")
Major languages: French (official), Fon, Yoruba
Currency: CFA franc = 100 centimes

1978 stamp depicting Samori Toure, hero of anticolonial resistance

GEOGRAPHY

With an area of 43,484 square miles (112,623 sq. km), Benin is one of Africa's smaller countries. It is a little larger in area than Tennessee in the United States (US).

Benin is a narrow country, and extends about 400 miles (640 km) from north to south. The coast, 77 miles (124 km) long, is lined by lagoons and has no natural harbors. Behind the coast is a broad plain with occasional hills. This region, which includes the marshy Lama Depression, is called the barre, or "clay country." In central Benin, the land rises to a series of low plateaus. The highest part of Benin reaches about 2,100 ft (640 m) in the Atakora Mountains in the northwest. In northeastern Benin, the land slopes down toward the valley of the Niger River.

The longest river is the Ouémé. This river flows south for 280 miles (450 km) to the Gulf of Guinea.

Benin has an equatorial climate. The rainfall is greatest in the central regions of the country. Rainforests once covered much of the south, but have been largely cleared. The rainfall decreases to the north, which has a marked dry season between November and March. Tropical savanna is the typical vegetation in the north.

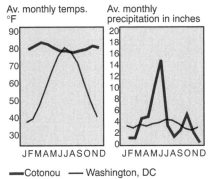

Av. monthly temps. °F
Av. monthly precipitation in inches

JFMAMJJASOND   JFMAMJJASOND

— Cotonou   — Washington, DC

ECONOMY

Chief farm products: Beans, cassava, cocoa, corn, coffee, cotton, millet, peanuts, rice, sorghum, sugar cane, yams
Chief mineral resources: Limestone, some offshore oil
Chief industrial products: Beverages, cement, palm oil, sugar, textiles
Employment:

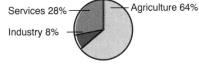

Services 28%   Agriculture 64%
Industry 8%

In the US, agriculture employs 3% of the work force, industry 25%, and services 72%
Exports: Cotton, energy, palm kernels and palm oil, manufactured goods
Per capita income: $370 (as compared with $25,860 in the US)

PEOPLE

Population: 5,246,000 (as compared with the US population of 260,529,000)
Major ethnic groups: Fon, Yoruba, Goun, Bariba
Religions: African religions (62%), Christianity (23%), Islam (12%)

SOCIAL FACTS

● The average life expectancy at birth is 50 years, as compared with 76 years in the US
● Only 41% of the people live in urban areas, as compared with about 76% in the US
● Benin was called Dahomey until 1975

● The historic Kingdom of Dahomey, with its capital at Abomey, existed long before the Europeans arrived
● African slaves took the worship of Dahomeyan gods – vodun (singular, vodu) – to the Americas. These gods are still venerated by some Brazilians. "Voodoo" is a corruption of "vodu"

KEY POINTS IN RECENT HISTORY

1960 Dahomey becomes independent from France (August 1)
1960s and 1970s The government changes frequently because of repeated military coups
1975 Dahomey is renamed Benin; it

becomes a one-party, Marxist-Leninist "people's republic" (socialist state)
1989 Marxism-Leninism is abandoned after years of economic decline
1990 A national conference discusses a new, multiparty constitution
1991 Benin holds its first multiparty

presidential elections; Nicéphore Soglo, a former World Bank executive, becomes president
1994 CFA franc is devalued by 50%
1996 Mathieu Kerekou, Benin's dictator from 1972 until 1990, defeats Soglo in elections and becomes president

*See **Peoples of West Africa** on the Fon and Yoruba*

Botswana

Location: Landlocked country in Southern Africa
Neighbors: Zimbabwe, South Africa, Namibia

Official name: Republic of Botswana
Divisions: Eleven districts, one city, and eight towns
Capital: Gaborone
Largest cities: Gaborone, Francistown, Selebi-Pikwe, Molepolole, Kanye (in order of size)

Flag: The flag consists of two blue stripes (top and bottom), with a black stripe, edged with white, in the center. The black-and-white feature is a symbol of racial harmony, while the blue represents much-needed rain

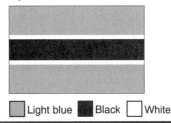

☐ Light blue ■ Black ☐ White

National anthem: "Fatshe leno la rona" ("Blessed noble land")
Major languages: English (official), Setswana (national)
Currency: Pula = 100 thebe

1966 stamp marking independence and depicting the National Assembly Building

GEOGRAPHY

With an area of 224,468 square miles (581,370 sq. km), Botswana is Africa's twenty-first largest country. It is about 1.4 times larger in area than California in the United States (US).

Botswana occupies part of the huge plateau that makes up most of Southern Africa. The average height of the flat or gently rolling land is around 3,300 ft (1,000 m) above sea level.

Large depressions in the north form inland drainage basins. The Okavango Swamps are supplied by the Okavango River, which rises (as the Cubango River) in Angola. Another depression, the Makgadikgadi Salt Pans, is supplied with water by the Botletle River, which flows from the Okavango Swamps when that area is flooded. These northern drainage basins are rich in wildlife. The Kalahari Desert in the southeast has practically no surface drainage.

Botswana has a dry, subtropical climate. The Kalahari has about 12 in. (30 cm) of rain a year and is really a semidesert, with grass and thorn scrub covering most of the land. The east has more rainfall and tropical savanna covers large areas. Droughts are common throughout the country.

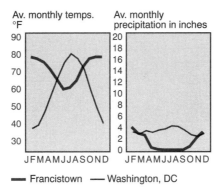

Av. monthly temps. °F

Av. monthly precipitation in inches

— Francistown — Washington, DC

ECONOMY

Chief farm products: Beef, corn, cotton, millet, roots and tubers, sorghum, vegetables
Chief mineral resources: Diamonds, copper, nickel, cobalt, coal
Chief industrial products: Chemicals, processed food, textiles, wood products and paper
Employment:

Services 34% — Agriculture 46%
Industry 20%

In the US, agriculture employs 3% of the work force, industry 25%, and services 72%
Exports: Diamonds, copper-nickel, beef products
Per capita income: $2,800 (as compared with $25,860 in the US)

PEOPLE

Population: 1,400,000 (as compared with the US population of 260,529,000)
Major ethnic groups: Tswana, Shona, Khoisan
Religions: Christianity (50%), African religions (49%)

SOCIAL FACTS

● The average life expectancy at birth is 68 years, as compared with 76 years in the US
● Only 30% of the people live in urban areas, as compared with about 76% in the US
● Botswana was once known as Bechuanaland

● Botswana is one of the most stable democracies in Africa
● 17% of the country is protected in national parks and reserves, the highest proportion in Africa
● Since 1971, mining has transformed Botswana's economy, which was formerly based on livestock raising

KEY POINTS IN RECENT HISTORY

1961 Seretse Khama forms the Bechuanaland (later Botswana) Democratic Party (BDP)
1966 Bechuanaland becomes independent from Britain as the Republic of Botswana (September 30);

Seretse Khama becomes the first president
1980 Seretse Khama dies and Dr Ketumile (Quett) Masire succeeds him as the head of the BDP
1980s Tension is caused by South African raids on the homes of African

National Congress (ANC) refugees
1984 The BDP wins the first elections after Khama's death
1994 The BDP wins national elections for the fifth time

See **Peoples of Southern Africa** on the Herero, Khoisan, and Tswana

© DIAGRAM

Burkina Faso

Location: Landlocked country in West Africa
Neighbors: Mali, Niger, Benin, Togo, Ghana, Ivory Coast

Official name: Democratic People's Republic of Burkina Faso
Divisions: Thirty provinces
Capital: Ouagadougou
Largest cities: Ouagadougou, Bobo-Dioulasso, Koudougou, Ouahigouya (in order of size)

Flag: The red and green flag, with a yellow star in the center, was adopted in 1984, when Upper Volta was renamed Burkina Faso. The three colors, taken from the flag of Ethiopia, symbolize African unity

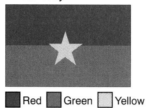

■ Red ■ Green □ Yellow

National anthem: "Against the shameful fetters"
Major languages: French (official), Moré
Currency: CFA franc = 100 centimes

1993 stamp depicting the red-fronted gazelle

GEOGRAPHY
With an area of 105,869 square miles (274,200 sq. km), Burkina Faso is Africa's twenty-eighth largest country. It is about the same size as Colorado in the United States (US).

The country consists of a large plateau, mostly between about 650 and 2,300 ft (200–700 m) above sea level. The highest point is the Aguille de Sindou, which reaches 2,352 ft (717 m) on the southwestern border with Mali. The soil in Burkina Faso is generally thin and infertile. Soil erosion has given many areas a barren, rocky appearance.

The chief rivers are the Black Volta, the Red Volta, and the White Volta, which flow southward into Lake Volta, in Ghana. However, in the northeast, small rivers flow into the Niger River. During droughts, some rivers stop flowing and parts of their courses become swamps.

Burkina Faso has a tropical climate. It is cool and dry between November and February, hot and dry from March to June, and hot and rainy for the rest of the year. The rainfall is greatest in the south. Tropical savanna with scattered forest occurs in the south, with stunted trees and thorn shrubs in the dry north.

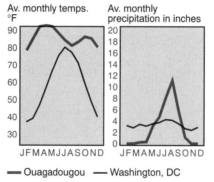

Av. monthly temps. °F

Av. monthly precipitation in inches

— Ouagadougou — Washington, DC

ECONOMY
Chief farm products: Corn, cotton, livestock, millet, peanuts, rice, shea nuts, sorghum, sugar cane
Chief mineral resources: Gold, silver, other unexploited minerals
Chief industrial products: Beverages, footwear, motorcycles and bicycles, processed food, textiles
Employment:

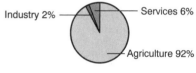

Industry 2% — Services 6%
Agriculture 92%

In the US, agriculture employs 3% of the work force, industry 25%, and services 72%
Exports: Raw cotton, live animals, manufactured goods, hides and skins
Per capita income: $300 (as compared with $25,860 in the US)

PEOPLE
Population: 10,046,000 (as compared with the US population of 260,529,000)
Major ethnic groups: Mossi, Fulani, Lobi, Bobo
Religions: African religions (45%), Islam (43%), Christianity (12%)

SOCIAL FACTS
● The average life expectancy at birth is 49 years, as compared with 76 years in the US
● Only 25% of the people live in urban areas, as compared with about 76% in the US
● Burkina Faso is a Mossi name, which means "land of the incorruptible men"

● Until 1984, Burkina Faso was known as Upper Volta, because it contained the headwaters of the Volta rivers
● Burkina Faso is heavily dependent on foreign aid and about two million of its citizens work abroad
● The north is part of the Sahel, a dry semidesert region south of the Sahara

KEY POINTS IN RECENT HISTORY
1919 France creates the colony of Upper Volta
1960 Upper Volta becomes independent (August 5) with Maurice Yameogo as president
1966 General Sangoulé Lamizana seizes power in a military coup

1978 Lamizana is elected president
1980 Colonel Saye Zerbo takes power after a military coup
1982 Another military coup brings Surgeon-Major Jean-Baptiste Ouedraogo to power
1983 Captain Thomas Sankara ousts Ouedraogo and becomes president

1987 Military leaders overthrow Sankara, who is replaced by Captain Blaise Compaoré
1991 Compaoré, the sole candidate, is elected president
1994 After pressure from France, the CFA franc, which is linked to the French franc, is devalued by 50%

*See **Peoples of West Africa** on the Bambara, Fulani, Malinke, and Mossi*

Burundi

Location: Landlocked country in East Africa
Neighbors: Rwanda, Tanzania, Zaire

Official name: Republic of Burundi
Divisions: Fifteen regions
Capital: Bujumbura
Largest cities: Bujumbura, Gitega, Bururi, Ngozi (in order of size)

Flag: The white circle in the center contains three red stars bordered in green. White bands extend from the circle to the corners separating red areas (above and below) and green (left and right)

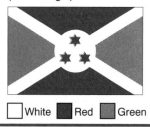

☐ White ■ Red ◼ Green

National anthem: "Uburundi bwacu" ("Dear Burundi")
Major languages: Rundi and French (both official), Swahili
Currency: Burundi franc = 100 centimes

1962 stamp marking independence, and depicting King Mwambutsa IV

GEOGRAPHY

With an area of 10,747 square miles (27,834 sq. km), Burundi is one of Africa's smaller countries. It is about the same size in area as Maryland in the United States (US.)

Western Burundi occupies part of the Great Rift Valley. The border with Zaire runs along the floor of the Rift Valley through Lake Tanganyika and along the Ruzizi River, which flows into it from the north. Overlooking the Rift Valley are high mountains, reaching 8,858 ft (2,700 m) in the north. which form part of the divide between the Congo (Zaire) and Nile river systems.

East of the mountains lie plateaus between about 5,000 and 6,500 ft (1,500–2,000 m) high. These plateaus descend toward the east along steep, steplike escarpments. Flowing northeast across the plateau is the Ruvuvu River, the most southerly tributary of the Nile.

Burundi has a tropical climate, though temperatures are moderated by the altitude. The rainfall is plentiful, especially on the mountains. May to August is the dry season. Forests grown on the mountains but they give way to wooded tropical savanna and more open grassland to the east.

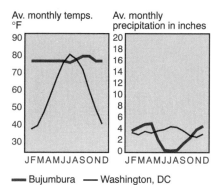

Av. monthly temps. °F

Av. monthly precipitation in inches

JFMAMJJASOND   JFMAMJJASOND

— Bujumbura   — Washington, DC

ECONOMY

Chief farm products: Bananas, beans, cassava, coffee, corn, cotton, livestock, peanuts, sorghum, sugar cane, sweet potatoes, tea, yams
Chief mineral resource: Gold
Chief industrial products: Beverages, footwear, leather goods, processed food, sugar, textiles
Employment:

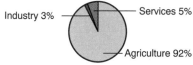

Industry 3% — Services 5%
Agriculture 92%

In the US, agriculture employs 3% of the work force, industry 25%, and services 72%
Exports: Coffee, hides and skins, cotton fabric
Per capita income: $160 (as compared with $25,860 in the US)

PEOPLE

Population: 6,200,000 (as compared with the US population of 260,529,000)
Major ethnic groups: Hutu, Tutsi, Twa
Religions: Christianity (79%), African religions (19%) Islam (2%)

SOCIAL FACTS

● The average life expectancy at birth is 50 years, as compared with 76 years in the US
● Only 7% of the people live in urban areas, as compared with about 76% in the US

● The minority Tutsi have controlled the region for hundreds of years
● Burundi is mainland Africa's second most densely populated country after neighboring Rwanda

KEY POINTS IN RECENT HISTORY

1916 Belgium occupies the former German territory of Ruanda-Urundi
1961 Urundi votes to break away from Ruanda-Urundi and become the independent Kingdom of Burundi
1962 Independence day (July 1)
1966 Burundi becomes a republic, with

a Tutsi, Michel Micombero, as president
1972 An unsuccessful Hutu revolt results in about 100,000 deaths
1976 Captain Jean-Baptiste Bagaza seizes power
1987 Major Pierre Buyoya takes power
1993 The newly elected Hutu president is killed; Tutsi-Hutu massacres follow

1994 Ethnic conflict follows the probable assassination of Burundi's and Rwanda's presidents in an airplane crash
1996 Burundi expels thousands of Rwandan Hutu refugees. Military coup led by Buyoya ousts president. Ethnic conlict erupts between Hutu and Tutsi

*See **Peoples of East Africa** on the Hutu and Tutsi*

© DIAGRAM

Cameroon

Location: West Africa
Neighbors: Nigeria, Chad, Central African Republic, Congo, Gabon, Equatorial Guinea

Official name: Republic of Cameroon
Divisions: Ten provinces
Capital: Yaoundé
Largest cities: Douala, Yaoundé, Garoua, Maroua, Bafoussam (in order of size)

Flag: The green, red, and yellow stripes symbolize African unity, because these colors come from the flag of Africa's oldest independent country, Ethiopia. The gold star was added in 1975

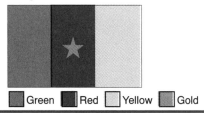

Green | Red | Yellow | Gold

National anthem: "O Cameroon, thou cradle of our fathers"
Major languages: French and English (both official), Fang
Currency: CFA franc = 100 centimes

Stamp marking the Union of African and Malagasy States in 1962

GEOGRAPHY

With an area of 183,569 square miles (475,442 sq. km), Cameroon is Africa's twenty-third largest country. It is a little larger in area than California in the United States (US).

Cameroon consists mainly of plateaus that slope down to the north to the Lake Chad basin. Lake Chad, which Cameroon shares with Nigeria, Niger, and Chad, is the largest lake. The southwest is mountainous. Near the coast is an active volcano, Mount Cameroon, which is the country's highest peak, at 13,353 ft (4,070 m).

The narrow coastal plain is crossed by two of the country's largest rivers, the Wouri and Sanaga. Another important river, the Benue, rises in the Adamawa plateau in central Cameroon. It flows north and then west to become a tributary of the Niger River in central Nigeria.

The south is hot and rainy, but inland temperatures are moderated by the altitude. The rainfall decreases to the north, which is hot and dry. Rainforests grow in the south, though farmers have cleared large areas. Tropical savanna is the main vegetation in central Cameroon, but the north is semidesert.

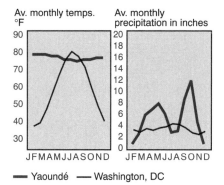

Av. monthly temps. °F

Av. monthly precipitation in inches

JFMAMJJASOND | JFMAMJJASOND

— Yaoundé — Washington, DC

ECONOMY

Chief farm products: Bananas, cassava, cocoa, coffee, cotton, lumber, millet, palm products, plantains, rice, sugar cane, yams
Chief mineral resources: Oil, tin
Chief industrial products: Aluminum, cement, petroleum products, processed food, wood products
Employment:

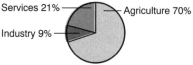

Services 21% — Agriculture 70%
Industry 9% —

In the US, agriculture employs 3% of the work force, industry 25%, services 72%
Exports: Oil, cocoa, sawn wood and logs, cotton, coffee
Per capita income: $680 (as compared with $25,860 in the US)

PEOPLE

Population: 12,780,000 (as compared with the US population of 260,529,000)
Major ethnic groups: Fang, Bamileke and Bamum, Dyula, Leda, and Basa
Religions: Christianity (77%), African religions (21%)

SOCIAL FACTS

● The average life expectancy at birth is 57 years, as compared with 76 years in the US
● Only 44% of the people live in urban areas, as compared with about 76% in the US
● Cameroon is known for its wooden masks and statues

● Cameroon is an ethnic crossroads, containing forest peoples, Bantu-speaking groups, and Sudanic peoples
● Some English-speaking Cameroonians favor secession
● Cameroon was named for the camarões (shrimps) found by the Portuguese in the Wouri River

KEY POINTS IN RECENT HISTORY

1960 French Cameroun becomes the independent Republic of Cameroon; Ahmadou Ahidjo becomes president
1961 Southern British Cameroons votes to join Nigeria; the north votes to join the Republic of Cameroon
1961 The southern part of British

Cameroons and the Republic of Cameroon combine to form the Federal Republic of Cameroon
1966 A one-party state is proclaimed
1972 Cameroon becomes a unitary (nonfederal) state
1982 Ahidjo resigns and Paul Biya becomes president

1990 The government legalizes opposition parties
1992 Multiparty elections take place; Biya is reelected president
1994 The CFA franc is devalued by 50% causing economic hardship
1995 Cameroon joins the Commonwealth of Nations

*See **Peoples of Central Africa** on the Baya, Fang, and Mbenga, Mbuti, and Twa*

Cape Verde

Location: Island nation in West Africa
Nearest mainland: Senegal

Official name: Republic of Cape Verde
Divisions: Ten islands and five islets
Capital: Praia
Largest cities: Praia, Mindelo (in order of size)

Flag: Adopted in 1992, the flag consists of a blue field, on the lower half of which are three stripes of white, red, and white. Superimposed are ten yellow stars arranged in a circle

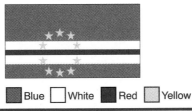

⬛ Blue ☐ White ⬛ Red ▨ Yellow

National anthem: "Sun, sweat, the green, and the sea"
Major languages: Portuguese (official), Creole
Currency: Escudo = 100 centavos

1976 stamp marking the first anniversary of Cape Verde's independence

GEOGRAPHY

With an area of 1,557 square miles (4,033 sq. km), Cape Verde is Africa's smallest country. It is a little larger than Rhode Island in the United States (US).

Cape Verde is a group of volcanic islands in the Atlantic Ocean. The Barlavento, or Windward, group consists of Santo Antão, São Vicente, Santa Luzia, São Nicolau, Sal, and Boa Vista. The Sotavento (Leeward) group of islands, in the south, are Brava, Fogo, São Tiago, and Maio. Santa Luzia and the five islets are uninhabited. The largest island is São Tiago, on which the capital, Praia, is located. This island contains more than three-quarters of the country's population.

The highest point on these mountainous islands, called Pico, is on Fogo island. It reaches 9,281 ft (2,829 m) above sea level.

Cape Verde has a warm, dry climate. Dry northeast trade winds blow for most of the year, but moister southwest winds bring some rain, mainly to São Tiago, from August until October. Sandstorms from the Sahara sometimes hit the islands. Much of the land is desert, with thorny shrubs in some areas.

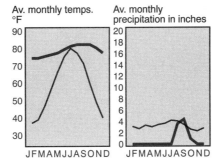

Av. monthly temps. °F
Av. monthly precipitation in inches

JFMAMJJASOND   JFMAMJJASOND

— Praia — Washington, DC

ECONOMY

Chief farm products: Bananas, cassava, coconuts, coffee, corn, fruits, livestock, plantains, sugar cane, sweet potatoes, vegetables
Chief mineral resources: Salt, pozzolana (volcanic rock used to make cement)
Chief industrial products: Beverages, processed food, rum and molasses
Employment:

Industry 30% — Agriculture 31%
Services 39% —

In the US, agriculture employs 3% of the work force, industry 25%, services 72%
Exports: Oil and oil products, fish
Per capita income: $840 (as compared with $25,860 in the US)

PEOPLE

Population: 381,000 (as compared with the US population of 260,529,000)
Major ethnic groups: Mixed origin: African and European
Religions: Christianity, including Roman Catholics (93%)

SOCIAL FACTS

● The average life expectancy at birth is 65 years, as compared with 76 years in the US
● Only 51% of the people live in urban areas, as compared with about 76% in the US
● Cape Verde has close historic links with Guinea-Bissau

● Severe droughts periodically cause famine and great hardship
● Many Cape Verdeans emigrate to find work; the money they send home is important in the country's economy
● The local Creole dialect contains words from Portuguese and various African languages

KEY POINTS IN RECENT HISTORY

1951 Portugal makes its colony of Cape Verde an overseas province
1956 Nationalists set up the Partido Africano de la Independência do Guiné e Cabo Verde (PAIGC) party; it calls for independence
1974 A military group overthrows the government in Portugal
1975 Cape Verde becomes an independent country
1981 The PAIGC is renamed the Partido Africano da Independência do Cabo Verde (PAICV); the removal of Guiné (Guinea) from the title reflects a rift with Guinea-Bissau's leaders
1990 Cape Verde's parliament abolishes the PAICV's sole right to rule
1991 Multiparty elections are won by the Movimento para a Democracia (MPD); António Mascarenhas Monteiro is elected president
1996 Cape Verde joins the Community of Portuguese-speaking Countries

© DIAGRAM

Central African Republic

Location:
Landlocked country in Central Africa
Neighbors: Chad, Sudan, Zaire, Congo, Cameroon

Official name: Central African Republic
Divisions: Sixteen prefectures and the autonomous commune of Bangui
Capital: Bangui
Largest cities: Bangui, Berbérati, Bouar, Bambari, Bossangoa, Carnot (in order of size)

Flag: The top two horizontal stripes of blue and white, together with the vertical red stripe, recall France's flag. The red and the horizontal green and yellow stripes symbolize African unity

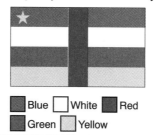

| ■ | Blue | □ | White | ■ | Red |
| ■ | Green | ▨ | Yellow | | |

National anthem: "La renaissance" ("Rebirth")
Major languages: French (official), Sango (national)
Currency: CFA franc = 100 cents

1960 stamp marking CAR joining the UN

GEOGRAPHY

With an area of 240,324 square miles (622,437 sq. km), Central African Republic (CAR) is Africa's nineteenth largest country. It is a bit smaller in area than Texas in the United States (US).

The country consists of a rolling plateau mostly between about 2,000 and 2,500 ft (600–760 m) above sea level. The highest point is Mount Toussoro, at 4,462 ft (1,360 m), in the northeast. The plateau is a major divide between the Congo (Zaire), Nile, and Lake Chad river basins. In the south, rivers drain into the Oubangui River, a tributary of the (Congo) Zaire River. The Oubangui and its tributary, the Mbomou River, form much of the country's border with Congo. They form a major waterway for trade. In the north, rivers feed the Chari River that flows north to Lake Chad. In the northeast, a number of rivers flow into the Nile River system.

The altitude moderates temperatures in this tropical country. The main rainy season is from June until October. The rainfall exceeds 60 in. (152 cm) in the south, but it is only 30 in. (76 cm) in the north. Rainforests grow in southern valleys, but wooded tropical savanna covers most of the land. Trees are fewer in the north.

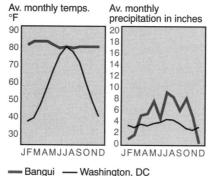

Av. monthly temps. °F

Av. monthly precipitation in inches

— Bangui   — Washington, DC

ECONOMY

Chief farm products: Bananas, cassava, coffee, corn, cotton, livestock, peanuts, sorghum, yams
Chief mineral resources: Copper, diamonds, gold, iron, uranium
Chief industrial products: Beverages, chemicals, clothing, metal products, textiles, tobacco, wood products
Employment:

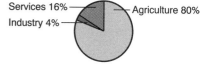

Services 16% — Agriculture 80%
Industry 4%

In the US, agriculture employs 3% of the work force, industry 25%, and services 72%
Exports: Diamonds, wood, cotton, tobacco, coffee, gold
Per capital income: $370 (as compared with $25,860 in the US)

PEOPLE

Population: 3,249,000 (as compared with the US population of 260,529,000)
Major ethnic groups: Baya , Banda, Mandija, Sara, Mbum
Religions: Christianity (68%), African religions (24%), Islam (8%)

SOCIAL FACTS

● The average life expectancy at birth s 49 years, as compared with 76 years in the US
● Only 39% of the people live in urban areas, as compared with about 76% in the US
● National parks and reserves make up

6% of the country
● Slavery greatly depleted the population of the region from the 1500s to the 1800s
● Farming is the main activity, but only 3% of the land is cultivated
● Sango, which is based on the Baya language, includes many French words

KEY POINTS IN RECENT HISTORY

1910 CAR (then called Oubangui-Chari) becomes part of the French Equatorial Africa colony
1960 CAR becomes independent (August 13) and David Dacko becomes the first president
1966 The army leader, Jean-Bédel

Bokassa, seizes power
1976 Bokassa makes himself emperor of the renamed Central African Empire; he rules as a dictator
1979 Bokassa is overthrown with French assistance and Dacko becomes president again
1981 Army officers remove Dacko and

General André Kolingba takes power
1992 The government introduces a multiparty constitution
1993 Multiparty elections take place and Ange-Félix Patassé beats eight candidates to become president
1994 CFA is devalued by 50%
1996 Bokassa dies

*See **Peoples of Central Africa*** on the Azande, Baya, Mbenga, Mbuti, and Twa

Chad

Location:
Landlocked country in West Africa
Neighbors: Libya, Sudan, Central African Republic, Cameroon, Nigeria, Niger
Official name: Republic of Chad
Divisions: Fourteen prefectures
Capital: N'Djamena
Largest cities: N'Djamena, Sarh, Moundou, Abéché, Koumra (in order of size)

Flag: The blue vertical stripe, left, represents the sky and hope; the yellow stripe, center, the Sun; and the red stripe, right, fire and unity. The flag was adopted in 1959 as Chad prepared for independence

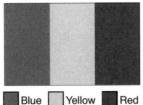

▮ Blue   ▯ Yellow   ▮ Red

National anthem: "People of Chad arise and to the task"
Major languages: French and Arabic (both official), Sara
Currency: CFA franc = 100 centimes

1976 stamp depicting decorated gourds and a ladle

GEOGRAPHY

With an area of 495,755 square miles (1,284,000 sq. km), Chad is Africa's fifth largest country. It is 1.2 times larger in area than California in the United States (US).

Northern Chad contains arid plateaus interspersed with rocky mountains. The highest peak, Emi Koussi, at 11,204 ft (3,415 m), is in the Tibesti Mountains in the northwest. The north contains sand dunes, gravel-strewn plains, and large areas of bare rock. The wadis (dry watercourses) are turned into fast-flowing rivers after heavy rainstorms.

The south contains a number of rivers, the most important being the Chari and Logone, which unite before flowing into Lake Chad. This lake, whose area varies greatly from season to season, is the country's largest and occupies an inland drainage basin. Chad shares it with Cameroon, Nigeria, and Niger.

Northern Chad is part of the Sahara and the climate is hot and almost rainless. Central Chad contains part of a semidesert region called the Sahel. In the south, where rain occurs from May until September, tropical savanna covers large areas. Some forests occur in the far south.

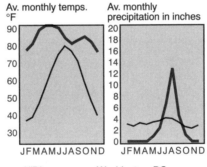

Av. monthly temps. °F

Av. monthly precipitation in inches

— N'Djamena   — Washington, DC

ECONOMY

Chief farm products: Beans, cassava, corn, cotton, livestock, millet, peanuts, rice, sugar cane, yams
Chief mineral resources: Salt, bauxite (aluminum ore), gold, and uranium
Chief industrial products: Beverages, cigarettes, cotton fabrics, hides and skins, processed food
Employment:

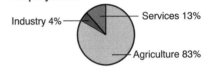

Industry 4% — Services 13%
— Agriculture 83%

In the US, agriculture employs 3% of the work force, industry 25%, and services 72%
Exports: Raw cotton, cattle and meat, hides and skins
Per capita income: $180 (as compared with $25,860 in the US)

PEOPLE

Population: 6,183,000 (as compared with the US population of 260,529,000)
Major ethnic groups: Sara, Bagirma and Kreish, Sudanic Arab
Religions: Islam (40%), Christianity (33%), African religions (27%)

SOCIAL FACTS

● The average life expectancy at birth is 48 years, as compared with 76 years in the US
● Only 21% of the people live in urban areas, as compared with about 76% in the US
● From the 700s until the 1800s, Chad was part of the Kanem-Borno Empire

● Conflict has occurred between the Muslim Arabs and Berbers in the north and the Black Africans, most of whom follow either Christianity or African religions
● In 1994 the International Court of Justice ruled against Libya's claim to the Aozou Strip in northern Chad

KEY POINTS IN RECENT HISTORY

1960 Chad becomes independent from France (August 11) with François Tombalbaye as the first president
1962 A group of northerners forms the Front de Libération National du Tchad (FROLINAT)

Mid-1960s Civil war breaks out
1971 Libya aids FROLINAT troops in their struggle
1973 Libya occupies the Aozou Strip
1975 A military group kills Tombalbaye and sets up a military regime; the civil war continues

1987 Government forces conquer the north, except for the Aozou Strip
1990 A rebel group overthrows the government; Idriss Déby becomes president; he seeks to unite the country and restore democratic institutions
1994 CFA is devalued by 50%

© DIAGRAM

*See **Peoples of West Africa** on the Fulani and Hausa*

Comoros

Location: Island nation in the Indian Ocean, off the coast of Southern Africa
Nearest countries: Mozambique, Madagascar

Official name: Federal Islamic Republic of the Comoros
Divisions: Three main islands
Capital: Moroni
Largest cities: Moroni, Fomboni, Mutsamudu (in order of size)

Flag: The white crescent on a green background represent the country's dominant religion, Islam. The four stars represent four islands – the three that make up the Comoros, and nearby Mayotte, which is a French dependency

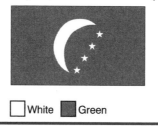

☐ White ■ Green

National anthem: "Udzima wa ya masiwa" ("The union of the islands")
Major languages: Comorian and French (both official), Swahili, Arabic
Currency: Comorian franc = 100 centimes

1977 stamp depicting a big-game fish

GEOGRAPHY

With an area of 719 square miles (1,862 sq. km), the Comoros is Africa's fourth smallest country. It is smaller in area than Rhode Island in the United States (US).

Geographically, the Comoros is a group of four islands in the Indian Ocean, between mainland Africa and northern Madagascar. The Comoros republic, however, includes only three of these islands – Njazidja (or Grande Comore), Mwali (or Mohéli), and Nzwani (or Anjouan). The people of the fourth island, Mayotte, in the southeast, voted to remain a French dependency.

The islands are volcanic in origin. The highest peak, Mont Kartala, which reaches 7,646 ft (2,331 m) above sea level, is on the largest island, Njazidja. This mountain is an active volcano. The mountainous areas are rocky, but the Comoros also has fertile lowlands.

The climate is tropical. Dry, cool conditions prevail from May until October, with a hot rainy season between November and April. The highest rainfall usually comes in January. Mangrove swamps border parts of the coast, but much of the forest inland has been cut down. Grasses and heather grow on the mountain slopes.

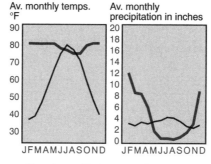

Av. monthly temps. °F
Av. monthly precipitation in inches

— Moroni — Washington, DC

ECONOMY

Chief farm products: Bananas, cassava, cloves. coconuts, coffee, copra, corn, rice, perfume oils, sisal, sweet potatoes, vanilla
Chief mineral resources: Sand, gravel
Chief industrial products: Beverages, plastics, textiles, wood products
Employment:

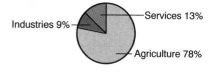

Industries 9% — Services 13% — Agriculture 78%

In the US, agriculture employs 3% of the work force, industry 25%, and services 72%
Exports: Vanilla, perfume oils, cloves
Per capita income: $560 (as compared with $25,860 in the US)

PEOPLE

Population: 485,000 (as compared with the US population of 260,529,000)
Major ethnic group: Comorians (of mixed African and Arab descent)
Religions: Islam (99.4%), Christianity (0.6%)

SOCIAL FACTS

● The average life expectancy at birth is 56 years, as compared with 76 years in the US
● Only 30% of the people live in urban areas, as compared with about 76% in the US
● Arab sultans ruled the islands from the 1400s until the 1800s

● The Comorians are descendants of Africans, Madagascans, Arabs, and Southeast Asians
● Comorian is a Bantu language, similar to Swahili – the lingua franca in East Africa
● From 1975 until 1995, the Comoros suffered seventeen coup attempts

KEY POINTS IN RECENT HISTORY

1947 France makes the Comoros an overseas territory
1961 The Comoros gain self-rule
1974 The people of three islands vote for independence, but Mayotte opts to remain under French rule

1975 The Comoros become independent (July 6) under President Ahmad Abdullah; a coup led by Ali Soilih overthrows Abdullah
1978 Abdullah regains power after a coup led by French mercenary Colonel Robert Denard

1989 Abdullah is assassinated; he is succeeded by Said Muhammad Djohar, head of the Supreme Court
1995 Djohar flees Comoros after failed coup attempt (led by Denard)
1996 Djohar returns; elections bring in new government

Congo

Location: Central Africa
Neighbors: Gabon, Cameroon, Central African Republic, Zaire, Cabinda (Angola)

Official name: Republic of Congo
Divisions: Nine prefectures
Capital: Brazzaville
Largest cities: Brazzaville, Pointe-Noire, Loubomo, Mossendjo (in order of size)

Flag: The flag has a diagonal pattern of green, yellow, and red. These are the colors of the flag of Ethiopia, and symbolize African unity. This flag was adopted in 1990, replacing the previous red (socialist) flag

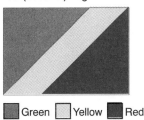

■ Green ☐ Yellow ■ Red

National anthem: "La congolaise"
Major languages: French (official), Kileta, Lingala, and Kongo
Currency: Lilangeni = 100 cents

1971 stamp commemorating the eighth anniversary of the 1963 revolution

GEOGRAPHY

With an area of 132,047 square miles (342,000 sq. km), Congo is Africa's twenty-sixth largest country. It is about twice as big as Texas in the United States (US).

Behind the coast, which is 100 miles (160 km) long, lies a narrow plain that extends inland to the steep Mayombe Escarpment. Beyond that lie a series of plateaus, between about 1,600 and 2,600 ft (500–800 m) above sea level. The highest point in the country is Mount Lékéti, at 3,412 ft (1,040 m).

The main river on the coastal plain is the Kouilou. Its main tributary, the Niari River, flows through a fertile region. Northern Congo consists of high plains crossed by many rivers that flow into the Congo (Zaire) River and one of its tributaries, the Oubangui. Many of the river valleys in the north flood annually and contain large areas of swamp.

Most of Congo has high temperatures and abundant rainfall. The cold, offshore Benguela Current lowers temperatures on the coast, which is the driest part of the country. The coastal plain is treeless, but tropical savanna covers the plateaus, with forests in the valleys. The north is largely forested.

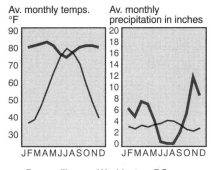

Av. monthly temps. °F
Av. monthly precipitation in inches

— Brazzaville — Washington, DC

ECONOMY

Chief farm products: Bananas, cassava, cocoa, coffee, corn, palm products, peanuts, sugar cane, yams
Chief mineral resources: Oil and natural gas, lead, zinc
Chief industrial products: Beverages, cement, fuel oils, processed food, textiles, wood products
Employment:

Services 36% — Agriculture 49%
Industry 15% —

In the US, agriculture employs 3% of the work force, industry 25%, and services 72%
Exports: Oil and oil products (90%), manufactured goods, raw materials
Per capita income: $620 (as compared with $25,860 in the US)

PEOPLE

Population: 2,600,000 (as compared with the US population of 260,529,000)
Major ethnic groups: Kongo, Teke, Mboshi, Mbete, Punu, Sango
Religions: Christianity (93%), African religions (5%)

SOCIAL FACTS

● The average life expectancy at birth is 51 years, as compared with 76 years in the US
● Only 58% of the people live in urban areas, as compared with about 76% in the US
● In 1970, Congo became the first declared communist country in Africa

● Brazzaville was named after the nineteenth-century French explorer Pierre Savorgnan de Brazza
● Congo was once called Congo (Brazzaville) to distinguish it from another Congo – Congo (Kinshasa), now called Zaire
● Dugout canoes are the main form of transportation in northern Congo

KEY POINTS IN RECENT HISTORY

1960 Congo becomes independent from France (August 15); Abbé Fulbert Youlou becomes the first president
1963 A socialist group led by Alphonse Massamba-Débat forces President Youlou to resign

1964 Congo adopts a one-party system of government
1968 A military group led by Captain Marien Ngouabi seizes power
1970 Congo declares itself a communist country
1977 Ngouabi is assassinated

1979 Colonel Denis Sassou-Nguesso becomes president
1990 Congo renounces communism
1991 Congo legalizes opposition political parties
1992 Sassou-Nguesso is defeated in national elections by Pascal Lissouba

*See **Peoples of Central Africa** on the Azande, Kongo, Mbenga, Mbuti, Teke, and Twa*

© DIAGRAM

Djibouti

Location: East Africa, on the Gulf of Aden
Neighbors: Somalia, Ethiopia, Eritrea

Official name: Republic of Djibouti
Divisions: Five administrative districts
Capital: Djibouti
Largest cities: Djibouti, Ali Sabieh, Tadjoura (in order of size)

Flag: The horizontal stripes of blue (top) and green symbolize the two main peoples, the Afar and the Somalis. The white triangle contains a red star, which represents unity and independence

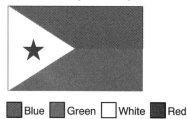

Blue ⬛ Green ⬛ White ☐ Red ⬛

National anthem: "Hinjinne u sara kaca" ("Arise with strength")
Major languages: Arabic and French (both official), Afar, Somali
Currency: Djibouti franc = 100 centimes

1978 stamp depicting a seashell

GEOGRAPHY

With an area of 8,958 square miles (23,201 sq. km), Djibouti is Africa's eighth smallest country. It is slightly smaller than New Hampshire in the United States (US).

Djibouti is located around the Gulf of Tadjoura, an inlet of the Gulf of Aden. Behind the narrow coastal plain, the land rises to highlands in the north, where Moussa Ali reaches 6,768 ft (2,063 m) above sea level. Volcanic plateaus occupy much of the central and southern regions of Djibouti.

The country includes Lake Assal, whose shoreline is Africa's lowest point on land, reaching 509 ft (155 m) below sea level. The largest lake in Djibouti is Lake Abbe on the Ethiopian border in the west. This lake is fed by the Awash River. The Awash flows through the Great Rift Valley, which cuts across Ethiopia and Djibouti.

The climate of Djibouti is hot and extremely dry. The annual rainfall is everywhere less than 20 in. (51 cm) and desert covers nearly 90% of the land. Only hardy grasses and thorn shrubs can survive there. The mountains contain some wooded areas and date palms and other plants grow on the plains and at oases, fertile pockets.

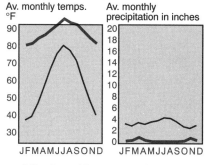

Av. monthly temps. °F

Av. monthly precipitation in inches

JFMAMJJASOND   JFMAMJJASOND

—— Djibouti   —— Washington, DC

ECONOMY

Chief farm products: Hides and skins, livestock (cattle, camels, goats, sheep), melons, meat, tomatoes, vegetables
Chief mineral resources: Salt, building materials
Chief industrial products: Beverages, furniture, electromechanical products
Employment:

Industry 11%
Services 14%
Agriculture 75%

In the US, agriculture employs 3% of the work force, industry 25%, and services 72%
Exports: Mainly reexports, live animals
Per capita income: $780 (as compared with $25,860 in the US)

PEOPLE

Population: 603,000 (as compared with the US population of 260,529,000)
Major ethnic groups: Somali, including Issa, Afar
Religions: Islam (96%), Christianity (4%)

SOCIAL FACTS

● The average life expectancy at birth is 48 years, as compared with 76 years in the US
● 82% of the people live in urban areas, as compared with about 76% in the US
● Djibouti is strategically placed at the southern end of the Red Sea

● Djibouti was formerly called French Somaliland and, later, the Territory of the Afars and the Issas
● Only about 1% of the land can be used for farming
● Rivalries between the Afar and the Somalis have caused problems in Djibouti

KEY POINTS IN RECENT HISTORY

1917 A railroad to Addis Ababa, Ethiopia, is completed, making Djibouti an important trading center
1947 Nationalists in what was then French Somaliland call for independence for the territory
1967 The country is renamed the

Territory of the Afars and the Issas
1977 The country becomes independent (June 26) as the Republic of Djibouti; Hassan Gouled Aptidon is the first president
1981 Hassan Gouled Aptidon is reelected president
1991 A coup attempt is defeated

1992 A constitution permitting four political parties is adopted; each party must have an ethnic balance
1993 Hassan Gouled Aptidon is again elected president, defeating three opponents

See **Peoples of East Africa** on the Afar and Somalis

Egypt

Location: North Africa, with coastlines on the Mediterranean and the Red Sea
Neighbors: Israel, Sudan, Libya

Official name: Arab Republic of Egypt
Divisions: Twenty-six governates
Capital: Cairo
Largest cities: Cairo, Alexandria, Giza, Shubra al Khayma, Port Said, Suez (in order of size)

Flag: The flag has three stripes of red, white, and black. The white stripe contains the national emblem, an eagle, which was the symbol of Saladin (Salah ad-Din), the great Muslim leader and warrior (1137–93)

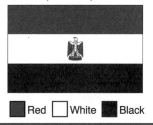

■ Red □ White ■ Black

National anthem: "Biladi, biladi" ("My homeland, my homeland")
Major languages: Arabic (official), Berber, English, French
Currency: Pound = 100 piastres

1951 stamp marking the royal wedding of King Farouk I and Queen Narriman

GEOGRAPHY

With an area of 386,095 square miles (1,000,000 sq. km), Egypt is Africa's twelfth largest country. It is nearly 1.5 times as big as Texas in the United States (US).

Egypt contains two main regions that are separated by the valley of the Nile, the world's longest river. To the west is the Libyan, or Western, Desert (part of the Sahara). This mainly plateau region contains depressions, including the Qattara Depression in the northwest, where Egypt's lowest point, 436 ft (133 m) below sea level, is located.

Eastern Egypt contains the Eastern Desert (also part of the Sahara) and the Sinai Peninsula, between the Suez Canal and the Gulf of Suez. The Sinai Peninsula contains Egypt's highest peak, Jabal Katherina, at 8,851 ft (2,698 m) above sea level.

Lake Nasser, a reservoir behind the Aswan High Dam, is the largest lake.

Egypt has a hot, dry climate. Summers (from May until October) are hot, but after dark, temperatures often fall quickly. Winters are mild. The average annual rainfall is about 8 in. (20 cm) on the Mediterranean coast, but it is much lower to the south. Plant life, including date palms, is confined to the fertile Nile Valley and desert oases, fertile pockets.

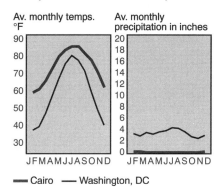

Av. monthly temps. °F

Av. monthly precipitation in inches

JFMAMJJASOND   JFMAMJJASOND

— Cairo — Washington, DC

ECONOMY

Chief farm products: barley, citrus fruits, cotton, dates, potatoes, rice, sorghum, sugar cane, wheat
Chief mineral resources: Oil and natural gas, phosphates, iron ore
Chief industrial products: Cars, cement, chemicals, cotton yarn, fertilizers, refrigerators, sugar, TV sets
Employment:

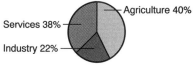

Agriculture 40%
Services 38%
Industry 22%

In the US, agriculture employs 3% of the work force, industry 25%, and services 72%
Exports: Oil and oil products, cotton goods, engineering and metal products
Per capita income: $720 (as compared with $25,860 in the US)

PEOPLE

Population: 61,636,000 (about a quarter of the US population of 260,529,000)
Major ethnic groups: Arabs
Religions: Islam (about 90%), Christianity – mainly Coptic Christians (about 10%)

SOCIAL FACTS

● The average life expectancy at birth is 62 years, as compared with 76 years in the US
● 45% of the people live in urban areas, as compared with about 76% in the US)
● Egypt is Africa's second most populous country after Nigeria

● Nearly all Egyptians live in the Nile Valley or along the Suez Canal
● Egypt is Africa's second most industrialized country
● Women have more rights in Egypt than in any other Arab country.
● Egyptian fundamentalists want to return to traditional Muslim culture

KEY POINTS IN RECENT HISTORY

1914 Egypt becomes a British protectorate
1922 Egypt becomes a nominally independent monarchy (February 28)
1948 Egypt is involved in the Arab-Israeli War (1948–9)

1954 Egypt becomes a republic
1956 Egypt nationalizes the Suez Canal; Britain, Israel, and France attack Egypt, but the United Nations ends the fighting and foreign troops withdraw
1967 Israel wins a short war against its Arab neighbors, including Egypt

1973 Renewed fighting between Israel and Arab nations, including Egypt
1979 Peace agreement is signed between Egypt and Israel
1991 Egyptian troops form part of the Allied military forces against Iraq in the Gulf War

*See **Peoples of North Africa** on the Arabs, Berbers, and Copts*

© DIAGRAM

Equatorial Guinea

Location: Central Africa
Neighbors: The mainland is bordered by Cameroon and Gabon

Official name: Republic of Equatorial Guinea
Divisions: Mainland Río Muni (or Mbini), plus Bioko and four other islands
Capital: Malabo
Largest cities: Malabo, Bata (in order of size)

Flag: The top horizontal stripe of green represents the country's natural resources, the white stripe stands for peace, and red stripe for the struggle for independence. The blue triangle represents the sea

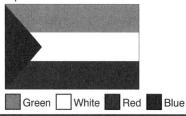

■ Green	□ White	■ Red	■ Blue

National anthem: "Let us journey, treading the pathways"
Major languages: Spanish (official), Fang, Creole
Currency: CFA franc = 100 centimes

1971 stamp marking the second anniversary of Equatorial Guinea's independence

GEOGRAPHY

With an area of 10,831 square miles (28,052 sq. km), Equatorial Guinea is Africa's eleventh smallest country. It is a little larger in area than Maryland in the United States (US).

The mainland part of Equatorial Guinea, called Río Muni or Mbini, makes up 93% of the country. It contains a narrow coastal plain, rising inland to a series of plateaus. The main river, also called Mbini, flows from east to west across the mainland.

The largest island is Bioko, which lies northwest of Río Muni. Bioko is a volcanic island and contains the country's highest point, Pico de Basilé (or Santa Isabel Mountain), which reaches a height of 9,869 ft (3,008 m) above sea level. Equatorial Guinea's capital, Malabo, on Bioko's north coast, stands on a natural harbor formed by a submerged volcanic crater.

The climate is hot, wet, and humid. Because of its rugged terrain, Bioko is especially rainy, but the country has a dry season from December until February. Río Muni has rainforests, with tropical savanna inland and mangrove swamps along the coast. Bioko's vegetation is varied, with vegetation zones determined by the altitude.

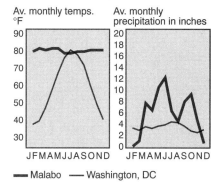

Av. monthly temps. °F

Av. monthly precipitation in inches

JFMAMJJASOND   JFMAMJJASOND

— Malabo   — Washington, DC

ECONOMY

Chief farm products: Bananas, cassava, cocoa, coconuts, coffee, lumber, palm kernels and palm oil, sweet potatoes
Chief mineral resources: Gold, oil (production began offshore in 1992), some unexploited metal reserves
Chief industrial products: Processed food, wood products
Employment:

Services 21% — Agriculture 77%
Industry 2% —

In the US, agriculture employs 3% of the work force, industry 25%, and services 72%.
Exports: Timber, cocoa, coffee
Per capita income: $420 (as compared with $25,860 in the US)

PEOPLE

Population: 386,000 (as compared with the US population of 260,529,000)
Major ethnic groups: Fang, Bubi, Ndowe, Annobonés
Religions: Christianity (89%), African religions (5%)

SOCIAL FACTS

● The average life expectancy at birth is 48 years, as compared with 76 years in the US
● Only 40% of the people live in urban areas, as compared with about 76% in the US
● Bioko was formerly called Fernando Póo and, briefly, Macías Nguema

● The Victorian writer and explorer Mary Kingsley praised the beauty of Bioko in her writings
● A small group of people, the Fernandinos, are Creoles descended from slaves freed by Britain in the nineteenth century
● Many Nigerian migrants work on Bioko

KEY POINTS IN RECENT HISTORY

1900 The mainland territories of what was then Spanish Guinea are fixed by the Treaty of Paris
1968 The country wins independence as Equatorial Guinea (October 12); Macías Nguema becomes president

1970 Equatorial Guinea becomes a one-party dictatorship
1979 Lt.-Col. Teodoro Obiang Nguema Mbasogo seizes power; Macías Nguema, accused of many crimes, including torture, murder, and persecution of foreigners, is executed

1992 A multiparty constitution is introduced
1993 The Democratic Party wins 68 of the 80 seats in parliment
1996 Obiang Nguema is reelected president amid allegations of vote-rigging

*See **Peoples of Central Africa** on the Fang*

Eritrea

Location: East Africa, facing the Red Sea
Neighbors: Djibouti, Ethiopia, Sudan

Official name: State of Eritrea
Divisions: Ten provinces, each with a governor
Capital: Asmera
Largest cities: Asmera, Aseb, Keren, Mitsiwa, Mendefera (in order of size)

Flag: The flag of Eritrea has three triangular segments. The top segment is green and the bottom one blue. The central segment, the largest of the three, is red and contains a yellow wreath and olive branch.

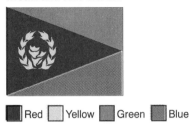

■ Red ☐ Yellow ■ Green ■ Blue

National anthem: "Eritrea, Eritrea, Eritrea"
Major languages: Tigrinya, Arabic (both official), Afar, Beja
Currency: Birr = 100 cents

1995 One of the first stamps from newly-independent Eritrea

GEOGRAPHY
With an area of 45,405 square miles (117,598 sq. km), Eritrea is one of Africa's smaller countries. It is about the same size as Pennsylvania in the United States (US).

The Red Sea coast extends northeast for about 620 miles (1,000 km) from the border with Djibouti to the border with Sudan. Behind the coastal plain, which is 10 to 40 miles (16–64 km) wide, the land rises to the central highlands and Eritrea's highest point, Mount Soira, which reaches a height of 9,885 ft (3,013 m) above sea level.

In the west, the land slopes down toward the Sudanese and Ethiopian borders. The country's lowest point, about 361 ft (110 m) below sea level, is located in the Danakil Depression in the southeast. Eritrea's main rivers, including the Baraka and Gash (or Marab), rise in the central highlands.

The coastal plain has a hot climate, with an average of only about 5 in. (13 cm) of rain per year, and the land is desert. The highlands are cooler and their average annual rainfall reaches around 24 in. (61 cm). The rainiest months are usually June and July. Extensive grasslands and forests occur in the uncultivated parts of the highlands.

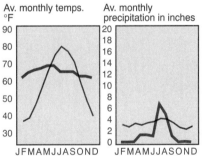

Av. monthly temps. °F

Av. monthly precipitation in inches

JFMAMJJASOND   JFMAMJJASOND

— Asmera — Washington, DC

ECONOMY
Chief farm products: Barley, dairy products, millet, sorghum, teff (a kind of grain), vegetables, wheat
Chief mineral resources: Salt, sand, some oil deposits
Chief industrial products: Beverages, glassware, leather goods, oil products, processed food, textiles
Employment:

Industry and services 20%

Agriculture 80%

In the US, agriculture employs 3% of the population, industry 25%, and services 72%
Exports: Beverages, leather goods, oil products, textiles
Per capita income: $115 (as compared with $25,860 in the US)

PEOPLE
Population: 3,482,000 (as compared with the US population of 260,529,000)
Major ethnic groups: Tigrinya, Tigre, Afar, Hedareb, Bilen
Religions: Christianity (about 50%), Islam (about 50%)

SOCIAL FACTS
● The average life expectancy at birth is 48 years, as compared with 76 years in the US
● Only 15% of the people live in urban areas, as compared with about 76% in the US
● Officially independent in 1993, Eritrea is Africa's youngest country

● Because of the disruption caused by civil war, adult illiteracy is high at about 80% of the population
● Women played an important part in the civil war, some as commanders, fighting alongside men
● Eritrea's economy depends heavily on overseas aid

KEY POINTS IN RECENT HISTORY
1941 British troops drive out Italian occupation forces and take over the government of Eritrea
1952 Eritrea becomes a self-governing part of Ethiopia
1961 Civil war breaks out
1962 Ethiopia declares Eritrea to be one of its provinces, making Ethiopia a unitary (nonfederal) state
1970 The Eritrean People's Liberation Front (EPLF) is formed to seek independence for Eritrea
1991 Ethiopia's government is overthrown by rebel forces; a government is set up to rule all of Ethiopia except for Eritrea: Eritrea is considered unofficially liberated
1993 Eritreans vote overwhelmingly for independence, which is officially achieved on May 24

*See **Peoples of East Africa** on the Afar*

© DIAGRAM

Ethiopia

Location: A landlocked nation in East Africa
Neighbors: Djibouti, Somalia, Kenya, Sudan, Eritrea

Official name: Ityo (Ethiopia)
Divisions: The 1995 constitution created nine provinces
Capital: Addis Ababa
Largest cities: Addis Ababa, Dire Dawa, Gonder, Nazret, Bahir Dahr, Debre Zeyit (in order of size)

Flag: Ethiopia's flag consists of three stripes of green (top), yellow (center), and red. In Africa, these colors now represent African unity, because Ethiopia is the continent's oldest independent nation

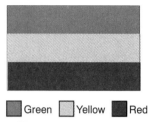

☐ Green ☐ Yellow ■ Red

National anthem: "In our Ethiopia, our civic pride is strong"
Languages: Amharic (official), Oromo, Tigrinya
Currency: Birr = 100 cents

Stamp marking the first session of the Economic Conference for Africa, in 1958

GEOGRAPHY
With an area of 435,523 square miles (1,128,000 sq. km), Ethiopia is Africa's tenth largest country. It is a little larger in area than California in the United States (US).

Ethiopia consists mainly of a high plateau, with lowlands in the east and south. Ethiopia's highest peak, Ras Dashen, reaches 15,157 ft (4,620 m) in the north. The plateau is split into two parts by the Great Rift Valley.

Lake Tana, the largest lake and source of the Blue Nile (called the Abay Wenz in Ethiopia), is also in the north. The Blue Nile, which has worn a huge canyon in the plateau, flows into Sudan, where it joins the White Nile at Khartoum. Other lakes are in the Great Rift Valley, the northern part of which is drained by the Awash River. The Awash provides hydroelectricity for Addis Ababa and water for irrigation.

The lowlands are hot and dry and large areas are uninhabited desert. Tropical forests grow in the hot and rainy southwest, but the altitude moderates the climate in the plateau regions. Grassland covers large areas in the cool highlands, where the rainfall is generally around 40 in. (102 cm) per year.

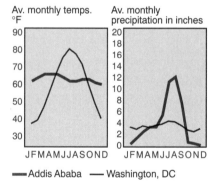

Av. monthly temps. °F
Av. monthly precipitation in inches

— Addis Ababa — Washington, DC

ECONOMY
Chief farm products: Barley, coffee, corn, hides and skins, oilseeds, sorghum, sugar cane, teff (a kind of grain), wheat
Chief mineral resources: Salt, limestone, gold
Chief industrial products: Beverages, cement, footwear, processed food, textiles
Employment:

Industry 2% — Services 12%
Agriculture 86%

In the US, agriculture employs 3% of the work force, industry 25%, and services 72%
Exports: Coffee, hides, gold, petroleum products
Per capita income: $100 (as compared with $25,860 in the US)

PEOPLE
Population: 54,900,000 (as compared with the US population of 260,529,000)
Major ethnic groups: Amhara, Oromo, Tigrinya, Gurage
Religions: Islam (45%), Christianity (40%), African religions (12%)

SOCIAL FACTS
● The average life expectancy at birth is 49 years, as compared with 76 years in the US
● Only 13% of the people live in urban areas, as compared with about 76% in the US
● Ethiopia has more than 70 languages and 200 dialects

● Ethiopia, formerly known as Abyssinia, is Africa's oldest independent country. Its empire lasted from Biblical times until 1974, when the emperor, Haile Selassie I, was overthrown
● The Ethiopian Orthodox (or Coptic) Church has inspired much art
● Many of Ethiopia's "Black Jews" – the Falasha – have emigrated to Israel

KEY POINTS IN RECENT HISTORY
1930 Ras Tafari becomes emperor as Haile Selassie I
1935 Italy invades Ethiopia
1941 The Italians are defeated by Ethiopian and British forces and Haile Selassie returns to the throne

1952 Eritrea becomes part of Ethiopia
1960s Fighting occurs as secessionist groups, including Somalis in the south, demand independence
1974 Haile Selassie is replaced by a socialist military government
1980s A major drought causes great

hardship; civil war breaks out
1991 Mengistu Haile Mariam, head of the government, is overthrown
1993 Eritrea becomes independent
1995 National elections are held under a new federal constitution

*See **Peoples of East Africa** on the Afar, Amhara, Falasha, Oromo, and Somalis*

Gabon

Location: Central Africa, facing the Atlantic Ocean
Neighbors: Equatorial Guinea, Cameroon, Congo

Official name: Gabonese Republic
Divisions: Nine provinces
Capital: Libreville
Largest cities: Libreville, Port-Gentil, Makoku, Lambaréné, Moanda (in order of size)

Flag: Of the three horizontal stripes, the green, top, represents the country's forests; the yellow, center, symbolizes the Equator (which runs through Gabon); and the blue, bottom, symbolizes the sea

■ Green □ Yellow ■ Blue

National anthem: "Uni dans la concorde" ("United in concord")
Major languages: French (official), Fang
Currency: CFA franc = 100 centimes

1965 stamp marking the fifth anniversary of independence and depicting President M'Ba

GEOGRAPHY

With an area of 103,347 square miles (267,668 sq. km), Gabon is Africa's twenty-ninth largest country. It is roughly the same size in area as Colorado in the United States (US).

Gabon's coast is 500 miles (800 km) long and lined with sandy beaches, lagoons, and swamps, Behind it is a narrow coastal plain and inland lie hills, plateaus, and low mountains. The highest point is Mount Iboundji, 3,904 ft (1,190 m) above sea level in the Massif du Chaillu in south-central Gabon.

Most of Gabon lies in the drainage basin of its chief river, the Ogooué. This river, 746 miles (1,201 km) long, rises in Congo and flows across Gabon to reach the sea near Port-Gentil, the chief port. It is navigable throughout the year below the town of Lambaréné. Numerous waterfalls and rapids make its upper course unnavigable.

The climate is hot, rainy, and humid. The rainy season is from October until May. During the dry season, from June until August, winds blow from the land to the sea and little rain falls. Tropical rainforests cover about 75% of Gabon, and merge into tropical savanna in the east and south.

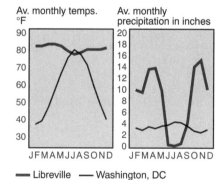

Av. monthly temps. °F

Av. monthly precipitation in inches

JFMAMJJASOND   JFMAMJJASOND

— Libreville — Washington, DC

ECONOMY

Chief farm products: Cassava, cocoa, coffee, corn, lumber, palm products, peanuts, sugar cane, yams
Chief mineral resources: Oil and natural gas, manganese, uranium
Chief industrial products: Beverages, cement, cigarettes, processed food, textiles, wood products
Employment:

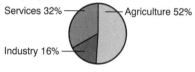

Services 32% — Agriculture 52%
Industry 16% —

In the US, agriculture employs 3% of the work force, industry 25%, and services 72%
Exports: Oil (80%), timber, manganese, uranium
Per capita income: $3,880 (as compared with $25,860 in the US)

PEOPLE

Population: 1,300,000 (as compared with the US population of 260,529,000)
Major ethnic groups: Fang, Mpongwe, Mbete, Punu
Religions: Christianity (96%), African religions (3%), Islam (1%)

SOCIAL FACTS

● The average life expectancy at birth is 54 years, as compared with 76 years in the US
● 49% of the people live in urban areas, as compared with about 76% in the US
● Gabon is one of Africa's most thinly populated countries

● Libreville (meaning "free town") was founded in 1849 by freed slaves
● Albert Schweitzer, who set up a sleeping sickness and leprosy hospital at Lambaréné, won the 1952 Nobel Peace Prize for his humanitarian work
● Some bands of tropical forest-foragers live in the southern forests

KEY POINTS IN RECENT HISTORY

1910 Gabon becomes a French colony within French Equatorial Africa
1960 Gabon becomes independent (August 17) and Léon M'Ba becomes the country's first president
1964 French troops restore M'Ba to power after a military coup

1967 M'Ba dies and is succeeded by Albert-Bernard (later, Omar) Bongo
1968 Gabon becomes a one-party state
1974 Work starts on the Trans-Gabon Railroad, which will open up the mineral-rich interior
1990 Opposition parties are legalized;

elections are won by the Parti Démocratique Gabonais (PDG), the former sole political party
1993 Presidential elections are held and Bongo is reelected for fourth time
1994 The CFA, which is linked to the French franc, is devalued by 50% causing hardship and civil unrest

*See **Peoples of Central Africa** on the Fang, Mbenga, Mbuti, Teke, and Twa*

© DIAGRAM

Gambia, The

Location: West Africa, facing the Atlantic Ocean
Neighbors: Gambia is almost completely enclosed by Senegal

Official name: Republic of The Gambia
Divisions: Thirty-five districts
Capital: Banjul
Largest cities: Greater Banjul, Serrekunda, Brikama, Bakau (in order of size)

Flag: The flag of Gambia consists of three horizontal colored bands. The red band, top, stands for the Sun; the blue (edged with white) in the center represents the Gambia River; the green, bottom, is for the land

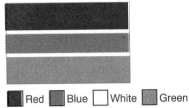

■ Red ■ Blue □ White ■ Green

National anthem: "For The Gambia, our homeland"
Major languages: English (official), Manding, Fulfulde, Wolof,
Currency: Dalasi = 100 butut

1975 Stamp marking the tenth anniversary of Gambia's independence

GEOGRAPHY

With an area of 4,361 square miles (11,295 sq. km), Gambia is the smallest country on the African mainland. It is slightly smaller in area than Connecticut in the United States (US).

Gambia is a long and narrow strip of land, running roughly 180 miles (290 km) from west to east, but it measures only between 15 and 30 miles (24–48 km) from north to south. It occupies the north and south banks of the Gambia River, which rises in Guinea and enters Gambia from Senegal. The river empties into the Atlantic Ocean at Banjul on Gambia's short coastline.

In the east, the Gambia River flows through a deep valley cut through a sandstone plateau. In the center of the country, flat, fertile terraces, called banto faros, border the river, but near the coast, saltwater has spread inland, spoiling the soils in the valley.

Gambia has a hot tropical climate. The summer months (especially June to October) are rainy, but winters, when a dusty wind called the harmattan blows from the Sahara, are dry. Mangrove swamps grow along the coast. Inland, much of the tropical savanna has been cleared to make farmland.

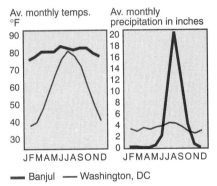

Av. monthly temps. °F / Av. monthly precipitation in inches

JFMAMJJASOND   JFMAMJJASOND

— Banjul   — Washington, DC

ECONOMY

Chief farm products: Bananas, cassava, cotton, livestock (cattle, goats and sheep), millet, palm kernels, peanuts, rice, sorghum
Chief mineral resources: sand, gravel
Chief industrial products: Beverages, chemicals, leather, palm-kernel oil, processed food, textiles
Employment:

Industry 8% — Services 10% — Agriculture 82%

In the US, agriculture employs 3% of the work force, industry 25%, and services 72%
Exports: Peanuts and peanut products, cotton, fish, hides and skins
Per capita income: $330 (as compared with $25,860 in the US)

PEOPLE

Population: 1,081,000 (as compared with the US population of 260,529,000)
Major ethnic groups: Malinke, Fulani, Wolof, Dyula, Soninke
Religions: Islam (95.4%), Christianity (3.7%), African religions (0.9%)

SOCIAL FACTS

● The average life expectancy at birth is 45 years, as compared with 76 years in the US
● Only 25%% of the people live in urban areas, as compared with about 76% in the US
● Tourism is a fast-developing industry in Gambia

● The African-American writer Alex Haley traced his ancestors back to Gambia in his novel *Roots*
● In the east, people from Senegal, called "strange farmers," help to plant the land and harvest the crops
● "The" was officially adopted as part of the country's name to further distinguish it from Zambia

KEY POINTS IN RECENT HISTORY

1965 Gambia becomes independent from Britain (February 18)
1970 Gambia becomes a republic; Sir Dawda Jawara becomes president
1981 Senegalese troops help Gambia to put down a rebellion

1982 Gambia and Senegal set up a confederation called Senegambia; it unites the countries' defense forces
1989 Senegambia is dissolved
1994 A military coup overthrows the government and Sir Dawda Jawara flees into exile; Lieutenant Yahya

Jammeh becomes president and chairman of an Armed Forces Provisional Council
1995 An attempted countercoup led by Vice-President Sana Sabally is foiled
1996 Jammeh wins presidential elections after retiring from military

*See **Peoples of West Africa** on the Bambara, Fulani, and Malinke*

Ghana

Location: West Africa, facing the Gulf of Guinea
Neighbors: Ivory Coast, Burkina Faso, Togo

Official name: Republic of Ghana
Divisions: Ten regions, each under a Regional Secretary
Capital: Accra
Largest cities: Accra, Kumasi, Tamale, Tema, Sekondi-Takoradi (in order of size)

Flag: The flag of Ghana has three horizontal stripes of red, yellow, and green. These colors are those of the Ethiopian flag and have come to symbolize African unity. In the center is a black star

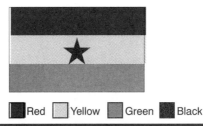

■ Red ☐ Yellow ■ Green ■ Black

National anthem: "God bless our homeland, Ghana"
Major languages: English (official), Akan, Moré, Ewe
Currency: Cedi = 100 pesewas

1959 stamp marking Africa Freedom Day

GEOGRAPHY

With an area of 91,985 square miles (238,240 sq. km), Ghana is one of Africa's smaller countries. It is a little smaller in area than Oregon in the United States (US).

The land is generally low-lying. The highest peak is Mount Afadjato, which reaches 2,904 ft (885 m) in the southeast, near the border with Togo. The north lies in the Volta River Basin, which is separated from the rivers that flow south into the Gulf of Guinea in the southwest by the Kwahu Plateau. This plateau forms a divide between the two river systems.

The Black and White Volta rivers, Ghana's main waterways, flow into Lake Volta, which lies behind the Akosombo Dam in the southeast. Lake Volta, 3,275 square miles (8,482 sq. km) in area, covers about 3.5% of Ghana and is one of the world's largest artificial lakes.

Ghana has a hot tropical climate. The southwest has rain throughout the year and rainforests grow there, but the southeast, around Accra, is much drier. The rainfall decreases to the north, which has a marked dry season. Tropical savanna with scattered trees in central Ghana merges into open grasslands in the far north.

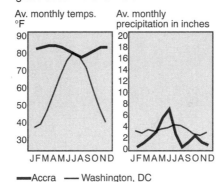

Av. monthly temps. °F

Av. monthly precipitation in inches

JFMAMJJASOND   JFMAMJJASOND
—Accra — Washington, DC

ECONOMY

Chief farm products: Cocoa, coconuts, corn, livestock, lumber, palm oil, peanuts, rice, sorghum, yams
Chief mineral resources: Bauxite (aluminum ore), manganese, gold, diamonds
Chief industrial products: Aluminum, cement, cocoa products, fuels, processed food, textiles
Employment:

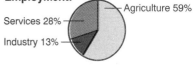

Agriculture 59%
Services 28%
Industry 13%

In the US, agriculture employs 3% of the work force, industry 25%, and services 72%
Exports: Cocoa, lumber, gold, manganese, industrial diamonds
Per capital income: $410 (as compared with $25,860 in the US)

PEOPLE

Population: 16,944,000 (as compared with the US population of 260,529,000)
Major ethnic groups: Akan, Mossi, Ewe, Ga-Adangme, Gurma
Religions: Christianity (63%), African religions (21%), Islam (16%)

SOCIAL FACTS

● The average life expectancy at birth is 58 years, as compared with 76 years in the US
● Only 36% of the people live in urban areas, as compared with 76% in the US
● Before 1957, Ghana was known as Gold Coast

● Ghana was the first Black African nation to win its independence
● Ghana is the name of a medieval African kingdom that lay to the northwest of present-day Ghana
● About 75 languages are spoken in Ghana, and many Ghanaians also speak English, the official language

KEY POINTS IN RECENT HISTORY

1947 Kwame Nkrumah forms the Convention People's Party, which calls for the independence of Gold Coast
1957 Gold Coast gains independence from Britain (March 6), with Nkrumah as prime minister; it is renamed Ghana

1960 Ghana becomes a republic and Nkrumah becomes president
1966 President Nkrumah is overthrown by military leaders
1969 Civilian rule is restored
1972 A military group again seizes power from the civilian government

1979 Flight Lieutenant Jerry Rawlings becomes head of state, but then steps down in favor of a civilian government
1981 Rawlings returns to power
1993 Civilian rule is restored under a new multiparty constitution, with Rawlings as the elected president

© DIAGRAM

*See **Peoples of West Africa** on the Asante, Ewe, and Mossi*

Guinea

Location: West Africa, facing the Atlantic Ocean
Neighbors: Guinea-Bissau, Senegal, Mali, Liberia, Sierra Leone

Official name: Republic of Guinea
Divisions: Thirty-three provinces and Conakry
Capital: Conakry
Largest cities: Conakry, Kankan, Labé, Kindia (in order of size)

Flag: The colors of the three vertical stripes – red, yellow, and green – are the same as those on the flag of Ethiopia, Africa's oldest independent nation. They symbolize African unity

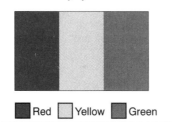

| ■ Red | □ Yellow | ■ Green |

National anthem: "People of Africa, the historic past"
Major languages: French (official), Fulfulde, Manding, Susu, Kissi
Currency: Guinean franc = 100 centimes

1959 stamp marking Guinea's independence and depicting President Sekou Touré

GEOGRAPHY

With an area of 94,926 square miles (245,849 sq. km), Guinea is Africa's thirtieth largest country. It is roughly the same size in area as Oregon in the United States (US).

Behind the coastline, which is 190 miles (300 km) long, is a swampy plain. Inland, the Futa Djallon plateau covers central Guinea. This region rises to heights of more than 3,000 ft (900 m) and contains much fine scenery. To the northeast, the land slopes gently down to the high plains of Upper Guinea. The Guinea Highlands in the southeast contain Mount Nimba, the highest peak. Located where Guinea's border meets those of Ivory Coast and Liberia, it reaches a height of 5,748 ft (1,752 m) above sea level.

Three major rivers rise in the Futa Djallon plateau. These are the Gambia, Niger, and Senegal rivers.

The climate is tropical. The rainy season is from May until October, and in the dry season, hot winds blow from the Sahara. Mangrove swamps grow on the coast, and there are rainforests inland, especially in the southeast. Tropical savanna is the main vegetation on the Futa Djallon plateau, with more-open grassland in the drier northeast.

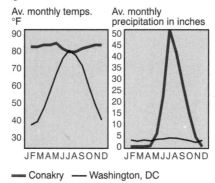

Av. monthly temps. °F
Av. monthly precipitation in inches

— Conakry   — Washington, DC

ECONOMY

Chief farm products: Bananas, cassava, coffee, corn, livestock, palm products, peanuts, sugar cane
Chief mineral resources: Bauxite (aluminum ore), diamonds, gold
Chief industrial products: Alumina, beverages, iron, plastics, processed food, textiles, tobacco
Employment:

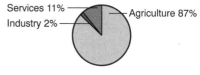

Services 11%
Industry 2%
Agriculture 87%

In the US, agriculture employs 3% of the work force, industry 25%, and services 72%
Exports: Bauxite, alumina, diamonds, gold, coffee, fish
Per capita income: $520 (as compared with $25,860 in the US)

PEOPLE

Population: 6,501,000 (as compared with the US population of 260,529,000)
Major ethnic groups: Fulani, Malinke, Susu, Kissi, Kpelle,
Religions: Islam (85%), African religions (5%), Christianity (1.5%)

SOCIAL FACTS

● The average life expectancy at birth is 44 years, as compared with 76 years in the US
● Only 29% of the people live in urban areas, as compared with about 76% in the US
● Guinea was once part of the medieval Mali and Songhay empires

● Griots, or storytellers, keep history alive by memorizing and reciting it
● Guinea is the world's second-largest producer of bauxite
● The name "Guinea" once applied to the entire West African coast; it now applies to three African countries: Guinea-Bissau, Equatorial Guinea, and Guinea

KEY POINTS IN RECENT HISTORY

1947 The nationalist political party, the Parti Démocratique de Guinée (PDG), is founded
1952 Sekou Touré becomes leader of the PDG
1958 Guineans vote for independence from France; France withdraws all its investment and stops aid; in a national crisis, Sekou Touré becomes president and introduces socialist policies
1980 An assassination attempt on Sekou Touré fails
1984 Sekou Touré dies and an army coup brings Col. Lansana Conté to power, heading a Military Committee; Conté introduces free-enterprise policies to revive the economy
1993 Conté is reelected president, defeating seven opponents

*See **Peoples of West Africa** on the Bambara, Fulani, and Malinke*

Guinea-Bissau

Location: West Africa, facing the Atlantic Ocean
Neighbors: Senegal, Guinea

Official name: Republic of Guinea-Bissau
Divisions: Eight regions
Capital: Bissau
Largest cities: Bissau, Bafata (in order of size)

Flag: The flag uses the three colors from the flag of Ethiopia, Africa's oldest independent country, with a red vertical stripe and two horizontal stripes of yellow (top) and green (bottom)

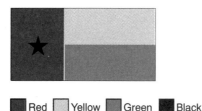

■ Red　□ Yellow　■ Green　■ Black

National anthem: As in Cape Verde – "Sun, sweat, the green, and the sea"
Major languages: Portuguese (official), Crioulo
Currency: Guinea-Bissau peso = 100 centavos

ESTADO DA GUINE-BISSAU

1976 stamp commemorating Amílcar Cabral, a former PAIGC leader

GEOGRAPHY

With an area of 13,945 square miles (36,117 sq. km), Guinea-Bissau is one of Africa's smaller countries. It is about 1.33 times as large as Maryland in the United States (US).

Guinea-Bissau is a low-lying country. The broad coastal plains are swampy and many of the flat islands in the Bijagós Archipelago and elsewhere are also waterlogged. Geologists believe that the coast was submerged in recent geological times, cutting off the islands from the mainland and creating drowned river valleys (called rias) along the coast.

The highest land, reaching a height of about 800 ft (240 m), is in the southeast. The ridges and hills found here are an extension of the Futa Djallon plateau in Guinea. The chief rivers are the Cacheu in the north, the Geba in the center, and the Corubal in the south.

The coast is hot and rainy, but inland it is drier. The dry season is from November until April. Mangrove swamps line parts of the coasts and the islands, with rainforests flourishing on the coastal plain. Inland, the forests merge into tropical savanna, with more-open grassland on higher ground.

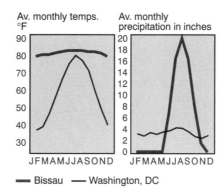

Av. monthly temps. °F

Av. monthly precipitation in inches

JFMAMJJASOND　　JFMAMJJASOND

— Bissau　— Washington, DC

ECONOMY

Chief farm products: Cashews, cassava, corn, lumber, millet, palm products, plantains, rice, sorghum, sugar cane, sweet potatoes
Chief mineral resources: Undeveloped reserves of bauxite (aluminum ore) and phosphate
Chief industrial products: Beverages, clothing, processed food
Employment:

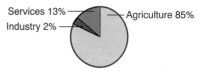

Services 13% — Agriculture 85%
Industry 2%

In the US, agriculture employs 3% of the work force, industry 25%, and services 72%
Exports: Cashews, peanuts, frozen fish
Per capita income: $240 (as compared with $25,860 in the US)

PEOPLE

Population: 1,050,000 (as compared with the US population of 260,529,000)
Major ethnic groups: Balante, Fulani, Malinke, Mandyako, Pepel
Religions: African religions (54%), Islam (38%), Christianity (8%)

SOCIAL FACTS

● The average life expectancy at birth is 38 years, as compared with 76 years in the US
● Only 22% of the people live in urban areas, as compared with about 76% in the US
● Slaves were taken from Guinea-Bissau to Cape Verde and Brazil

● Guinea-Bissau was formerly called Portuguese Guinea
● Guinean and Cape Verdean people collaborated in opposing Portuguese rule, but a movement to unite the two countries failed in 1977
● The lingua franca Crioulo contains African and Portuguese words

KEY POINTS IN RECENT HISTORY

1951 Portuguese Guinea becomes an overseas province of Portugal
1956 Nationalists form the Partido Africano da Independência do Guiné e Cabo Verde (PAIGC); it demands freedom for Cape Verde and Guinea-Bissau

1963 The war for independence begins
1973 By now, nationalists control 75% of the country
1974 Guinea-Bissau wins independence (September 10) with Luiz Cabral as president
1980 Major João Bernardo Vieira seizes power from Cabral

1984 A new constitution creates a new National People's Assembly and a Council of State
1991 The law making the PAIGC the sole political party is abolished
1994 Vieira wins presidential elections
1996 Guinea joins the Community of Portuguese-speaking Countries

*See **Peoples of West Africa** on the Bambara and Malinke*

© DIAGRAM

Ivory Coast

Location: West Africa, facing the Gulf of Guinea
Neighbors: Liberia, Guinea, Mali, Burkina Faso, Ghana

Official name: République de la Côte d'Ivoire
Divisions: Forty-nine departments
Capital: Yamoussoukro
Largest cities: Abidjan, Man, Bouaké, Yamoussoukro, Daloa (in order of size)

Flag: The vertical orange stripe, left, represents the savanna country in northern Ivory Coast; the white stripe, center, represents peace and unity; and the green stripe, right, represents the forests in the south

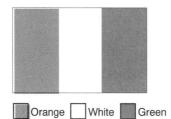

☐ Orange ☐ White ☐ Green

National anthem: "L'Abidjanaise ("Hail, o land of hope")
Major languages: French (official), Akan, Dyula
Currency: CFA franc = 100 cents

Stamp marking the 1963 Conference of African Heads of State

GEOGRAPHY

With an area of 124,504 square miles (322,464 sq. km), Ivory Coast is Africa's twenty-seventh largest country. It is a little larger than New Mexico in the United States (US).

The country's coastline, 315 miles (507 km) long, changes in character from east to west. In the east, sand bars hold back lagoons, while the west has a rocky, cliff-lined coast. Abidjan, the chief port, stands on a lagoon in the east. A canal links the lagoon to the sea.

The narrow coastal plain, up to 40 miles (64 km) wide, gives way to plateaus inland. The plateaus rise in the west to the country's highest point, Mount Nimba, which reaches 5,748 ft (1,752 m). The principal rivers are the Bandama, which is 300 miles (480 km) long; the Cavally, which forms part of the border with Liberia; the Komoé; and the Sassandra.

The south is hot throughout the year, with two main rainy seasons – from May until July and in October and November. The north is much drier, with one rainy season and a marked dry season. A rainforest once covered much of the south, but farmers have cut down large areas of it. Tropical savanna covers most of the north.

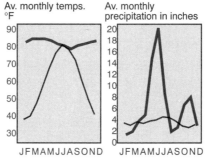

Av. monthly temps. °F — Av. monthly precipitation in inches

JFMAMJJASOND   JFMAMJJASOND

—Abidjan —Washington, DC

ECONOMY

Chief farm products: Cassava, coffee, corn, cotton, livestock, lumber, palm products, rice, sugar cane, yams
Chief mineral resources: Diamonds, oil, gold
Chief industrial products: Beverages, cement, oil products, processed food, textiles, wood products
Employment:

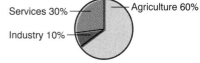

Services 30% — Agriculture 60%
Industry 10%

In the US, agriculture employs 3% of the work force, industry 25%, services 72%
Exports: Cocoa, oil products, wood and wood products, coffee, cotton
Per capita income: $610 (as compared with $25,860 in the US)

PEOPLE

Population: 13,780,000 (as compared with the US population of 260,529,000)
Major ethnic groups: Akan, Voltaic, Malinke, Kru, Southern Mande
Religions: Islam (39%), Christianity (27%), African religions (17%)

SOCIAL FACTS

● The average life expectancy at birth is 56 years, as compared with 76 years in the US
● Only 43% of the people live in urban areas, as compared with about 76% in the US
● More than 60 languages and dialects are spoken in Ivory Coast

● Ivory was a major export from the 1400s until the 1800s
● Abidjan is one of the world's most expensive cities
● The new capital, Yamoussoukro, contains the world's largest church: the Basilica of Our Lady of Peace
● Ivory Coast is also known as Côte d'Ivoire

KEY POINTS IN RECENT HISTORY

1960 Ivory Coast becomes independent from France (August 7) Félix Houphouët-Boigny becomes the first president .
1980 An attempted coup fails
1983 Parliament agrees to build a new

capital at Yamoussoukro, Houphouët-Boigny's birthplace
1990 Pope John Paul II dedicates Yamoussoukro's huge new basilica
1990 The government introduces a multiparty constitution
1990 The first multiparty elections are

held; Houphouët-Boigny is reelected for the seventh time
1993 Houphouët-Boigny dies; his successor is Henri Konan-Bédie
1994 CFA franc is devalued by 50%
1995 Konan-Bédie's party wins a majority in the National Assembly

*See **Peoples of West Africa** on the Asante, Malinke, and Mossi*

Kenya

Location: East Africa, facing the Indian Ocean
Neighbors: Ethiopia, Somalia, Tanzania, Uganda, Sudan

Official name: Republic of Kenya
Divisions: Seven provinces and Nairobi district
Capital: Nairobi
Largest cities: Nairobi, Mombasa, Kisumu, Nakuru, Machakos, Meru, Eldoret (in order of size)

Flag: The flag has three stripes of black, red (edged with white), and green. In the center is a Maasai warrior's shield and crossed spears. The shield and spears represent the defense of freedom

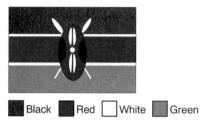

| ■ Black | ■ Red | □ White | ■ Green |

National anthem: "Ee Mungu nguvu yetu" ("Oh God of all Creation")
Major languages: Swahili (official), English, Kikuyu, Maa
Currency: Shilling = 100 cents

Stamp marking Kenyatta Day, 1978

GEOGRAPHY

With an area of 224,961 square miles (582,647 sq. km), Kenya is Africa's twenty-second largest country. It is about twice as big as Arizona in the United States (US).

Behind the narrow coastal plain, the land rises in a series of plateaus to a highland region in the southwest. The highlands slope down to Lake Victoria, Kenya's largest lake, which Kenya shares with Tanzania and Uganda. Rising above the plateau is Kenya's highest peak, the extinct volcano Mount Kenya, at 17,057 ft (5,199 m) above sea level.

An arm of the steep-sided Great Rift Valley cuts across Kenya from north to south. This huge trough contains several lakes, including Naivasha and Nakuru in the south and Turkana in the north. The Athi and Tana, Kenya's two main rivers, drain into the Indian Ocean.

Kenya lies on the equator and the coast is hot and humid. The generally dry plateaus, covered mainly by tropical savanna, are cooler. The weather is especially pleasant in the rainier southwest highlands, where some forests grow. Only 15% of Kenya gets a reliable annual rainfall of 30 in. (76 cm). The north is mainly desert.

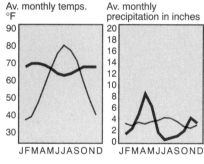

Av. monthly temps. °F
Av. monthly precipitation in inches
— Nairobi — Washington, DC

ECONOMY

Chief farm products: Bananas, beef, coffee, corn, pineapples, sisal, sugar cane, tea, wheat
Chief mineral resources: Soda ash, fluorspar
Chief industrial products: Cement, chemicals, petroleum products, processed food, textiles, vehicles
Employment:

Services 13%
Industry 7%
Agriculture 80%

In the US, agriculture employs 3% of the work force, industry 25%, services 72%
Exports: Tea, coffee, fruits and vegetables, petroleum products
Per capita income: $250 (as compared with $25,860 in the US)

PEOPLE

Population: 26,000,000 (about a tenth of the US population of 260,529,000)
Major ethnic groups: Kikuyu, Luhya, Luo, Kamba, Kalenjin
Religions: Christianity (73%), African religions (19%), Islam (6%)

SOCIAL FACTS

● The average life expectancy at birth is 59 years, as compared with 76 years in the US
● Only 27% of the people live in urban areas, as compared with about 76% in the US
● 75% of Kenyans live in the southwestern highland region

● 51% of Kenyans are under 15 years of age; in the US, only about 22% are under 15 years of age
● Fossils of some of the earliest of human ancestors have been found near Lake Turkana
● Many tourists visit Kenya to see its magnificent wildlife

KEY POINTS IN RECENT HISTORY

1920 Kenya becomes a British colony
1952 Mau Mau rebellion (1952–6) begins and the Kikuyu leader Jomo Kenyatta is convicted of being its leader
1963 Kenya becomes independent (December 12)

1964 Kenya becomes a republic and Kenyatta becomes president
1978 Kenyatta dies and is succeeded by Daniel arap Moi
1982 Kenya becomes a one-party state, ruled by the Kenya African National Union (KANU)

1991 Under pressure from aid donors, the government legalizes opposition parties
1992 Elections are held; Moi reelected; KANU remains the majority party, but accusations of autocratic rule continue

*See **Peoples of East Africa** on the East African Asians, Kikuyu, Maasai, Oromo, Somalis, and Swahili*

© DIAGRAM

Lesotho

Location:
Landlocked country in Southern Africa
Neighbors: Lesotho is completely surrounded by South Africa

Official name: Kingdom of Lesotho
Divisions: Eleven districts
Capital: Maseru
Largest cities: Maseru, Maputsoe, Teyateyaneng, Mafeteng, Butha-buthe (in order of size)

Flag: The white, blue, and green flag of Lesotho was adopted in 1987. The white area occupying the upper diagonal half of the flag contains a brown emblem that represents a Basotho shield, a spear, and a club.

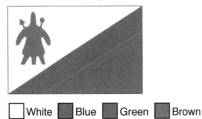

☐ White ■ Blue ■ Green ■ Brown

National anthem: "Lesotho, land of our fathers"
Major languages: Sesotho, English (both official), Zulu, Xhosa
Currency: Loti = 100 lisente

1966 stamp marking the independence of the Kingdom of Lesotho

GEOGRAPHY

With an area of 11,720 square miles (30,355 sq. km), Lesotho is Africa's twelfth smallest country. It is a little larger in area than Maryland in the United States (US).

Lesotho is a mountainous country, where all the land is above 3,300 ft (1,000 m). The highest point, Thabana Ntlenyana, reaches 11,424 ft (3,482 m) in the northeast. It is the highest point in Southern Africa. The mountains form part of the Drakensberg range, which is made up of the eroded southeast corner of the high plateau that makes up most of Southern Africa.

The Orange River rises in the northeast and flows across southern Lesotho, through South Africa, and into the Atlantic Ocean. The main centers of population are in the lower Orange River Valley and on the western lowlands, where the capital, Maseru, is located.

The climate is greatly influenced by the altitude. The mountains are snow-capped in winter and temperatures sometimes fall below freezing on the western lowlands. Summers are warm, and the average rainfall is around 28 in. (71 cm) a year. Mountain grassland covers most of Lesotho, with trees, such as willows, in sheltered areas.

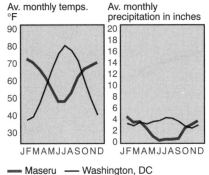

Av. monthly temps. °F

Av. monthly precipitation in inches

JFMAMJJASOND   JFMAMJJASOND

— Maseru — Washington, DC

ECONOMY

Chief farm products: Beans, cattle, corn, hides and skins, mohair, sorghum, wool, wheat
Chief mineral resources: Diamonds, sand and gravel
Chief industrial products: Beverages, chemicals, clothing, leather goods, processed food, textiles,
Employment:

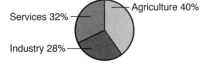

Services 32%
Agriculture 40%
Industry 28%

In the US, agriculture employs 3% of the work force, industry 25%, and services 72%
Exports: Manufactured goods, food and live animals, raw materials
Per capita income: $720 (as compared with $25,860 in the US)

PEOPLE

Population: 1,899,000 (as compared with the US population of 260,529,000)
Major ethnic groups: Sotho, Zulu
Religions: Christianity (about 93%), African religions (about 7%)

SOCIAL FACTS

● The average life expectancy at birth is 61 years, as compared with 76 years in the US
● Only 22% of the people live in urban areas, as compared with about 76% in the US
● About 60% of working-age men are employed in South Africa's mines

● Most Sotho people live in villages; the center of the village is the kgotla (meeting place or court)
● Because Lesotho is so mountainous, less than 12% of the land is suitable for farming
● Many houses are painted in bright colors and striking designs

KEY POINTS IN RECENT HISTORY

1966 Basutoland becomes independent from Britain (October 4) as the Kingdom of Lesotho
1979 Opposition parties are banned, their leaders are arrested, and the constitution is suspended

1986 Military leaders overthrow the civilian government
1990 King Moshoeshoe II is removed from office and his son, Letsie III, is installed as monarch
1993 Multiparty elections held, returning Lesotho to civilian rule

1995 Moshoeshoe II is restored as King of Lesotho
1996 Moshoeshoe II is killed in a car crash and Letsie III returns to the throne

*See **Peoples of Southern Africa** on the Sotho, Zulu, and Xhosa*

Liberia

Location: West Africa, facing the Atlantic Ocean
Neighbors: Sierra Leone, Guinea, Ivory Coast

Official name: Republic of Liberia
Divisions: Thirteen counties
Capital: Monrovia
Largest cities: Monrovia, Buchanan, Yekepa, Tubmanburg (in order of size)

Flag: The flag was inspired by the US Stars and Stripes. The eleven red and white stripes represent the eleven men who signed Liberia's Declaration of Independence in 1847. The white star is set on a blue field

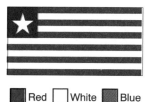

■ Red   □ White   ■ Blue

National anthem: "All hail, Liberia, hail"
Major languages: English (official), Mende, Kwa
Currency: Liberian dollar = 100 cents

1952 stamp honoring the United Nations (UN)

GEOGRAPHY

With an area of 42,990 square miles (111,344 sq. km), Liberia is one of Africa's smaller countries. It is a little larger in area than Ohio in the United States (US).

Behind the coastline, which is 350 miles (560 km) long, lies a coastal plain between 15 and 25 miles (24–40 km) wide. Inland, the ground rises to low hills and plateaus. The highest point is Mount Nimba, which reaches a height of 5,748 ft (1,752 m) on Liberia's border with Ivory Coast and Guinea.

The chief rivers are the Cavally, which forms part of the border with Ivory Coast, and the Mano and Morro rivers that form the border with Sierra Leone. The St. Paul River reaches the sea near Monrovia. A hydroelectric power station at rapids on the St. Paul River is a major source of electricity for Liberia.

Liberia has a tropical climate, with high temperatures and the heavy rainfall. The coast has a relatively dry season from December until March. The rainfall diminishes inland, where the dry season is longer. Rainforests cover about 40% of the land and there is tropical savanna in the drier interior.

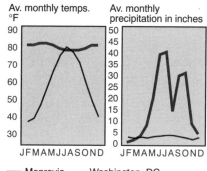

Av. monthly temps. °F

Av. monthly precipitation in inches

JFMAMJJASOND   JFMAMJJASOND

— Monrovia   — Washington, DC

ECONOMY

Chief farm products: Bananas, cassava, cocoa, coffee, fruits, livestock, palm products, rice, rubber, sugar cane, sweet potatoes
Chief mineral resources: Iron ore, diamonds, gold
Chief industrial products: Beverages, cement, palm oil
Employment:

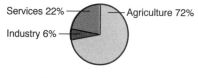

Services 22%   Agriculture 72%
Industry 6%

In the US, agriculture employs 3% of the work force, industry 25%, and services 72%
Exports: Iron ore, rubber, wood, diamonds, gold, coffee
Per capita income: $675 (as compared with $25,860 in the US)

PEOPLE

Population: 2,719,000 (as compared with the US population of 260,529,000)
Major ethnic groups: Kpelle, Bassa, Grebo, Gio, Kru, Mano
Religions: Christianity (68%), Islam (14%), African religions (18%)

SOCIAL FACTS

● The average life expectancy at birth is 57 years, as compared with 76 years in the US
● Only 44% of the people live in urban areas, as compared with about 76% in the US
● Liberia's name comes from the Latin word "liber," meaning "free"

● Monrovia was founded in 1822 by the American Colonization Society
● Descendants of the original freed slaves who settled in Monrovia are called Americo-Liberians
● Americo-Liberians dominated the government until 1980, when people from local ethnic groups seized power

KEY POINTS IN RECENT HISTORY

1926 The American Firestone Company sets up huge rubber plantations in Liberia
1944 William Tubman, an Americo-Liberian, becomes president
1971 William Tolbert becomes

president when Tubman dies
1979 People demonstrate against price rises
1980 President Tolbert is assassinated; an army sergeant, Samuel Doe, becomes president
1989 Civil war breaks out between

various ethnic groups
1990 Doe is assassinated; rival leaders declare themselves president
1995 A cease-fire holds after the heads of warring factions join in a transitional government
1996 Fighting recurs in Monrovia

*See **Peoples of West Africa** on the Mende*

© DIAGRAM

Libya

Location: North Africa, facing the Mediterranean Sea
Neighbors: Egypt, Chad, Niger, Algeria, Tunisia

Official name: Great Socialist People's Libyan Arab Jamahiriya
Divisions: About 1,500 communes
Capital: Tripoli
Largest cities: Tripoli, Benghazi, Misratah, Zawiyah (in order of size)

Flag: Libya's plain green flag, the world's simplest, symbolizes Islam and the country's commitment to creating a green revolution (based on irrigation) in agriculture. The flag was officially adopted in 1977

□ Green

National anthem: "Allahu Akbar" ("God is great")
Major languages: Arabic (official), Berber
Currency: Dinar = 100 dirhams

1978 Stamp marking International Antiapartheid Year

GEOGRAPHY

With an area of 679,180 square miles (1,759,069 sq. km), Libya is Africa's fourth largest country. It is two and a half times as large in area as Texas in the United States (US).

Desert landscapes dominate all of Libya apart from the narrow coastal regions in the northeast and northwest. The Sahara covers most of Libya and it contains huge areas of sand dunes and bare rocky mountains, which rise to Bette Peak in the south, near the Chad border. Bette Peak is Libya's highest point at 7,500 ft (2,286 m) above sea level.

Under the barren desert are huge aquifers – layers of rock saturated with water. Water from the aquifers appears at the surface at oases, and engineers have tapped many aquifers and piped water to the north. This scheme is called the "Great Man-made River Project."

The northeast and northwest coasts have hot, dry summers and mild, moist winters – the typical climate of Mediterranean lands. But most of Libya is hot desert, with an average yearly rainfall of 4 in. (10 cm) or less. Scrub and woodland grow in the coastal regions, while date palms flourish around oases in the desert.

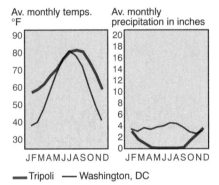

Av. monthly temps. °F
Av. monthly precipitation in inches

JFMAMJJASOND   JFMAMJJASOND

— Tripoli — Washington, DC

ECONOMY

Chief farm products: Barley, citrus fruits, dates, livestock (sheep, goats, camels, cattle), olives, onions, potatoes, tomatoes, watermelons, wheat
Chief mineral resources: Oil and natural gas
Chief industrial products: Cement, oil products, steel
Employment:

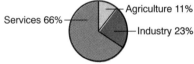

Services 66% — Agriculture 11%
Industry 23%

In the US, agriculture employs 3% of the work force, industry 25%, and services 72%
Exports: Oil and oil products
Per capita income: $8,365 (as compared with $25,860 in the US)

PEOPLE

Population: 5,225,000 (as compared with the US population of 260,529,000)
Major ethnic groups: Arab, Berber
Religions: Islam (97% of Libyans are Sunni Muslims)

SOCIAL FACTS

● The average life expectancy at birth is 63 years, as compared with 76 years in the US
● About 85% of the people live in urban areas, as compared with about 76% in the US
● The first people to settle in Libya were the Berbers

● The Arabic language was introduced into Libya in the 600s
● Tripoli was once a base for Barbary pirates, or corsairs; the US fought a war against the corsairs in the early 1800s
● Libya is known for its active support of radical movements around the world

KEY POINTS IN RECENT HISTORY

1911 Italy conquers northern Libya
1942 Britain and France take over Libya during World War II
1951 Libya becomes an independent kingdom (December 24), formed from three provinces – Cyrenaica, Fezzan, and Tripolitania

1969 Army officers declare Libya to be a republic; Col. Muammar al Qaddafi becomes head of the government
1977 Libya becomes a one-party socialist jamahiriya, or "state of the masses" – every adult is supposed to have a share in policy-making

1986 The United States bombs Libya as a reprisal for alleged Libyan involvement in terrorist activities
1994 The International Court of Justice rejects Libya's claims to the Aozou Strip in Chad; Libya becomes increasingly isolated internationally

*See **Peoples of North Africa** on the Arabs, Berbers, and Tuareg*

Madagascar

Location: Island country off the southeast coast of Southern Africa
Nearest mainland: Mozambique

Official name: Democratic Republic of Madagascar
Divisions: Six provinces
Capital: Antananarivo
Largest cities: Antananarivo, Toamasina, Antsirabe, Mahajanga, Fianarantsoa (in order of size)

Flag: The white of the vertical stripe, and the red and green of the horizontal stripes, are colors used on historic flags of Southeast Asia, reflecting the country's ancient ties with that region

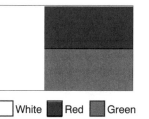

☐ White ■ Red ■ Green

National anthem: "Ry tanindrazanay malalaô" ("O our beloved fatherland")
Major languages: Malagasy (official), French
Currency: Malagasy franc = 100 centimes

1962 stamp marking the UNESCO Conference on Higher Education in Africa

GEOGRAPHY

With an area of 226,658 square miles (587,042 sq. km), Madagascar is Africa's twentieth largest country. It is about 1.4 times larger than California in the United States (US).

Madagascar consists of one large island and many tiny ones dotted around it. The length of the coastline of the main island is about 2,600 miles (4,180 km). The east coast is narrow and the land rises steeply to the central highlands, which reach heights of about 2,000 to 4,000 ft (600–1,200 m) above sea level, but several mountains tower above this level. The highest point is Maromokotro, in the north, which reaches 9,436 ft (2,876 m).

Western Madagascar consists of low plateaus and broad plains. The longest rivers, including the Mangoky and Onilahy, flow across the region into the Mozambique Channel, which separates Madagascar from Mozambique.

The lowlands are hot and wet except in the south, where deserts occur. In the highlands, the altitude moderates temperatures. Grassland and scrub occur in the south. Rainforest once covered much of central Madagascar, but deforestation has meant that tropical savanna and open grassland are now the main vegetation types.

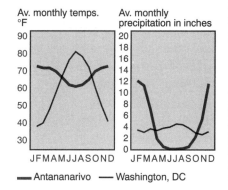

Av. monthly temps. °F
Av. monthly precipitation in inches

JFMAMJJASOND   JFMAMJJASOND

— Antananarivo   — Washington, DC

ECONOMY

Chief farm products: Bananas, cassava, cloves, coffee, corn, cotton, fruits, livestock, rice, sweet potatoes, taro (an edible tuber), vanilla
Chief mineral resources: Chromite (chromium ore), salt, mica
Chief industrial products: Beverages, cement, palm oil, processed food
Employment:

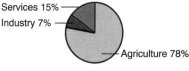

Services 15%
Industry 7%
Agriculture 78%

In the US, agriculture employs 3% of the work force, industry 25%, and services 72%
Exports: Vanilla, shrimp, coffee, cloves and clove oil, cotton fabrics
Per capita income: $200 (as compared with $25,860 in the US)

PEOPLE
Population: 13,100,000 (as compared with the US population of 260,529,000)
Major ethnic groups: Madagascans, including Merina and Betsimisaraka
Religions: Christianity (51%), African religions (47%), Islam (2%)

SOCIAL FACTS
● The average life expectancy at birth is 52 years, as compared with 76 years in the US.
● Only 26% of the people live in urban areas, as compared with about 76% in the US
● Madagascar is the world's fourth largest island

● Madagascans are of mixed African and Southeast Asian descent
● The official language, Malagasy, resembles Malay and Indonesian, with Arabic, Bantu, and European words
● Deforestation has caused widespread soil erosion
● Cyclones (tropical storms) frequently hit Madagascar

KEY POINTS IN RECENT HISTORY
1960 Madagascar becomes independent from France (June 26) as the Malagasy Republic; Philibert Tsiranana becomes president
1972 Army officers seize power; Gabriel Ramanantsoa becomes president

1975 The country's name is changed from Malagasy Republic to the Republic of Madagascar; Didier Ratsiraka becomes leader of the country's ruling Supreme Revolutionary Council
1982 A fourth attempted coup against Ratsiraka fails

1991 After much unrest, an interim government is formed to introduce a new multiparty constitution
1993 Professor Albert Zafy defeats Ratsiraka in presidential elections

*See **Peoples of Southern Africa** on Madagascans*

© DIAGRAM

Malawi

Location:
Landlocked country in East Africa
Neighbors: Tanzania, Mozambique, Zambia

Official name: Republic of Malawi
Divisions: Three regions and twenty-four districts
Capital: Lilongwe
Largest cities: Blantyre, Lilongwe, Mzuzu, Zomba (in order of size)

Flag: A rising Sun on the top black stripe, added in 1964 when Malawi became independent, represents the beginning of a new era for the country. The other stripes are red, center, and green, bottom

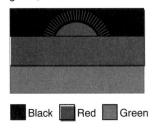

■ Black ■ Red ■ Green

National anthem: "O God bless our land of Malawi"
Major languages: Chichewa and English (both official)
Currency: Kwacha = 100 tambala

Stamp depicting Malawi's first coinage, 1964

GEOGRAPHY

With an area of 45,747 square miles (118,484 sq. km), Malawi is one of Africa's smaller countries. It is a little larger in area than Tennessee in the United States (US).

Malawi includes part of Lake Malawi, which is called Nyasa in neighboring Tanzania and Niassa in Mozambique. This lake, one of the world's deepest at more than 2,300 ft (700 m), occupies part of the floor of the Great Rift Valley and covers a total area of about 11,000 square miles (28,500 sq. km). Malawi's chief river, the Shire, flows south from Lake Malawi to the Zambezi River.

West of the deep Great Rift Valley, the land rises to plateaus at about 2,500 to 4,000 ft (760–1,200 m) above sea level. The land rises to more than 8,000 ft (2,400 m) in the north, but the country's highest peak, Mulanje, which reaches 9,843 ft (3,000 m), is in the southeast.

The Great Rift Valley is hot and humid, but the highlands have a pleasant, much cooler climate. The average annual rainfall ranges from around 70 in. (178 cm) in the highlands to 30 in. (76 cm) in the lowlands. Open grassland and tropical savanna cover most of Malawi, with woodland in river valleys and other wet areas.

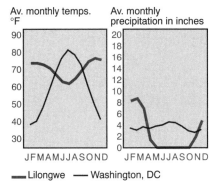

Av. monthly temps. °F

Av. monthly precipitation in inches

— Lilongwe — Washington, DC

ECONOMY

Chief farm products: Bananas, cassava, corn, cotton, livestock, peanuts, potatoes, sorghum, sugar cane, tea, tobacco
Chief mineral resources: Limestone and marble
Chief industrial products: Beverages, cement, chemicals, processed food, textiles, tobacco
Employment:

Industry 5% — Services 8% — Agriculture 87%

In the US, agriculture employs 3% of the work force, industry 25%, and services 72%
Exports: Tobacco, tea, sugar, cotton
Per capita income: $170 (as compared with $25,860 in the US)

PEOPLE

Population: 9,500,000 (as compared with the US population of 260,529,000)
Major ethnic groups: Maravi (including Nyanja, Chewa, Tonga)
Religions: Christianity (64%), African religions (19%), Islam (16%)

SOCIAL FACTS

● The average life expectancy at birth is 44 years, as compared with 76 years in the US
● Only 13% of the people live in urban areas, as compared with about 76% in the US
● Malawi has one of Africa's highest rates of HIV infection

● Malawi is heavily dependent on foreign aid; most aid was suspended in the early 1990s because of the country's poor human rights record
● Malawi was a center of the slave trade in the early 1800s
● Tourism is an expanding industry in Malawi

KEY POINTS IN RECENT HISTORY

1953 Britain makes Nyasaland part of the Central African Federation (CAF) despite African protests against white-minority domination
1963 CAF is dissolved and Nyasaland prepares for independence

1964 Nyasaland becomes independent as Malawi (July 6)
1966 Malawi becomes a republic; the prime minister, Dr Hastings Kamuzu Banda, becomes the first president
1971 Banda becomes president-for-life and Malawi adopts a one-party system

1993 A multiparty system is restored
1994 Bakili Muluzi defeats Banda in presidential elections
1995 Banda is charged with the murder of four of his former cabinet ministers. He is later acquitted

Mali

Location: Landlocked country in West Africa

Neighbors: Algeria, Niger, Burkina Faso, Ivory Coast, Guinea, Senegal, Mauritania

Official name: Republic of Mali
Divisions: Eight regions
Capital: Bamako
Largest cities: Bamako, Ségou, Mopti, Sikasso, Gao (in order of size)

Flag: The colors of the three vertical stripes – green, yellow, and red – are those of the flag of Ethiopia, Africa's oldest independent nation. As on several other African flags, the colors symbolize African unity

Green | Yellow | Red

National anthem: "A ton appel, Mali" ("At your call, Mali")
Major languages: French (official), Manding, Fulfulde, Songhay
Currency: CFA franc = 100 cents

1961 stamp marking Mali's independence and its admission into the United Nations (UN)

GEOGRAPHY

With an area of 478,821 square miles (1,240,142 sq. km), Mali is Africa's eighth largest country. It is 1.8 times larger in area than Texas in the United States (US).

Mali is a largely flat country. The main highland region is the Adrar des Ifôghas in the northeast, but the highest point is Hombori Tondo, which reaches 3,798 ft (1,158 m) and is in the south, near the Burkina Faso border.

The chief river is the Niger, which makes a large loop, called the Niger Bend, through south-central Mali. In the Niger Bend, the river divides into several channels. The region also contains numerous small lakes. Niger's other main river is the Senegal, in the west. The south, with its rivers providing water for irrigation, contrasts with the desert landscapes and empty wadis (dry watercourses) in the north.

Mali has a hot tropical climate. The south has an average annual rainfall of 40 in. (102 cm) or more, with the rainy season from May until October, but the north has 4 in. (10 cm) or less. The north lacks plants except around oases. Central Mali belongs to a semidesert zone called the Sahel, and tropical savanna occurs in the south.

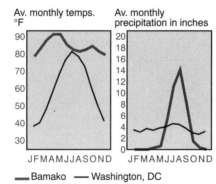

Av. monthly temps. °F | Av. monthly precipitation in inches

JFMAMJJASOND | JFMAMJJASOND

— Bamako — Washington, DC

ECONOMY

Chief farm products: Cassava, corn, cotton, livestock, millet, peanuts, rice, sorghum, sugar cane, sweet potatoes, yams
Chief mineral resources: Limestone, phosphates, gold, diamonds
Chief industrial products: Beverages, cement, processed food, textiles
Employment:

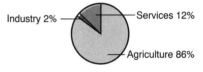

Industry 2% — Services 12%
Agriculture 86%

In the US, agriculture employs 3% of the work force, industry 25%, and services 72%
Exports: Cotton and cotton products, live animals, gold, diamonds
Per capita income: $250 (as compared with $25,860 in the US)

PEOPLE

Population: 10,462,000 (as compared with the US population of 260,529,000)
Major ethnic groups: Bambara, Malinke, Dyula, Fulani, Dogon
Religions: Islam (90%), African religions (9%), Christianity (1%)

SOCIAL FACTS

● The average life expectancy at birth is 40 years, as compared with 76 years in the US
● Only 26% of the people live in urban areas, as compared with about 76% in the US
● Only about 2% of the land in Mali is cultivated

● Mali was part of three major medieval African civilizations: the Empire of Ghana, Empire of Mali, and Songhay
● Timbuktu (modern Tombouctou) was a great Islamic center of learning in the 1300s
● Prolonged and severe droughts in the Sahel in the 1970s and 1980s caused great suffering

KEY POINTS IN RECENT HISTORY

1959 The French colony of Soudan unites with Senegal to form the Federation of Mali
1960 The Federation breaks up and Soudan becomes the independent Republic of Mali (June 20)

1968 A military coup sweeps Modibo Keita, Mali's first president, from power; he is succeeded by Lt. Moussa Traoré
1974 Mali becomes a one-party state
1991 A coup brings Lt.-Col. Amadou Toumani Touré to power
1992 Multiparty elections are held and

Alpha Oumar Konaré becomes president
1993 A coup to restore Traoré to power is unsuccessful
1994 CFA franc, which is linked to the French franc, is devalued by 50%. This causes widespread economic hardship

*See **Peoples of West Africa** on the on the Bambara, Dogon, Fulani, and Malinke*

© DIAGRAM

Mauritania

Location: West Africa, facing the Atlantic Ocean
Neighbors: Western Sahara, Algeria, Mali, Senegal

Official name: Islamic Republic of Mauritania
Divisions: Twelve regions and the capital district
Capital: Nouakchott
Largest cities: Nouakchott, Nouadhibou, Kaédi, Kiffa (in order of size)

Flag: The green color of the flag and the yellow star and crescent are symbols of Islam, the country's official religion. The flag was officially adopted in 1959, one year before the country became independent

| Green | Yellow |

National anthem: The national anthem has no words
Major languages: Arabic (official), Soninke, Wolof
Currency: Ouguiya = 5 khoums

1976 stamp celebrating the reunification of Mauritania with southern Western Sahara

GEOGRAPHY
With an area of 395,955 square miles (1,025,519 sq. km), Mauritania is Africa's eleventh largest country. It is about 1.5 times larger in area than Texas in the United States (US).

Mauritania is a mainly low-lying country, with flat coastal plains and rocky plateaus at about 600 to 900 ft (200–300 m) above sea level. A few isolated peaks rise above the plateaus. These include Mauritania's highest point, Kediet Ijill, which is a huge mass of hematite (an iron ore) and reaches 3,002 ft (915 m).

Northern Mauritania is part of the Sahara and is thinly populated. Its features include drifting sand dunes, bare rocky areas, and wadis (dry watercourses). The chief river is the Senegal, which forms the southeast border with Senegal. Most Mauritanians live in the south of the country.

Mauritania has a hot, dry climate, though temperatures often fall from about 100 °F (38 °C) in the afternoon to 45 °F (7 °C) at night. The north is almost rainless, but the south has 12 to 15 in. (30–38 cm) of rain a year. The desert in the north merges into the semidesert Sahel, with tropical savanna in the far south of the country.

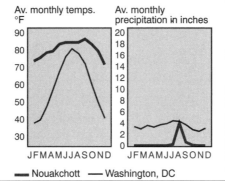

Av. monthly temps. °F

Av. monthly precipitation in inches

JFMAMJJASOND   JFMAMJJASOND

━ Nouakchott   ━ Washington, DC

ECONOMY
Chief farm products: Beans, corn, dates, gum arabic, livestock (cattle, sheep, goats), millet, peanuts, pulses, rice, sorghum, sweet potatoes
Chief mineral resources: Iron ore, gypsum (calcium sulfate)
Chief industrial products: Dairy products, meat, hides and skins
Employment:

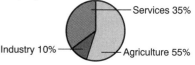

Services 35%
Industry 10%
Agriculture 55%

In the US, agriculture employs 3% of the work force, industry 25%, and services 72%
Exports: Iron ore, fish (both ocean and freshwater)
Per capita income: $480 (as compared with $25,860 in the US)

PEOPLE
Population: 2,217,000 (as compared with the US population of 260,529,000)
Major ethnic groups: Moors, Black Africans
Religions: Islam (99.4%), Christianity (0.4%)

SOCIAL FACTS
● The average life expectancy at birth is 51 years, as compared with 76 years in the US
● Only 52% of the people live in urban areas, as compared with about 76% in the US
● Mauritania is a very sparsely populated country

● Mauritanian Moors include White Moors or Bidanis (who are of Arab-Berber origin) and Black Moors or Sudanis (of Black African origin)
● Historically, White Moors were divided into two castes: warriors and marabouts (scholars or priests)
● Droughts in the 1970s and 1980s caused great hardship

KEY POINTS IN RECENT HISTORY
1903 France makes Mauritania a protectorate (colony)
1960 Mauritania becomes independent (November 28) with Moktar Ould Daddah as president
1965 Mauritania is a one-party state

1976 Mauritania occupies the southern third of Western (formerly Spanish) Sahara and Morocco takes the north; Western Saharan guerrillas launch a war for independence
1978 Military leaders overthrow President Ould Daddah

1979 Mauritania gives up its claims to Western Sahara; Morocco takes the entire territory
1991 Mauritania adopts a democratic multiparty constitution
1992 The people elect Maawiya Ould Sid' Ahmad Taya as president

*See **Peoples of West Africa** on the Moors*

Mauritius

Location: Island country in the Indian Ocean, to the east of Southern Africa
Nearest country: Madagascar

Official name: Republic of Mauritius
Divisions: The islands of Mauritius, Rodrigues, and some smaller islands
Capital: Port Louis
Largest cities: Port Louis, Beau Bassin-Rose Hill (in order of size)

Flag: The four horizontal bands, from top to bottom, are red, for the struggle for independence; blue, for the ocean; yellow, for sunlight and the bright future; and green, for agriculture and the country's lush vegetation

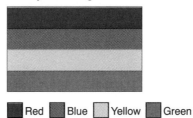

■ Red ■ Blue □ Yellow ■ Green

National anthem: "Glory to thee, motherland"
Major languages: English (official), Creole, French
Currency: Mauritian rupee = 100 cents

1971 stamp commemorating the twenty-fifth anniversary of Plaisance Airport

GEOGRAPHY

With an area of 788 square miles (2,041 sq. km), Mauritius is Africa's third smallest country. It is about two-thirds the size of Rhode Island in the United States (US).

Mauritius consists of one large island, Mauritius, which covers 720 square miles (1,865 sq. km). Rodrigues, with an area of 40 square miles (104 sq. km), lies about 340 miles (550 km) to the east. The two small islands of Agalega lie 580 miles (930 km) to the north, and the Cargados Carajos Shoals are about 250 miles (400 km) to the north.

Mauritius, a volcanic island, rises to a central plateau ringed by some higher areas. The highest point, the Piton de la Petite Rivière-Noire, reaches 2,711 ft (826 m). Of the rivers flowing off the plateau, the largest are the Grand River South East, 25 miles (40 km) long, and the Grand River North West.

The climate is tropical, though the altitude moderates temperatures. The hottest part of the year is from December until April. The rainfall ranges from about 200 in. (508 cm) a year in the north to about 35 in. (89 cm) in the southwest. Mauritius is densely populated and most of its forest has been cleared to make way for farms.

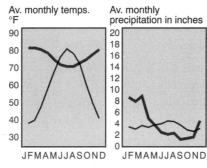

Av. monthly temps. °F
Av. monthly precipitation in inches

JFMAMJJASOND   JFMAMJJASOND

— Port Louis   — Washington, DC

ECONOMY

Chief farm products: Bananas, corn, livestock, peanuts, pineapples potatoes, sugar cane, tea, tobacco, vegetables
Chief mineral resources: Sand, salt
Chief industrial products: Beverages, sugar and molasses, tea
Employment:

Services 40%
Agriculture 17%
Industry 43%

In the US, agriculture employs 3% of the work force, industry 25%, and services 72%
Exports: Clothing and textiles, sugar, yarns, diamonds and synthetic gemstones
Per capita income: $3,150 (as compared with $25,860 in the US)

PEOPLE

Population: 1,111,000 (as compared with the US population of 260,529,000)
Major ethnic groups: Indo-Pakistanis, Creoles, Chinese
Religions: Hinduism (50%), Christianity (32%), Islam (16%)

SOCIAL FACTS

● The average life expectancy at birth is 70 years, as compared with 76 years in the US
● Only 41% of the people live in urban areas, as compared with about 76% in the US
● Mauritius was colonized first by France and then by Britain

● Mauritius claims the island of Diego Garcia in the British Indian Ocean Territory
● The population increased quickly after the eradication of malaria
● Mauritius is a tax haven: from 1992 through 1995, the number of offshore (mainly Indian) registered companies rose from ten to more than 2,500

KEY POINTS IN RECENT HISTORY

1968 Mauritius becomes independent from Britain as a constitutional monarchy (March 12), with Queen Elizabeth II as head of state; Sir Seewoosagur Ramgoolam heads the government as prime minister

1982 Elections are won by the Mouvement Militant Mauricien (MMM) and Aneerood Jugnauth becomes the prime minister
1983 Jugnauth founds a new party, the Mouvement Socialiste Mauricien (MSM), which wins the elections

1987 The MSM is returned to power
1991 The MSM wins a third election
1992 Mauritius becomes a republic on March 12; Cassam Uteem becomes the first president, while Jugnauth continues as prime minister

Morocco

Location: North Africa, facing the Mediterranean Sea and Atlantic Ocean
Neighbors: Algeria, Western Sahara

Official name: Kingdom of Morocco
Divisions: Thirty-six provinces and eight prefectures
Capital: Rabat
Largest cities: Casablanca, Rabat, Fez, Marrakech, Meknès, Kenitra (in order of size)

Flag: The flag of Morocco is a plain red color and features a green, five-pointed star at its center. This star is also a part of the country's coat of arms, which depicts the Atlas Mountains, the Sun, a crown, and two lions

☐ Green ■ Red

National anthem: "Fountain of freedom, source of light"
Major languages: Arabic (official), Berber, French, Spanish
Currency: Dirham = 100 centimes

1960 stamp marking the inauguration of the Arab League Center

GEOGRAPHY

With an area of 175,115 square miles (453,546 sq. km), Morocco is Africa's twenty-fourth largest country. It is about the same size as Washington state in the United States (US).

Most Moroccans live on the fertile coastal plains in the north and west. Mountain ranges occupy much of the interior, and the High Atlas Mountains, which run across the country from southwest to northeast, contain Morocco's highest peak, Djebel Toubkal, at 13,665 ft (4,165 m). Other ranges include the Anti Atlas range in the south, the Middle Atlas in the center, and the Rif Atlas in the north.

Most of Morocco's rivers flow from the mountains to the Atlantic Ocean or vanish in the Sahara, a region of sand, bare rock, and stony plains in the south. The Moulouya is the main river flowing into the Mediterranean.

The coastal lowlands have hot, dry summers and mild, moist winters. Uncultivated areas have typical Mediterranean scrub vegetation. The cooler, wetter mountain regions contain forests of cedar, fir, and juniper, with grasslands at higher levels. In the hot, dry Sahara, date palms grow around the scattered oases.

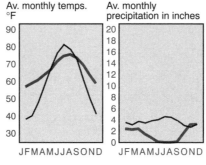

Av. monthly temps. °F

Av. monthly precipitation in inches

JFMAMJJASOND   JFMAMJJASOND

— Rabat — Washington, DC

ECONOMY

Chief farm products: Barley, citrus fruits, corn, dairy products, meat, vegetables, wheat
Chief mineral resources: Phosphates, copper, lead, zinc
Chief industrial products: Cement, chemicals, metal products, olive oil, sugar, textiles, vehicles, wine
Employment:

Agriculture 45%
Services 30%
Industry 25%

In the US, agriculture employs 3% of the work force, industry 25%, and services 72%
Exports: Phosphate rock and phosphates, food products, textiles
Per capita income: $1,140 (as compared with $25,860 in the US)

PEOPLE

Population: 26,488,000 (about a tenth of the US population of 260,529,000)
Major ethnic groups: Arab, Berber
Religions: Islam (98.7%), Christianity (1.1%)

SOCIAL FACTS

● The average life expectancy at birth is 65 years, as compared with 76 years in the US
● Only 48% of the people live in urban areas, as compared with about 76% in the US
● The Berbers live mainly in the mountain areas

● Morocco claims authority over Western (formerly Spanish) Sahara, a region to its south some 102,703 square miles (266,000 sq. km) in area, but its claim is disputed
● Morocco produces excellent leather goods, metalware, pottery, and rugs
● The University of Kairaouin, Fez, was founded in 859 and is the world's oldest

KEY POINTS IN RECENT HISTORY

1956 Morocco, divided into French and Spanish territories in 1912, gains its independence from France (March 2) and Spain (April 7), becoming a sultanate
1957 The Sultan takes the title of King Muhammad V

1961 Hassan II succeeds Muhammad V
1976 Spain withdraws from Western Sahara, which is partitioned between Morocco and Mauritania
1979 Mauritania withdraws from Western Sahara; Morocco annexes the entire territory

1982 The Sahrawi Arab Democratic Republic, proclaimed by Western Saharan opponents of Moroccan rule, joins the Organization of African Unity
1990s The United Nations attempts to hold a referendum in Western Sahara to decide the territory's future

*See **Peoples of North Africa** on the Arabs, Berbers, and Tuareg*

Mozambique

Location: Southern Africa, facing the Indian Ocean
Neighbors: South Africa, Swaziland, Zimbabwe, Zambia, Malawi, Tanzania
Official name: Republic of Mozambique
Divisions: Ten provinces and Maputo
Capital: Maputo
Largest cities: Maputo, Beira, Nampula, Nacala (in order of size)

Flag: The flag's green stripe symbolizes fertile land, the black stripe (edged with white) represents Africa, the yellow stripe stands for minerals. The red triangle contains a star with a rifle, a hoe, and a book

| | Green | | Black | | White | | Yellow | | Red |

National anthem: "Viva, viva a Frelimo" ("Long live Frelimo")
Major languages: Portuguese (official), Makua, Shona, Tsonga
Currency: Metical = 100 centavos

1980 stamp marking the independence of neighboring Zimbabwe

GEOGRAPHY

With an area of 309,496 square miles (801,592 sq. km), Mozambique is Africa's sixteenth largest country. It is nearly twice as big in area as California in the United States (US).

The coastline is bordered by coral reefs, with swamps and sand dunes along the shore. Southern Mozambique has the broadest coastal plains in Africa, and the port of Maputo has the country's only natural harbor. Plains cover nearly half of Mozambique, with hill country and plateaus inland. The mountain regions are along the western borders. The highest peak is Mount Binga, which reaches 7,992 ft (2,436 m) near the Zimbabwe border.

The chief river is the Zambezi. The Cahora Bassa Dam, which has been built across this river, has a major hydroelectric power station that exports electricity to South Africa.

The coast has a tropical climate, but inland it is cooler and less humid. Summers (November–March) are wet and hot, while winters are relatively mild and dry. The average annual rainfall varies from 20 to 50 in. (51–127 cm) Patches of rainforest occur on the plains, but tropical savanna is the most common type of vegetation.

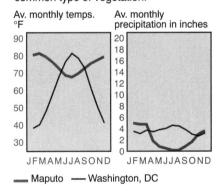

Av. monthly temps. °F
Av. monthly precipitation in inches

JFMAMJJASOND   JFMAMJJASOND

— Maputo   — Washington, DC

ECONOMY

Chief farm products: Bananas, cashew nuts, cassava, corn, cotton, livestock, palm products, peanuts, rice, sorghum, sugar cane
Chief mineral resources: Bauxite (aluminum ore), coal, salt
Chief industrial products: Beverages, cement, processed food, textiles
Employment:

Industry 9% — Services 8%
Agriculture 83%

In the US, agriculture employs 3% of the work force, industry 25%, and services 72%
Exports: Shrimp, cashew nuts, cotton, sugar, lobster
Per capita income: $90 (as compared with $25,860 in the US)

PEOPLE
Population: 15,500,000 (as compared with the US population of 260,529,000)
Major ethnic groups: Makua, Tsonga, Malawi, Shona, Yao
Religions: African religions (48%), Christianity (39%), Islam (13%)

SOCIAL FACTS
● The average life expectancy at birth is 46 years, as compared with 76 years in the US
● Only 33% of the people live in urban areas, as compared with about 76% in the US
● Mozambique was once a major slave-trading area

● Mozambique is the world's poorest country in terms of per capita GNP
● Most Portuguese left Mozambique after independence in 1975
● Mozambique's railroads link neighboring landlocked countries, such as Zimbabwe, with its seaports and are a major source of revenue

KEY POINTS IN RECENT HISTORY
1961 The Frente de Libertação de Moçambique (Frelimo) is formed
1964 Frelimo launches a guerrilla war against Portuguese colonial rule
1974 A coup occurs in Portugal; the new leaders negotiate with Frelimo

1975 Mozambique becomes an independent one-party state (June 25)
1980s A guerrilla force, the Resistência Nacional Moçambicana Movement (Renamo), fights government forces
1990 Opposition parties are allowed
1992 A cease-fire is signed

1994 Multiparty elections are won by Frelimo; Renamo states that it will cooperate with the government
1995 Mozambique joins the Commonwealth of Nations
1996 Mozambique joins the Community of Portuguese-speaking Countries

*See **Peoples of Southern Africa** on the Afrikaners and Swazi*

© DIAGRAM

Namibia

Location: Southern Africa, facing the Atlantic Ocean
Neighbors: Angola, Zambia, Botswana, South Africa

Official name: Republic of Namibia
Divisions: Thirteen regions and ninety-three local government areas
Capital: Windhoek
Largest cities: Windhoek, Swakopmund, Rundu, Rehoboth, Keetmanshoop (in order of size)

Flag: The flag of Namibia features a red diagonal stripe, with white borders, running from bottom left to top right. This stripe separates a blue triangle with a yellow Sun, top left, from a green triangle, bottom right

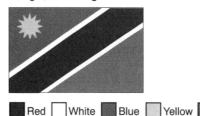

■ Red ☐ White ■ Blue ▨ Yellow ■ Green

National anthem: "Namibia, land of the brave"
Major languages: English (official), Ovambo, Kavango, Afrikaans, Herero
Currency: Dollar = 100 cents

1990 stamp marking Namibia's independence and depicting President Sam Nujoma

GEOGRAPHY

With an area of 318,261 square miles (824,293 sq. km), Namibia is Africa's fifteenth largest country. It is about 1.2 times as large as Texas in the United States (US).

Behind the narrow coastal plain, Namibia forms part of the Southern Plateau, which makes up most of Southern Africa. Central Namibia lies mainly between about 3,000 and 6,500 ft (900–2,000 m) above sea level, though Brandberg, Namibia's highest point, reaches 8,465 ft (2,580 m) on the west of the plateau. In eastern Namibia, the land descends to the Kalahari basin.

The Orange River borders South Africa in the south, while the Kunene and Okavango rivers form parts of the northern border with Angola. In the far northeast, the Zambezi River flows along the border with the Caprivi Strip, a narrow corridor of land linking Namibia with Zambia.

Namibia has a warm, dry climate. North-central Namibia has about 20 in. (51 cm) of rain a year, and the tropical savanna provides a habitat for many animals. The rainfall on the plateau decreases to the south. The coastal Namib Desert is one of the world's bleakest areas. The Kalahari Desert, in the east, is actually a semidesert.

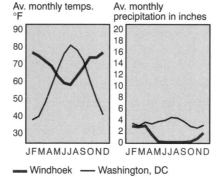

Av. monthly temps. °F
Av. monthly precipitation in inches

—— Windhoek —— Washington, DC

ECONOMY

Chief farm products: Corn, dairy products, livestock, millet, sorghum, vegetables, wheat, wool
Chief mineral resources: Diamonds, uranium, copper, gold, lead, zinc
Chief industrial products: Cut diamonds, karakul sheep pelts, refined metals, processed food, textiles
Employment:

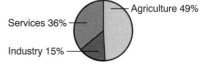

Services 36%
Industry 15%
Agriculture 49%

In the US, agriculture employs 3% of the work force, industry 25%, and services 72%
Exports: Diamonds and other minerals; farm products, including cattle
Per capita income: $1,970 (as compared with $25,860 in the US)

PEOPLE

Population: 1,565,000 (as compared with the US population of 260,529,000)
Major ethnic groups: Ovambo, Kavango, Herero, whites, Nama
Religions: Christianity (90%), including Lutheran (51.2%)

SOCIAL FACTS

● The average life expectancy at birth is 59 years, as compared with 76 years in the US
● Only 36% of the people live in urban areas, as compared with about 76% in the US
● The whites in Namibia are of Dutch, English, and German descent

● The earliest inhabitants of Namibia were the Khoisan
● Namibia is sparsely populated, because it is one of the world's driest countries
● Northern Namibia's Skeleton Coast was the scene of many shipwrecks

KEY POINTS IN RECENT HISTORY

1915 South Africa takes South West Africa (Namibia) from Germany
1920 The League of (later, United) Nations gives South Africa a mandate to govern South West Africa

1945 South Africa refuses a United Nations (UN) request that South West Africa be placed under UN trusteeship
1948–89 Form of apartheid in practice
1966 Guerrilla warfare begins
1969 The UN declares South African

rule in South West Africa to be illegal
1990 Namibia independent (March 21); Sam Nujoma becomes president
1994 Walvis Bay, a South African enclave (external territory) on the Namibian coast, is returned to Namibia

*See **Peoples of Southern Africa** on the Afrikaners, Herero, Khoisan, and Ovambo*

Niger

Location:
Landlocked country in West Africa
Neighbors: Algeria, Libya, Chad, Nigeria, Benin, Burkina Faso, Mali

Official name: Republic of Niger
Divisions: Eight departments
Capital: Niamey
Largest cities: Niamey, Zinder, Maradi, Tahoua, Agadez (in order of size)

Flag: The orange stripe, top, represents the Sahara and the white stripe stands for the Niger River, with the circle symbolizing the Sun. The green stripe at the bottom represents the grasslands in the south of the country

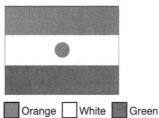

■ Orange □ White ■ Green

National anthem: "By the banks of the mighty great Niger"
Major languages: French (official), Hausa, Songhay, Arabic
Currency: CFA franc = 100 centimes

1961 stamp marking the first anniversary of Niger's admission into the United Nations

GEOGRAPHY

With an area of 489,191 square miles (1,267,000 sq. km), Niger is Africa's sixth largest country. It is 1.8 times larger in area than Texas in the United States (US).

Southern Niger consists of plains that slope down to the Lake Chad basin in the southeast. The northern two-thirds of the country consists of plateaus, which are broken by the volcanic Aïr Mountains. These mountains contain Niger's highest point, Mount Gréboun, which reaches 6,552 ft (1,997 m) above sea level. Northern Niger forms part of the Sahara, though the Aïr Mountains have a little more annual rainfall than the surrounding plateaus.

The chief river is the Niger, which flows from Mali through Niger and into Nigeria in the southwest. The Niger Valley, which contains the capital, Niamey, is the country's most fertile and most heavily populated region.

Niger is one of the world's hottest countries. The north is extremely arid and the rainfall is unreliable in the south. From March until May, a hot, dusty wind, the harmattan, blows from the Sahara over the south. The north is desert, but the Sahel in the south is semidesert. Tropical savanna occurs in the far south of the country.

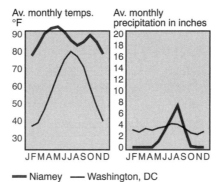

Av. monthly temps. °F

Av. monthly precipitation in inches

JFMAMJJASOND   JFMAMJJASOND

━━ Niamey ━━ Washington, DC

ECONOMY

Chief farm products: Cassava, corn, cotton, livestock, millet, peanuts, rice, sorghum, sugar cane, sweet potatoes, tobacco, vegetables, wheat
Chief mineral resources: Uranium, natron (sodium carbonate), phosphates, salt, gold
Chief industrial products: Beverages, cement, processed food, textiles
Employment:

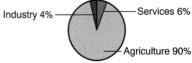

Industry 4% — Services 6%
— Agriculture 90%

In the US, agriculture employs 3% of the work force, industry 25%, and services 72%
Exports: Uranium, live animals, beverages, tobacco
Per capita income: $230 (as compared with $25,860 in the US)

PEOPLE

Population: 8,846,000 (as compared with the US population of 260,529,000)
Major ethnic groups: Hausa, Zerma-Songhay, Tuareg, Fulani
Religions: Islam (98.6%), African religions (1.4%)

SOCIAL FACTS

● The average life expectancy at birth is 46 years, as compared with 76 years in the US
● Only 22% of the people live in urban areas, as compared with about 76% in the US
● Droughts have caused great hardship since the 1960s

● Mobile "tent schools" provide education for the children of nomads
● 85% of the people live by farming, but only 3% of the land is farmed
● Tuareg in northern Niger have conducted guerrilla warfare in an attempt to achieve self-rule

KEY POINTS IN RECENT HISTORY

1906 France fixes Niger's boundaries
1946 The Parti Progressiste Nigérien (PPN) is formed under Hamani Diori
1960 Niger becomes independent, with Diori as president

1974 A military coup overthrows Diori; Lt.-Col. Seyni Kountché becomes head of a military government
1987 Kountché dies; Col. Ali Saïbou succeeds him
1992 A multiparty constitution is

approved by a referendum
1993 Mahamane Ousmane is elected as president
1994 CFA franc is devalued by 50%
1995 Opposition parties win elections, defeating the parties loyal to Ousmane

*See **Peoples of West Africa** on the Fulani and Hausa*

© DIAGRAM

Nigeria

Location: West Africa, on the Gulf of Guinea
Neighbors: Benin, Niger, Chad, Cameroon

Official name: Federal Republic of Nigeria
Divisions: Thirty states and the Federal Capital Territory
Capital: Abuja
Largest cities: Lagos, Ibadan, Kano, Ogbomosho (in order of size)

Flag: The Nigerian flag has three broad vertical stripes of equal width. The two outer stripes are of green, which represents agriculture. The stripe in the center is white, which stands for unity and peace

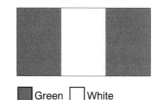

🟩 Green ⬜ White

National anthem: "Arise O compatriots, Nigeria's call obey"
Major languages: English (official), Hausa, Yoruba, Igbo, Fulfulde
Currency: Naira = 100 kobo

1961 Stamp marking Nigeria's admission into the Universal Postal Union

GEOGRAPHY

With an area of 356,669 square miles (923,769 sq. km), Nigeria is Africa's fourteenth largest country. It is about 1.33 times bigger than Texas in the United States (US).

Northern Nigeria consists of high plains and plateaus, which are drained by the Niger and Benue rivers. But in the northeast, rivers drain into Lake Chad, which occupies an inland drainage basin. Lake Chad, which Nigeria shares with Niger, Chad, and Cameroon, is the country's largest lake.

Southern Nigeria contains hilly regions and broad plains. The land rises to the southeast, with highlands along the border with Cameroon. Nigeria's highest point, Vogel Peak, reaches 6,669 ft (2,033 m) in these highlands. Nigeria's coastline, which contains many lagoons and the huge Niger delta, is 478 miles (769 km) long.

Nigeria has a tropical climate. The south, which is hot and rainy throughout the year, was once covered by dense rainforests, but large areas have been cleared for farming. The north is hotter and drier, with a dry season from November until March. Tropical savanna merges into thorn scrub in the far north.

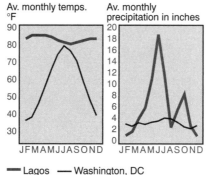

Av. monthly temps. °F
Av. monthly precipitation in inches

JFMAMJJASOND   JFMAMJJASOND

— Lagos   — Washington, DC

ECONOMY

Chief farm products: Beans, beef and hides, cocoa, cassava, corn, cotton, millet, palm products, peanuts, rice, rubber, yams
Chief mineral resources: Oil and natural gas
Chief industrial products: Cement, chemicals, fertilizers, food products, textiles, vehicles
Employment:

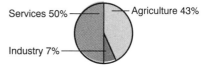

Services 50% — Agriculture 43%
Industry 7%

In the US, agriculture employs 3% of the work force, industry 25%, and services 72%
Chief export: Oil (98%)
Per capita income: $280 (as compared with $25,860 in the US)

PEOPLE
Population: 108,467,000 (as compared with the US population of 260,529,000)
Major ethnic groups: Hausa, Yoruba, Igbo, Fulani
Religions: Islam 48%; Christianity 34%; African religions 18%

SOCIAL FACTS
● The average life expectancy at birth is 52 years, as compared with 76 years in the US
● Only 38% of the people live in urban areas, as compared with about 76% in the US
● Nigeria has the highest population in Africa

● Nigeria's external debts are the highest in Africa
● Conflict exists between northerners, who are mainly Muslim, and southerners, who are Christians or followers of African religions
● Nigeria's great artistic and historical centers include Nok, Ife, Oyo, and Benin

KEY POINTS IN RECENT HISTORY
1914 Britain forms the colony of Nigeria
1960 Nigeria becomes an independent federation (October1)
1966 Military leaders overthrow the civilian government
1967 Civil war breaks out and the eastern state of Biafra proclaims its independence
1970 Civil war ends with Biafra's defeat
1979 Civilian rule is restored
1983 A military group overthrows the elected civilian government and sets up a military regime

1993 Presidential elections are annulled and military rule continues
1995 Writer Ken Saro-Wiwa and eight other Ogoni activists are executed by the military government. As a result, Nigeria's membership of the Commonwealth is suspended

See **Peoples of West Africa** on the Fulani, Hausa, Igbo, and Yoruba

Rwanda

Location: Landlocked country in East Africa
Neighbors: Uganda, Tanzania, Burundi, Zaire

Official name: Republic of Rwanda
Divisions: Ten prefectures
Capital: Kigali
Largest cities: Kigali, Ruhengeri, Butare, Gisenyi (in order of size)

Flag: The red, yellow, and green stripes symbolize African unity; they are the colors of the flag of Ethiopia, Africa's oldest independent nation. The "R" in the center distinguishes Rwanda's flag from that of Guinea

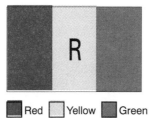

⬛ Red ⬜ Yellow ⬛ Green

National anthem: "My Rwanda, Rwanda who gave me birth"
Major languages: Rwanda and French (both official), Swahili
Currency: Rwanda franc = 100 centimes

1962 stamp marking independence and depicting President Kayibanda

GEOGRAPHY
With an area of 10,169 square miles (26,338 sq. km), Rwanda is Africa's ninth smallest country. It is a little larger in area than Vermont in the United States (US).

The Great Rift Valley, which cuts through western Rwanda, contains part of the country's largest lake, Kivu. Overlooking the Rift Valley are mountains, including Mount Karisimbi in the northwest. This mountain, Rwanda's highest, reaches a height of 14,787 ft (4,507 m). The mountains bordering the Rift Valley form part of the divide between the Congo (Zaire) and Nile river systems. Eastern Rwanda consists of a series of plateaus that slope down to the Kagera River Valley in the east. The Kagera, which flows into Lake Victoria, is one of the most remote sources of the Nile River.

Rwanda has an equatorial climate, though the altitude moderates temperatures. The hottest region is the Rift Valley floor, while the rainiest places are the mountains in the west. The rainforests in the west once spread over the eastern plateaus, but they have been largely cleared for farming

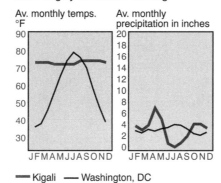

Av. monthly temps. °F
Av. monthly precipitation in inches

— Kigali — Washington, DC

ECONOMY
Chief farm products: Bananas, beans, cassava, coffee, corn, livestock, peanuts, potatoes, pyrethrum (a plant used in insecticides), tea, tobacco
Chief mineral resources: Tin ore, tungsten ore, gold, natural gas
Chief industrial products: Blankets, cement, processed food, soap
Employment:

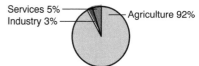

Services 5%
Industry 3%
Agriculture 92%

In the US, agriculture employs 3% of the work force, industry 25%, and services 72%
Exports: Coffee, tea, pyrethrum
Per capita income: $80 (as compared with $25,860 in the US)

PEOPLE
Population: 7,800,000 (as compared with the US population of 260,529,000)
Major ethnic groups: Hutu, Tutsi, Twa
Religions: Christianity (74%), African religions (17%), Islam (9%)

SOCIAL FACTS
● The average life expectancy at birth is 47 years, as compared with 76 years in the US
● Only 6% of the people live in urban areas, as compared with 76% in the US
● The Tutsi people have ruled the area

for hundreds of years, often treating the Hutu like serfs in the past
● Rwanda is mainland Africa's most densely populated country
● Soil erosion, a serious problem in Rwanda, has helped to make the country one of the world's poorest

KEY POINTS IN RECENT HISTORY
1916 Belgium occupies the former German territory of Ruanda-Urundi
1961 Following a Hutu rebellion against the Tutsi monarchy, the people of Ruanda vote in a referendum to make their country a republic
1962 Independence is achieved for the new Republic of Rwanda (July 1);

Grégoire Kayibanda becomes president
1973 General Juvénal Habyarimana overthrows Kayibanda
1983 Habyarimana elected president
1990 10,000 guerrillas of Tutsi-based Front Patriotique Rwandais (FPR) invade northeast Rwanda from Uganda starting a civil war
1991 Tension between Hutu and Tutsi

is increased by conflict. A multiparty system of government is introduced
1993 One million refugees flee conflict in Rwanda, many Tutsi civilians and moderate Hutu are massacred by other Rwandans. Cease-fire is declared
1994 Habyarimana dies in plane crash; assassination is suspected; war erupts. Pasteur Bizimungu becomes president

© DIAGRAM

*See **Peoples of East Africa** on the Hutu and Tutsi*

São Tomé and Príncipe

Location: Island country off the coast of Central Africa **Nearest mainland country:** Gabon

Official name: Democratic Republic of São Tomé and Príncipe
Divisions: Two main islands and several islets
Capital: São Tomé
Largest cities: São Tomé, Trinidade, São Antonio (in order of size)

Flag: The two stripes of green, the yellow stripe, center, and the red triangle use the three colors of the flag of Ethiopia, Africa's oldest independent nation. The black stars represent the two main islands

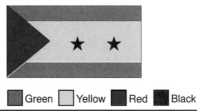

■ Green □ Yellow ■ Red ■ Black

National anthem: "Total independence, glorious song of the people"
Major languages: Portuguese (official), Creole, Fang
Currency: Dobra = 100 céntimos

REPÚBLICA DEMOCRÁTICA
12 de Julio de 1976 · L'Aniversario
independencia Nacional 12$50
DE SÃO TOMÉ E PRÍNCIPE

1976 stamp marking the first anniversary of independence

GEOGRAPHY

With an area of 372 square miles (963 sq. km), São Tomé and Príncipe is Africa's second smallest independent country after Seychelles. It is less than a third of the size of Rhode Island in the United States (US).

São Tomé, the country's main island, makes up about 86% of the total area. Measuring about 21 miles (34 km) wide and 32 miles (52 km) long, it consists of the remains of extinct volcanoes. Fertile plains formed from volcanic ash lie in the south, but the island is largely mountainous. The highest point, Pico de São Tomé, reaches 6,640 ft (2,024 m) on the western side of the island.

Príncipe is another volcanic island. It is roughly rectangular in shape, measuring about 5 miles (8 km) wide and 11 miles (18 km) long. Its highest point is 3,107 ft (947 m) above sea level. The country's other islands are tiny.

The climate is tropical, but temperatures are moderated by altitude and by the cold Benguela Current, which flows north along the western coast of Africa. The rainfall is abundant, though a marked dry season occurs from June until September. Rainforest covers the higher land, but farmers have cleared most of the forest on the lower slopes.

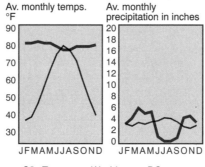

Av. monthly temps. °F
Av. monthly precipitation in inches

JFMAMJJASOND   JFMAMJJASOND

— São Tome   — Washington, DC

ECONOMY

Chief farm products: Bananas, cassava, cocoa, coconuts, coffee, copra, livestock, palm oil, sweet potatoes, yams
Chief mineral resources: Some quarrying for construction materials
Chief industrial products: Bricks, processed food, soap, textiles, wood products
Employment:

Services 69% — Agriculture 28%
— Industry 3%

In the US, agriculture employs 3% of the work force, industry 25%, and services 72%
Exports: Cocoa (60%), copra, coffee, bananas, palm oil
Per capita income: $250 (as compared with $25,860 in the US)

PEOPLE

Population: 125,000 (as compared with the US population of 260,529,000)
Major ethnic groups: Mixed Black African and European ancestry
Religions: Christianity (100%)

SOCIAL FACTS

● The average life expectancy at birth is 68 years, as compared with 76 years in the US
● Only 45% of the people live in urban areas, as compared with about 76% in the US
● About 95 percent of the population lives on São Tomé island

● São Tomé was a Portuguese slave-trading center in the 1500s
● Most farms produce crops for export; food has to be imported
● Most of the people are descendants of slaves, contract laborers and European settlers; they are called "filhos da terra" ("sons of the land")

KEY POINTS IN RECENT HISTORY

1953 Portuguese troops kill hundreds of workers during a protest
1972 The country's nationalist party is named the Movimento de Libertação de São Tomé e Príncipe (MLSTP)
1975 The country becomes independent from Portugal (July 12) and

the MLSTP leader, Manuel Pinto da Costa, an economist, becomes president
1983–4 An acute drought occurs
1990 A new constitution makes the formation of opposition parties legal
1991 The MLSTP is defeated in elections and da Costa retires; Miguel

Trovoada becomes the new president
1994 The MLSTP regains power when it wins 27 out of the 55 seats in the National Assembly
1996 São Tomé and Príncipe joins the Community of Portuguese-speaking Countries

Senegal

Location: West Africa, facing the Atlantic Ocean
Neighbors: Mauritania, Mali, Guinea, Guinea-Bissau, Gambia

Official name: Republic of Senegal
Divisions: Ten regions
Capital: Dakar
Largest cities: Dakar, Thiès, Kaolack, Ziguinchor, Saint-Louis (in order of size)

Flag: The green, yellow, and red vertical stripes symbolize African unity; these are the colors of the flag of Ethiopia, Africa's oldest independent nation. The green star symbolizes Islam

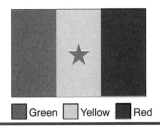

■ Green ☐ Yellow ■ Red

National anthem: "All pluck the koras, strike the balafons"
Major languages: French (official), Wolof, Fulfulde, Manding
Currency: CFA franc = 100 centimes

1970 stamp marking the twenty-fifth anniversary of the United Nations (UN)

GEOGRAPHY

With an area of 75,955 square miles (196,723 sq. km), Senegal is Africa's thirty-third largest country. It is about the same size as South Dakota in the United States (US).

Senegal's coastline, which is 310 miles (499 km) long, is lined with sandy beaches, with high sand dunes in the north and mangrove swamps in parts of the south. The capital, Dakar, stands on a volcanic promontory, Cape Verde. Inland are rolling plains, and the land rises in the southeast to a height of 1,634 ft (498 m), the country's highest elevation. This area is an extension of the Futa Djallon plateau in Guinea.

Major rivers include the Senegal, which forms the northern border, and the Casamance in the south. The Gambia River flows from northern Guinea through Senegal into Gambia, a narrow country surrounded by Senegal.

Senegal has a tropical climate, with a rainy season from July until October. The northeast has a desert climate, but northwestern and central Senegal are part of the semidesert Sahel. Tropical savanna occurs in the far south. Forests grow only in the river valleys.

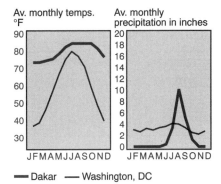

Av. monthly temps. °F
Av. monthly precipitation in inches
JFMAMJJASOND JFMAMJJASOND
— Dakar — Washington, DC

ECONOMY

Chief farm products: Cassava, corn, cotton, livestock, millet, peanuts, rice, sorghum
Chief mineral resources: Phosphates
Chief industrial products: Beverages, cement, fish products, processed food and edible oils, fertilizers
Employment:

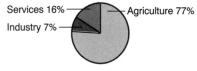

Services 16% — Agriculture 77%
Industry 7% —

In the US, agriculture employs 3% of the work force, industry 25%, and services 72%
Exports: Canned fish, phosphates, fresh fish, peanut oil, shellfish, cotton
Per capita income: $600 (as compared with $25,860 in the US)

PEOPLE

Population: 8,300,000 (as compared with the US population of 260,529,000)
Major ethnic groups: Wolof, Fulani, Tukolor, Serer, Dyula
Religions: Islam (94%) Christianity (5%), African religions (1%)

SOCIAL FACTS

● The average life expectancy at birth is 50 years, as compared with 76 years in the US
● Only 42% of the people live in urban areas, as compared with about 76% in the US
● Dakar is a major African seaport

● In colonial times, Dakar was the capital, main port, and industrial center of French West Africa, which included eight countries
● Many Senegalese belong to brotherhoods (Islamic groups), headed by marabouts (religious leaders), who have much political influence

KEY POINTS IN RECENT HISTORY

1959 Senegal unites with French Soudan to form the Federation of Mali
1960 Senegal leaves the federation and becomes independent (June 20)
1966–74 Senegal is governed by a one-party system
1980 Senegal's first president, Léopold Sédar Senghor, resigns; Abdou Diouf becomes president
1981 Senegalese troops help to put down a rebellion in Gambia
1982 Senegal and Gambia form a confederation called Senegambia
1989 Senegambia is dissolved
1993 Diouf is reelected president for the third time; his Parti Socialiste wins the majority of the seats in the National Assembly
1994 CFA franc, which is linked to the French franc, is devalued by 50% causing widespread economic hardship and civil unrest

*See **Peoples of West Africa** on the Bambara, Fulani, and Malinke

Seychelles

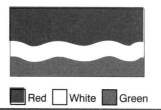

Location: Island country in the Indian Ocean, off the coast of East Africa
Nearest mainland: Mainland Africa lies about 1,000 miles (1,600 km) to the west

Official name: Republic of Seychelles
Divisions: 115 islands in two main groups, the Granitic and Coralline
Capital: Victoria
Largest city: Victoria

Flag: The red stripe, top, represents revolution and progress; the wavy white stripe symbolizes the Indian Ocean; and the green stripe, bottom, stands for agriculture. The flag was first introduced in 1977

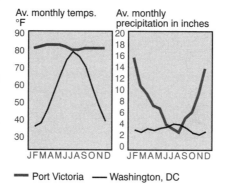

▦ Red ☐ White ▦ Green

National anthem: "With courage and discipline, we have broken down all barriers"
Major languages: French, English (both official), Creole
Currency: Seychelles rupee = 100 cents

1976 stamp marking both the independence of Seychelles and the US Bicentenary

GEOGRAPHY

With an area of 176 square miles (456 sq. km), Seychelles is Africa's smallest nation. It is about one-seventh of the size in area of Rhode Island in the United States (US).

The 32 islands in the Granitic group cover a total area of 92 square miles (238 sq. km). These mountainous islands, which are mostly surrounded by sandy beaches, include the largest island, Mahé, which makes up one-third of the country. Mahé contains the highest point in Seychelles, at 2,893 ft (882 m) above sea level. The Granitic Islands contain many rocky areas where farming is difficult.

The 83 Coralline, or Outer, Islands are low-lying. They include circular atolls made of coral, which has built up on sunken volcanic mountains. Other islands are coral reefs jutting up above the sea. Many of the Coralline Islands are uninhabited.

The climate is tropical, though the highlands are cooler than the humid coasts. The rainfall is moderate to heavy, being greatest on the south-facing slopes of the Granitic Islands, which lie in the paths of the prevailing southeast trade winds. The vegetation is lush, but most of the original rainforest has been cleared.

Av. monthly temps. °F / Av. monthly precipitation in inches

JFMAMJJASOND   JFMAMJJASOND

— Port Victoria   — Washington, DC

ECONOMY

Chief farm products: Bananas, cassava, cinnamon, coconuts, copra, livestock, sugar cane, sweet potatoes, tea, vegetables, yams
Chief mineral resources: Guano
Chief industrial products: Beverages, canned fish, petroleum products
Employment:

Agriculture 9%
Industry 18%
Services 73%

In the US, agriculture employs 3% of the work force, industry 25%, and services 72%
Exports: Petroleum products, canned tuna and other fish, cinnamon, food, beverages, tobacco, chemicals
Per capital income: $6,680 (as compared with $25,860 in the US)

PEOPLE

Population: 72,000 (as compared with the US population of 260,529,000)
Major ethnic groups: Creole, Indian, Madagascans, Chinese, English
Religions: Christianity (97%), Hinduism

SOCIAL FACTS

● The average life expectancy at birth is 72 years, as compared with 76 years in the US
● About 53% of the people live in urban areas, as compared with about 76% in the US
● More than 80% of the people live on Mahé island

● Most people are Creoles, of mixed African and European descent; the Creole language used in the Seychelles is considered to be a French dialect
● The islands were uninhabited when they were first discovered in the early 1500s
● Tourism is a major and expanding industry in Seychelles

KEY POINTS IN RECENT HISTORY

1976 Seychelles becomes independent from Britain (June 29); James Mancham, leader of the Democratic Party, becomes the first president
1979 A military coup ousts Mancham and the opposition leader, France-Albert René, becomes president
1977 René's Seychelles People's Progressive Front (SPPF) becomes the sole party; the government pursues Marxist policies
1981 A coup attempt fails
1984 René is reelected president

1989 René is reelected president
1991 The government legalizes opposition parties and relaxes its socialist policies
1993 René is reelected president and the SPPF wins 28 of the 33 seats in the People's Assembly

Sierra Leone

Location: West Africa, facing the Atlantic Ocean
Neighbors: Guinea, Liberia

Official name: Republic of Sierra Leone
Divisions: Four provinces
Capital: Freetown
Largest cities: Freetown, Koidu-New Sembehun, Bo, Kenema, Makeni (in order of size)

Flag: The green stripe, top, symbolizes agriculture; the white stripe, center, stands for peace; and the blue stripe, bottom, represents the waters of the Atlantic Ocean

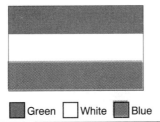

Green ▢ White ▢ Blue

National anthem: "High we exalt thee, realm of the free"
Major languages: English (official), Mende, Temne, Krio
Currency: Leone = 100 cents

1975 stamp marking the first anniversary of the Mano River Union

GEOGRAPHY

With an area of 27,699 square miles (71,740 sq. km), Sierra Leone is one of Africa's smaller countries. It is a little smaller in area than South Carolina in the United States (US).

Deep estuaries and swamps occur along the northern coast, but lagoons border the southern shore. Freetown, which stands on the rocky Sierra Leone peninsula, has one of West Africa's finest natural harbors.

Behind the coast is a broad plain, extending up to 100 miles (160 km) inland in the north, but plateaus and mountains make up about half of the country. The mountains rise to Mount Mansa, which reaches 6,391 ft (1,948 m) above sea level near the northeastern border. Many rivers flow across Sierra Leone, running generally from northeast to southwest. They include the Great and Little Scarcies, Rokel, Jong, Sewa, Moa, and Mano.

The climate is tropical, with rains from April until November. January and February are dry in the south. In the north, the dry season runs from December until March. Swamps lie along the coast, but inland the rainforest has been largely cut down, giving way to grasslands and low bush. Tropical savanna occurs in the north.

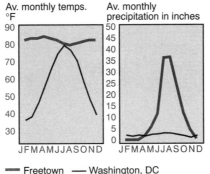

Av. monthly temps. °F
Av. monthly precipitation in inches

JFMAMJJASOND   JFMAMJJASOND

— Freetown   — Washington, DC

ECONOMY

Chief farm products: Cassava, cocoa, coffee, corn, livestock, millet, palm oil and kernels, peanuts, plantains, rice, sorghum, sweet potatoes
Chief mineral resources: Bauxite (aluminum ore), rutile (titanium ore), diamonds, gold
Chief industrial products: Beverages, furniture, processed food, salt
Employment:

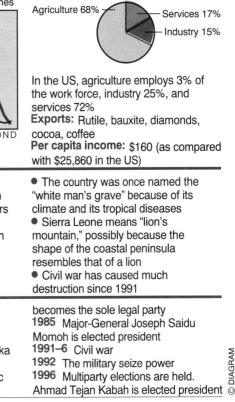

Agriculture 68% — Services 17%
— Industry 15%

In the US, agriculture employs 3% of the work force, industry 25%, and services 72%
Exports: Rutile, bauxite, diamonds, cocoa, coffee
Per capita income: $160 (as compared with $25,860 in the US)

PEOPLE

Population: 4,402,000 (as compared with the US population of 260,529,000)
Major ethnic groups: Mende, Temne, Limba, Kono, Bullom-Sherbro, Fulani
Religions: Islam (60%), African religions (30%), Christianity (10%)

SOCIAL FACTS

- The average life expectancy at birth is 40 years, as compared with 76 years in the US
- Only 35% of the people live in urban areas, as compared with about 76% in the US
- Freetown was set up in 1787 as a settlement for freed slaves

- The country was once named the "white man's grave" because of its climate and its tropical diseases
- Sierra Leone means "lion's mountain," possibly because the shape of the coastal peninsula resembles that of a lion
- Civil war has caused much destruction since 1991

KEY POINTS IN RECENT HISTORY

1952 Dr Milton Margai of the Sierra Leone People's Party is elected prime minister
1961 Sierra Leone becomes independent from Britain (April 27)
1964 Milton Margai dies and his brother

Albert becomes prime minister
1967 A military coup overthrows the civilian government
1968 Civilian rule is restored with Siaka Stevens as prime minister
1971 The country becomes a republic
1978 The All People's Congress

becomes the sole legal party
1985 Major-General Joseph Saidu Momoh is elected president
1991–6 Civil war
1992 The military seize power
1996 Multiparty elections are held. Ahmad Tejan Kabah is elected president

*See **Peoples of West Africa** on the Mende*

© DIAGRAM

Somalia

Location: East Africa, facing the Gulf of Aden and the Indian Ocean
Neighbors: Kenya, Ethiopia, Djibouti

Official name: Somali Democratic Republic
Divisions: Eighteen regions
Capital: Mogadishu
Largest cities: Mogadishu, Hargeisa, Kismatu, Berbera, Merca (in order of size)

Flag: The blue flag is based on that of the United Nations (UN). The five points of the white star represent regions where Somalis live, namely the former British and Italian Somalilands, Kenya, Ethiopia, and Djibouti

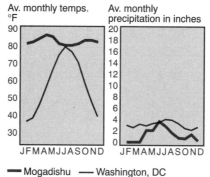 Blue White

Major languages: Somali and Arabic (both official); English, Italian
Currency: Somali shilling = 100 cents

1967 stamp marking the visit of King Faisal of Saudi Arabia

GEOGRAPHY

With an area of 246,201 square miles (637,658 sq. km), Somalia is Africa's eighteenth largest country. It occupies the Horn of Africa and in area is a little smaller than Texas in the United States (US).

In the north, a narrow coastal plain facing the Gulf of Aden extends to the tip of the Horn of Africa. Behind this hot and arid plain, which is called the Guban (meaning "burned"), lie mountains that rise to a height of 7,900 ft (2,408 m) at Surud Ad mountain, Somalia's highest peak.

Central and southern Somalia, facing the Indian Ocean, consist of low plateaus and plains, which are generally between 300 and 400 ft (90–120 m) above sea level. The only permanent rivers, the Juba and Shebelle, are in the south. These rivers rise in Ethiopia and they provide valuable water for drinking and irrigation.

Somalia has a tropical climate, but the altitude moderates temperatures in the north. The average annual rainfall seldom exceeds 20 in. (51 cm), even in the wetter south, and is also unreliable. Semidesert and dry grassland cover much of the land, with tropical wooded savanna in parts of the south.

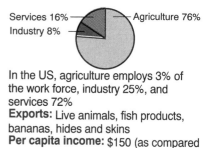

Av. monthly temps. °F / Av. monthly precipitation in inches

— Mogadishu — Washington, DC

ECONOMY

Chief farm products: Bananas, citrus fruits, corn, cotton, dates, livestock, rice, sorghum, sugar cane
Chief mineral resources: Deposits of many minerals have been found
Chief industrial products: Beverages, hides and skins, processed food, petroleum products, textiles
Employment:

Services 16% — Agriculture 76%
Industry 8%

In the US, agriculture employs 3% of the work force, industry 25%, and services 72%
Exports: Live animals, fish products, bananas, hides and skins
Per capita income: $150 (as compared with $25,860 in the US)

PEOPLE

Population: 8,775,000 (as compared with the US population of 260,529,000)
Major ethnic groups: Somalis, divided into several clans; some Arabs and Bantu-speaking people
Religions: Islam (99.8%)

SOCIAL FACTS

● The average life expectancy at birth is 49 years, as compared with 76 years in the US
● Only 25% of the people live in urban areas, as compared with about 76% in the US
● The Somalis have a rich oral literature

● The Somali language did not have a written form until the early 1970s
● Somali-speaking people live in Djibouti, Ethiopia, and Kenya; some Somalis would like to create a Greater Somalia to include these people
● Somalis are divided into clans; clan rivalries have led to civil war

KEY POINTS IN RECENT HISTORY

1905 Italy takes over southern Somalia (northern Somalia is a British protectorate)
1941 During World War II, Britain occupies Italian Somaliland
1960 The two Somalilands unite to form independent Somalia (July 1)
1969 A military regime is set up
1970s Somalia supports Somali-speaking guerrillas in Ethiopia
1988 Somalia and Ethiopia sign a peace treaty
1991 Civil war occurs; the north "secedes," but it is not recognized internationally as a sovereign state
1993–4 US Marines sent by the United Nations oversee food distribution
1995 Somalia has no effective central government, and political power is in the hands of clan leaders

*See **Peoples of East Africa** on the Somalis*

South Africa

Location: Southern Africa, facing both the Indian and Atlantic oceans
Neighbors: Namibia, Botswana, Zimbabwe, Mozambique, Swaziland, Lesotho
Official name: Republic of South Africa
Divisions: Nine provinces
Capitals: Pretoria (administrative), Cape Town (legislative), Bloemfontein (judicial)
Largest cities: Cape Town, Johannesburg, Durban, (in order of size)

Flag: The South African flag combines the red, white, and blue colors of the flags of the former colonial power Britain and of the Boer republics with the green, black, and gold of African nationalist organizations

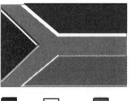

■ Red □ White ■ Blue ■ Green ■ Black ■ Gold

National anthem: "Nkosi sikelel'i, Afrika" ("God bless Africa")
Major languages: Afrikaans, English, Ndebele, Sesotho, Tsonga, Setswana, Tshivenda, Xhosa, Zulu (all official)
Currency: Rand = 100 cents

1986 stamp marking the twenty-fifth anniversary of the Republic of South Africa

GEOGRAPHY

With an area of 473,290 square miles (1,225,816 sq. km), South Africa is Africa's ninth largest country. It is nearly twice as big in area as Texas in the United States (US).

South Africa contains part of the huge plateau that makes up most of Southern Africa. The plateau is ringed by the Great Escarpment (a zone of cliffs and mountains). The Drakensberg range, part of the Great Escarpment, contains South Africa's highest peak, Champagne Castle, which rises to 11,073 ft (3,375 m). In the southwest, the plateau is bordered by the Cape ranges, which are separated by valleys. The coastal plains are mainly narrow.

Parts of two deserts, the Kalahari and the Namib, are located in the west. The longest river is the Orange, which rises in Lesotho and flows 1,300 miles (2,090 km) to the Atlantic Ocean.

The climate is mild and sunny, though the highlands are much cooler than the coastal lowlands. The Cape region has hot, dry summers and mild, moist winters, and scrub, called fynbos, covers some areas. Only 25% of South Africa has over 25 in. (64 cm) of rain per year. Grasslands cover large areas, and forests cover only 3% of the land.

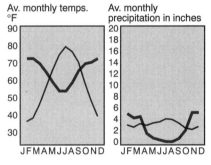

Av. monthly temps. °F

Av. monthly precipitation in inches

JFMAMJJASOND JFMAMJJASOND

— Pretoria — Washington, DC

ECONOMY

Chief farm products: Apples, beef, citrus fruits, corn, potatoes, tobacco, sugar cane, wheat, wool
Chief mineral resources: Coal, copper, diamonds, gold, uranium
Chief industrial products: Chemicals, iron, steel, machinery, metal products, processed food, textiles, vehicles
Employment:

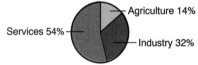

Services 54% — Agriculture 14%
— Industry 32%

In the US, agriculture employs 3% of the work force, industry 25%, and services 72%
Exports: Gold, metals and metal products, diamonds, food products
Per capita income: $3,040 (as compared with $25,860 in the US)

PEOPLE

Population: 40,500,000 (as compared with the US population of 260,529,000)
Major ethnic groups: Zulu, Sotho, Tswana, Venda, Ndebele, Xhosa, Afrikaner, Cape Colored, Cape Malay, European, Khoisan, Asian, Swazi
Religions: Christianity (78%), African religions (10.5%)

SOCIAL FACTS

● The average life expectancy at birth is 64 years, as compared with 76 years in the US
● Only 50% of the people live in urban areas, as compared with about 76% in the US
● The most widely spoken of the official languages are Zulu and Xhosa

● South Africa is the continent's most developed and richest country, but most of the wealth is in the hands of the white minority.
● Afrikaans is a language that developed from Dutch; it was spoken by people once called Boers but now called Afrikaners

KEY POINTS IN RECENT HISTORY

1910 Union of South Africa is formed
1912 South African Native National Congress – renamed African National Congress (ANC) in 1923 – is formed
1934 South Africa approves independence from Britain

1948 National Party is elected to power by the whites-only electorate and apartheid is officially introduced
1961 South Africa becomes a republic
1986 State of emergency declared as opposition to apartheid mounts
1989 F. W. de Klerk becomes president

and starts to ease apartheid laws
1990 ANC leader Nelson Mandela is released after twenty-six years in prison
1991 Apartheid laws abolished
1994 ANC wins multiracial elections and Mandela becomes president
1996 New constitution adopted

© DIAGRAM

*See **Peoples of Southern Africa** on the Afrikaners, Cape Coloreds, Cape Malays, Indian South Africans, Khoisan, Ndebele, Xhosa, and Zulu*

Sudan

Location: North Africa, facing the Red Sea
Neighbors: Ethiopia, Kenya, Zaire, Central African Republic, Chad, Libya, Egypt

Official name: Republic of Sudan
Divisions: Twenty-six states
Capital: Khartoum
Largest cities: Khartoum (including Omdurman and Khartoum North), Port Sudan (in order of size)

Flag: The red, white, and black horizontal stripes are colors associated with the Pan-Arab movement. The green triangle is a symbol of Islam. Sudan adopted this flag in 1969

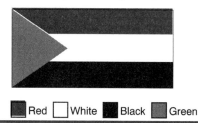

■ Red □ White ■ Black ■ Green

National anthem: "Nahnu djundullah" ("We are god's army")
Major languages: Arabic (official), Nuer, Beja, Dinka, Koalib, Tegali, Katla, Tumtum, Shilluk
Currency: Dinar = 10 Sudanese pounds

1969 Stamp marking the fifth anniversary of the African Development Bank

GEOGRAPHY

With an area of 967,245 square miles (2,505,155 sq. km), Sudan is Africa's largest country. It is 3.6 times larger in area than Texas in the United States (US).

Most of Sudan is flat, but there is a hilly region behind the Red Sea coastline, which is 400 miles (640 km) long. In west-central Sudan, a badland region of ancient lavas and compacted volcanic ash rises more than 10,000 ft (3,000 m) above sea level. Sudan's highest point is Mount Kinyeti, at 10,456 ft (3,187 m).

The chief rivers are the Nile, the world's longest, and its tributaries, the Bahr al Arab, the Blue Nile, and the Atbara. In the south, where the Nile winds through a vast swamp called the Sudd, the river is called the Bahr al Jabal. It is called the White Nile between the Sudd and Khartoum, where it is joined by the Blue Nile and becomes simply the Nile.

Temperatures are high throughout the year. The land north of Khartoum has a desert climate, but heavy rains occur in the far south. The north is desert, except along the Nile Valley and at oases. Central Sudan is a dry grassland where farming depends on irrigation. Tropical savanna, rainforest, and swamp occur in the south.

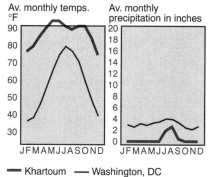

Av. monthly temps. °F

Av. monthly precipitation in inches

JFMAMJJASOND   JFMAMJJASOND

— Khartoum   — Washington, DC

ECONOMY

Chief farm products: Cotton, gum arabic, livestock, millet, peanuts, sesame seeds, sugar cane, wheat
Chief mineral resources: Chromite (chromium ore), gold, gypsum, salt
Chief industrial products: Cement, fertilizers, hides and skins, processed food, textiles
Employment:

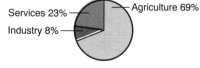

Services 23% Agriculture 69%
Industry 8%

In the US, agriculture employs 3% of the work force, industry 25%, and services 72%.
Exports: Cotton, sesame seeds, sheep and lambs, gum arabic, hides and skins
Per capita income: $675 (as compared with $25,860 in the US)

PEOPLE

Population: 27,361,000 (as compared with the US population of 260,529,000)
Major ethnic groups: Arab, Dinka, Nuba, Beja, Nuer, Azande, Bari, Fur
Religions: Islam (75%), African religions (17%), Christianity (8%)

SOCIAL FACTS

● The average life expectancy at birth is 54 years, as compared with 76 years in the US
● Only 24% of the people live in urban areas, as compared with about 76% in the US
● Khartoum is a center of Islamic fundamentalism

● Conflict between Muslim northerners and mainly Christian southerners has gone on for hundreds of years
● Sudan's Muslim leaders have been accused of trying to destabilize Egypt, Eritrea, Libya, and Uganda
● Nearly all of Sudan's Christians are Black Africans who live in in the south of the country

KEY POINTS IN RECENT HISTORY

1956 Sudan becomes independent (January 1) from Anglo-Egyptian rule
1958 An army group seizes power
1964 Civil war breaks out between the north and the mainly Christian south
1969 Col. Gaafar Muhammad al Nimeri seizes power
1972 The government grants southern Sudan regional autonomy, ending the civil war
1983 Nimeri introduces Sharia (Islamic holy) law throughout Sudan and the civil war starts again

1985 A military group overthrows Nimeri
1989 Another coup brings Brig. Omar Hassan Ahmad al Bashir to power; he abolishes all political parties
1990s The civil war continues with sporadic fighting in the south

*See **Peoples of North Africa** on the Arabs, Baggara, Beja, Dinka, Nuba, Nuer, and Shilluk*

Swaziland

Location: Landlocked country in Southern Africa
Neighbors: Mozambique, South Africa

Official name: Kingdom of Swaziland
Divisions: Four regions
Capital: Mbabane
Largest cities: Mbabane, Manzini, Nhlangano, Piggs Peak, Siteki (in order of size)

Flag: The flag of Swaziland has horizontal blue stripes at the top and bottom. Thin yellow stripes separate these from the central red stripe, which contains a warrior's shield, two assegais (spears), and a fighting stick

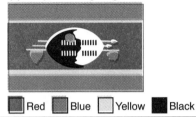

■ Red ■ Blue ▢ Yellow ■ Black ▢ White

National anthem: "O Lord our God, bestower of blessings upon the Swazi"
Major languages: Swazi, English (both official), Zulu
Currency: Lilangeni = 100 cents

1968 stamp depicting a Swazi warrior

GEOGRAPHY

With an area of 6,704 square miles (17,363 sq. km), Swaziland is Africa's seventh smallest country. It is a little larger in area than Hawaii in the United States (US).

Swaziland's land regions run north-south. The Highveld in the west covers 30% of Swaziland and includes Mount Emlembe, the country's highest point at 6,109 ft (1,862 m). To the east lies the Middleveld, which is from 1,150 to 3,300 ft (350–1,000 m) above sea level. The Middleveld makes up 28% of the land, and the third region, the Lowveld, makes up another 33%. Here the average height is around 900 ft (270 m). The fourth region is the Lebombo Mountains along the Mozambique border in the east. These mountains reach a height of about 2,600 ft (790 m). The chief rivers are the Komati, the Umbeluzi, the Great Usutu, and the Ingwavuma.

Swaziland has a subtropical climate, though the altitude moderates the climate. While the Lowveld is hot and fairly dry, the Highveld has warm summers, cool winters, and abundant rainfall. Grasslands cover about two-thirds of the country, and pine forests planted by Europeans cover large areas in the Highveld.

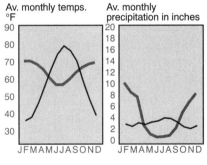

Av. monthly temps. °F

Av. monthly precipitation in inches

JFMAMJJASOND   JFMAMJJASOND

— Mbabane   — Washington, DC

ECONOMY

Chief farm products: Citrus fruits, corn, cotton, livestock, pineapples, sorghum, sugar cane, vegetables
Chief mineral resources: Asbestos, diamonds, quarry stone
Chief industrial products: Cement, beverages, fertilizers, processed food, sugar, textiles, wood pulp
Employment:

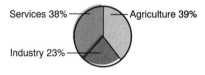

Services 38% — Agriculture 39%

Industry 23%

In the US, agriculture employs 3% of the work force, industry 25%, and services 72%
Exports: Sugar, wood and wood products, canned fruit, diamonds
Per capita income: $1,100 (as compared with $25,860 in the US)

PEOPLE

Population: 906,000 (as compared with the US population of 260,529,000)
Major ethnic groups: Swazi, Zulu, Tsonga
Religions: Christianity (77%), African religions (21%)

SOCIAL FACTS

- The average life expectancy at birth is 58 years, as compared with 76 years in the US.
- Only 29% of the people live in urban areas, as compared with about 76% in the US
- Swaziland is one of three independent monarchies in Africa

- Swaziland's economy is closely linked to that of South Africa
- Mbabane is the national capital, but the nearby village of Lobamba is the royal capital
- The Swazi kingdom was founded in the nineteenth century by Sobhuza I and Mswati I, after whom the country was named

KEY POINTS IN RECENT HISTORY

1902 Britain takes control of Swaziland at the end of the Anglo-Boer War
1968 Swaziland becomes independent (September 6)
1973 King Sobhuza II abolishes the

constitution, suspends parliament, and abolishes all political parties
1979 A new parliament is set up, but Sobhuza retains powers of veto
1982 King Sobhuza dies; his heir, named in 1983, is the fifteen-year-old

Prince Makhosetive
1986 Prince Makhosetive is installed as King Mswati III
1993 Swaziland holds its first democratic multiparty elections

*See **Peoples of Southern Africa** on the Swazi and Zulu*

© DIAGRAM

Tanzania

Location: East Africa, facing the Indian Ocean
Neighbors: Mozambique, Malawi, Zambia, Burundi, Rwanda, Uganda, Kenya
Official name: United Republic of Tanzania
Divisions: Twenty-five regions
Capital: Dodoma
Largest cities: Dar es Salaam, Mwanza, Dodoma, Tanga (in order of size)

Flag: The flag of Tanzania has five diagonal stripes. These stripes are green, representing agriculture; gold, which represents minerals; black, which symbolizes the people; gold again; and blue, for the ocean

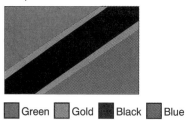

■ Green ■ Gold ■ Black ■ Blue

National anthem: "Mungu ibariki Afrika" ("God bless Africa")
Major languages: Swahili, English (official), 120 African languages
Currency: Shilling = 100 cents

Stamp marking the International Year of the Child, 1979

GEOGRAPHY
With an area of 364,900 square miles (945,087 sq. km), Tanzania is Africa's thirteenth largest country. It is nearly 1.34 times as big in area as Texas in the United States (US).

Behind the narrow coastal plain on the Indian Ocean, the land rises in a series of plateaus. Rising above the plateaus in the northeast is Africa's highest peak, a dormant volcano called Kilimanjaro, at 19,341 ft (5,895 m) above sea level.

Two arms of the Great Rift Valley cross Tanzania. In the west, the Rift Valley is deep and contains Lake Tanganyika. The other arm, through central Tanzania, is not as deep, and contains lakes Natron and Manyara in the north. Tanzania's largest lake, Victoria, is shared with Kenya and Uganda and its chief river is the Rufiji. The largest of Tanzania's offshore islands, Zanzibar and Pemba, are made of coral.

The coast and the islands have a hot, humid climate. The plateaus and mountains are cooler and drier, and Kilimanjaro, although near the equator, is always snowcapped. Mangrove swamps are found on the coast. Inland, miombo (wooded tropical savanna) covers large areas. Grassland occurs in the drier regions.

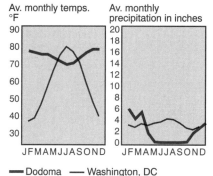

Av. monthly temps. °F / Av. monthly precipitation in inches

— Dodoma   — Washington, DC

ECONOMY
Chief farm products: Bananas, beef, cloves, coconuts, coffee, corn, millet, rice, sisal, sorghum, sugar cane, tobacco, wheat
Mineral resources: Diamonds, gold
Chief industrial products: Petroleum and chemical products, processed food, textiles
Employment:

Services 10% — Agriculture 85%
Industry 5%

In the US, agriculture employs 3% of the work force, industry 25%, and services 72%
Exports: Coffee, manufactured goods, cotton, minerals, tea, tobacco
Per capita income: $140 (as compared with $25,860 in the US)

PEOPLE
Population: 28,800,000 (about a ninth of the US population of 260,529,000)
Major ethnic groups: Nyamwezi, Sukuma, Swahili, Haya
Religions: African religions (35%), Islam (35%), Christianity (30%)

SOCIAL FACTS
● The average life expectancy at birth is 51 years, as compared with 76 years in the US
● Only 24% of the people live in urban areas, as compared with about 76% in the US
● Tanzania, though poor, has one of Africa's highest literacy rates

● About 13% of Tanzania is protected in reserves and national parks
● Though Tanzania has many ethnic groups (about 120), it has not suffered from ethnic conflicts
● The beautiful carvings and masks made by the Makonde people of Tanzania are among Africa's finest and best-known artworks

KEY POINTS IN RECENT HISTORY
1918 Britain takes over Tanganyika (formerly German East Africa)
1961 Tanganyika becomes independent (December 9)
1962 Tanganyika becomes a republic; Dr Julius Nyerere is elected president

1964 Tanganyika and Zanzibar, which became independent from Britain in 1963 (December 10), unite to form Tanzania
1965 Tanzania becomes a one-party state and pursues Ujamaa policies (a form of rural socialism)

1985 New president, Ali Hassan Mwinyi, aims to reduce state control
1992 A democratic multiparty constitution is introduced
1993 Regional parliaments are set up for mainland Tanganyika and Zanzibar
1995 Multiparty elections take place

See **Peoples of East Africa** on the East African Asians, Maasai, Nyamwezi, and Swahili

Togo

Location: West Africa, facing the Gulf of Guinea
Neighbors: Ghana, Burkina Faso, Benin

Official name: Republic of Togo
Divisions: Five regions
Capital: Lomé
Largest cities: Lomé, Sokodé, Kpalimé, Atakpamé, Tsévié, Bassari (in order of size)

Flag: The three horizontal stripes of green stand for agriculture, the yellow for minerals, and the red square for blood shed during the struggle for independence. The white star stands for purity

◼ Green ☐ Yellow ◼ Red ☐ White

National anthem: "Let us sweep aside all ill feelings that foil the national unity"
Major languages: French (official), Ewe, Akan
Currency: CFA franc = 100 centimes

1977 stamp depicting a crocodile and highlighting endangered wildlife

GEOGRAPHY

With an area of 21,925 square miles (56,786 sq. km), Togo is one of Africa's smaller countries. It is just over twice the size of Maryland in the United States (US).

Togo is a narrow country, measuring about 360 miles (580 km) from north to south. The coastline on the Gulf of Guinea is only 40 miles (64 km) long, while the greatest east-west distance is only 90 miles (145 km).

The country is divided into two main regions by the Togo-Atakora Mountains, which extend diagonally across the country from the southwest to the northeast. South of the mountains is a plateau that descends to a narrow but densely populated coastal plain. To the north is another low plateau region. The highest point in Togo is Mount Agou in the southwest. This mountain reaches 3,235 ft (986 km) above sea level.

The climate is tropical, with high temperatures throughout the year. The main rainy season is from March until July, with a lesser rainy season in October and November. The north is drier, with one rainy season. Tropical savanna covers most of Togo, with some patches of rainforest in the center of the country.

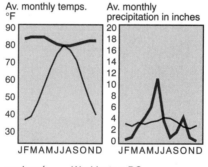

Av. monthly temps. °F

Av. monthly precipitation in inches

— Lomé — Washington, DC

ECONOMY

Chief farm products: Bananas, cassava, cocoa, coffee, corn, cotton, kola nuts, livestock, millet, palm oil and kernels, peanuts, rice, sorghum, yams
Chief mineral resources: Phosphates, iron ore, limestone
Chief industrial products: Beverages, cement, processed food, textiles
Employment:

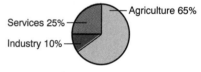

Services 25% — Agriculture 65%
Industry 10% —

In the US, agriculture employs 3% of the work force, industry 25%, and services 72%
Exports: Phosphates, cotton, lime and cement
Per capita income: $320 (as compared with $25,860 in the US)

PEOPLE
Population: 4,010,000 (as compared with the US population of 260,592,000)
Major ethnic groups: Ewe, Tem-Kabre, Gurma, Kebu-Akposo, Yoruba
Religions: African religions (59%), Christianity (28%), Islam (12%)

SOCIAL FACTS
- The average life expectancy at birth is 55 years, as compared with 76 years in the US
- Only 30% of the people live in urban areas, as compared with about 76% in the US
- The port of Lomé also handles trade for Niger and Burkina Faso

- From the 1400s until the 1800s, Togo was called "the coast of slaves"
- Togo is an Ewe word meaning "behind the sea"; the Ewe form the largest single ethnic group
- Germany, France, and Britain all once colonized Togo

KEY POINTS IN RECENT HISTORY
1919 After World War I, the League of Nations partitions the former German Togoland between Britain and France
1957 British Togoland joins Ghana, which becomes independent
1960 French Togoland becomes the

independent Republic of Togo (April 27); Sylvanus Olympio becomes the first president
1963 Olympio is assassinated; his successor is Nicolas Grunitzky
1967 Army officers led by Gnassingbe Eyadéma seize power

1992 Togo adopts a new constitution
1994 The Rassemblement du Peuple Togolais (RPT), formerly the sole party, sets up a coalition government with one of the opposition parties. CFA franc, which is linked to the French franc, is devalued by 50%

See **Peoples of West Africa** on the Asante, Ewe, and Yoruba

© DIAGRAM

Tunisia

Location: North Africa, facing the Mediterranean Sea
Neighbors: Libya, Algeria

Official name: Republic of Tunisia
Divisions: 23 governorates
Capital: Tunis
Largest cities: Tunis, Sfax, L'Ariana, Bizerte, Djerba, Gabès, Sousse, Kairouan (in order of size)

Flag: The white circle in the center of the flag contains two symbols of Islam – the crescent and the star. The flag dates from 1835 and is based on that of Turkey, but it did not become Tunisia's national flag until 1956

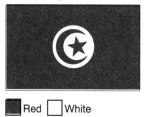

■ Red □ White

National anthem: "Humata al hima" ("Defenders of the homeland")
Major languages: Arabic (official), French, Berber
Currency: Dinar = 1,000 millimes

1978 stamp marking International Antiapartheid Year

GEOGRAPHY

With an area of 63,360 square miles (164,102 sq. km), Tunisia is Africa's thirty-fourth largest country. It is a little larger in area than Georgia in the United States (US).

The eastern ranges of the Atlas Mountains, which run through Morocco and Algeria, extend into northern Tunisia. The country's highest point, Mount Chambi, is in the southern branch of the Atlas Mountains, which is called the Tebessa Mountains. Mount Chambi reaches a height of 5,066 ft (1,544 m) above sea level.

Fertile plains lie to the north and east of the Atlas ranges, but to the south, the land descends in a series of plateaus into the barren Sahara. Central Tunisia contains several depressions, which are salt pans. The largest is the Chott Djerid. Tunisia has only one permanent river, the Medjerda in the north.

Northern Tunisia has hot, dry summers and mild, rainy winters, the climate of Mediterranean lands. The rainfall decreases to the south. Forests of cork oak and other trees grow in the mountains, but the northern plains support only scrub vegetation. Dry grassland in central Tunisia merges into desert in the south.

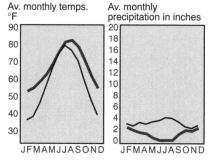

Av. monthly temps. °F

Av. monthly precipitation in inches

JFMAMJJASOND   JFMAMJJASOND

— Tunis   — Washington, DC

ECONOMY

Chief farm products: Almonds, barley, citrus fruits, dates, grapes, livestock, olive oil, sugar beets, vegetables, wheat
Chief mineral resources: Oil and natural gas, phosphates, iron ore
Chief industrial products: Cement, phosphoric acid, processed food
Employment:

Agriculture 28%
Services 39%
Industry 33%

In the US, agriculture employs 3% of the work force, industry 25%, and services 72%
Exports: Clothing and accessories, oil and oil products, olive oil
Per capita income: $1,790 (as compared with $25,860 in the US)

PEOPLE

Population: 8,733,000 (as compared with the US population of 260,529,000)
Major ethnic groups: Arab, Berber, French, Italian
Religions: Islam (99.4%), Christianity, Judaism

SOCIAL FACTS

● The average life expectancy at birth is 68 years, as compared with 76 years in the US
● Only 57% of the people live in urban areas, as compared with about 76% in the US
● More than three million tourists visit Tunisia every year

● Kairouan in Tunisia is the fourth holiest city of Islam, after Mecca, Medina, and Jerusalem; Kairouan was founded in 671
● The site of ancient Carthage is just north of the city of Tunis
● Tunisia's educational system is one of the best in Africa

KEY POINTS IN RECENT HISTORY

1934 Habib Bourguiba sets up the nationalist Néo-Destour (New Constitution) Party, later called the Parti Socialiste Destourien (PSD)
1956 Tunisia becomes independent from France as a monarchy (March 20);

Bourguiba is prime minister
1957 Tunisia becomes a republic; Bourguiba becomes president
1987 The prime minister, Zine al Abidine Ben Ali, removes Bourguiba from office and becomes president
1988 Opposition parties are allowed

1989 Ben Ali, leader of the Rassemblement Constitutionnel Démocratique (formerly the PSD), is elected president
1992 A fundamentalist Islamic group, Nahda, is banned
1994 Ben Ali is reelected unopposed

*See **Peoples of North Africa** on the Arabs and Berbers*

Uganda

Location: Landlocked nation in East Africa
Neighbors: Tanzania, Rwanda, Zaire, Sudan, Kenya

Official name: Republic of Uganda
Divisions: Thirty-eight districts
Capital: Kampala
Largest cities: Kampala, Jinja, Mbale, Masaka, Gulu, Entebbe, Soroti, Mbarara (in order of size)

Flag: The six horizontal stripes on the flag of Uganda are, from top to bottom, black, yellow, red, black, yellow, and red. The bird depicted within the white central disk is a crested crane, Uganda's national emblem

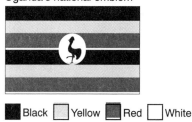

■ Black ▢ Yellow ■ Red ▢ White

National anthem: "Oh, Uganda, may God uphold thee"
Major languages: Swahili, English (both official), Ganda, Luo, Nyoro
Currency: Shilling = 100 cents

cordia abyssinica 5c

1969 stamp depicting Ugandan flowers

GEOGRAPHY

With an area of 93,074 square miles (241,061 sq. km), Uganda is one of Africa's smaller countries. It is about the same size as Oregon in the United States (US).

Uganda lies mainly on the high East African plateau, east of an arm of the Great Rift Valley that contains lakes Edward and Albert. However, Uganda's largest lake, Victoria, is not in the Rift Valley but occupies a shallow depression in the plateau. The highest mountains are in the southwestern Ruwenzori Range, where Margherita Peak reaches a height of 16,762 ft (5,109 m) above sea level.

The chief river of Uganda is the Nile, which is the only outlet of Lake Victoria. Called the Victoria Nile when it leaves the lake, it flows through lakes Kyoga and Albert before flowing north, as the Albert Nile, into Sudan.

Uganda is on the equator and the climate is always warm. The wettest regions lie north of Lake Victoria. Some rainforest grows in the south of the country, but much of the original forest is now farmland. Wooded tropical savanna covers much of the center and north. Strange giant herbs grow to tree size along the Ruwenzori Range.

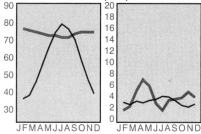

Av. monthly temps. °F

Av. monthly precipitation in inches

JFMAMJJASOND   JFMAMJJASOND

— Kampala — Washington, DC

ECONOMY

Chief farm products: Bananas, beans, cassava, coffee, corn, cotton, meat, sugar cane, tea, tobacco
Chief mineral resources: Gold, copper, tungsten
Chief industrial products: Beverages, cement, footwear, processed food, textiles
Employment:

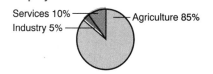

Services 10%
Industry 5%
Agriculture 85%

In the US, agriculture employs 3% of the work force, industry 25%, and services 72%.
Exports: Coffee, cotton, gold, tea, tobacco, copper
Per capita income: $190 (as compared with $25,860 in the US)

PEOPLE

Population: 18,600,000 (as compared with the US population of 260,529,000)
Major ethnic groups: Ganda, Teso, Nkole, Soga, Gisu, Chiga, Lango
Religions: Christianity (78%), African religions, Islam

SOCIAL FACTS

● The average life expectancy at birth is 42 years, as compared with 76 years in the US
● Only 12% of the people live in urban areas, as compared with about 76% in the US
● Uganda has one of the world's highest rates of HIV infection

● Rivalries between people of the diverse ethnic groups has led to much bloodshed and instability
● Most Ugandan Asians were forced to leave the country in the early 1970s
● Before Europeans arrived, much of Uganda was divided into centralized kingdoms, such as Buganda, Bunyoro, Ankole, and Toro

KEY POINTS IN RECENT HISTORY

1962 Uganda becomes independent from Britain (October 9); Dr Milton Obote becomes prime minister
1963 The Kabaka (king) of Buganda is elected head of state
1966 Obote dismisses the kabaka; he becomes president, and abolishes the four kingdoms of Toro, Ankole, Buganda, and Bunyoro
1971 Idi Amin Dada seizes power
1972 Ugandan Asians expelled by Amin
1979 Tanzanian troops and Ugandan rebels invade and overthrow Amin

1980 Obote is restored to power; a guerrilla war breaks out
1985 Obote is overthrown
1986 Guerrilla leader Yoweri Museveni takes power and restores order
1993 The four kingdoms are restored, but only as cultural institutions

© DIAGRAM

*See **Peoples of East Africa** on the East African Asians, Ganda, Karamojong, and Nyoro*

Zaire

Location: Central Africa, facing the Atlantic Ocean
Neighbors: Congo, Central African Republic, Sudan, Uganda, Rwanda, Burundi, Zambia, Angola
Official name: Republic of Zaire
Divisions: Ten regions and Kinshasa
Capital: Kinshasa
Largest cities: Kinshasa, Lubumbashi, Mbuji-Mayi, Kisangani, Kananga (in order of size)

Flag: The flag of Zaire has a plain green background with a yellow disk at its center. The blazing torch depicted within the yellow disk symbolizes Zaire's revolutionary spirit

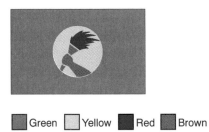

■ Green	□ Yellow	■ Red	■ Brown

National anthem: "Zaireans, in peace found again, are a united people"
Major languages: French (official), Luba, Kongo, Lingala
Currency: Zaire = 100 makuta

1973 stamp marking Zaire's Third International Fair, Kinshasa

GEOGRAPHY

With an area of 905,568 square miles (2,345,412 sq. km), Zaire is Africa's third largest country. It is 3.4 times larger in area than Texas in the United States (US).

Zaire lies mainly within the Congo (Zaire) River Basin. This river is Africa's second longest, with a length of about 2,900 miles (4,660 km). It carries more water than any other river in the world apart from the Amazon.

The land rises to the east, where mountains border the Great Rift Valley. Zaire's highest point is Margherita Peak, 16,762 ft (5,109 m), in the Ruwenzori Range on the Uganda border. There are other highlands are in the south.

The Great Rift Valley contains lakes Tanganyika (Zaire's largest), Kivu, Edward, and Albert. Zaire's eastern border runs through these lakes.

Northern Zaire has an equatorial climate, with high temperatures and heavy rainfall. Rainforests cover much of the land, but the south has a marked dry season, and there, the forests give way to tropical savanna. Zaire's highlands have a cooler climate and zones of vegetation based on altitude.

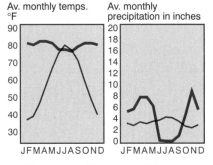

Av. monthly temps. °F
Av. monthly precipitation in inches

— Kinshasa   — Washington, DC

ECONOMY

Chief farm products: Bananas, cassava, coffee, corn, cotton, palm oil, peanuts, rice, rubber, timber
Chief mineral resources: Copper, diamonds, oil, gold, silver
Chief industrial products: Beverages, cement, chemicals, footwear, processed food, textiles, tires
Employment:

Services 19%
Industry 13%
Agriculture 68%

In the US, agriculture employs 3% of the work force, industry 25%, and services 72%
Exports: Copper, industrial diamonds, oil, coffee
Per capita income: $220 (as compared with $25,860 in the US)

PEOPLE

Population: 42,540,000 (as compared with the US population of 260,529,000)
Major ethnic groups: Luba, Kongo, Mongo, Azande
Religions: Christianity (94.5%), African religions (3%), Islam (1%)

SOCIAL FACTS

● The average life expectancy at birth is 52 years, as compared with 76 years in the US
● Only 29% of the people live in urban areas, as compared with about 76% in the US
● The province of Kasai uses a different currency from the rest of Zaire; it has

refused to adopt the new zaire notes and still uses the old ones
● In 1971, many names were Africanized; Léopoldville became Kinshasa and President Joseph-Désiré Mobutu became Mobutu Sese Seko
● Secessionist groups, especially in the mineral-rich Shaba (previously Katanga) region, have caused political instability

KEY POINTS IN RECENT HISTORY

1908 Zaire becomes a Belgian colony, known as Belgian Congo
1960 Zaire gains its independence (June 30); it is called Congo (Kinshasa) to distinguish it from its neighbor, Congo (Brazzaville)
1960–3 Civil (First Shaba) War

1965 General Joseph-Désiré Mobutu becomes president and puts down rebellions
1970 Mobutu declares the country to be a one-party state
1971 Congo (Kinshasa) is renamed Republic of Zaire
1990 Mobutu announces that Zaire will

eventually become a multiparty state once again
1991 Mobutu sets up a national conference to draft a new multiparty constitution but postpones elections
1996 Rwanda/Burundi conflict spreads to Tutsi of eastern Zaire and refugee crisis and civil disorder follow

*See **Peoples of Central Africa** on the Azande, Bemba, Chokwe, Kongo, Kuba, Luba, Lunda, Mbenga, Mbuti, Mongo, Teke, and Twa*

Zambia

Location: Landlocked country in Central Africa
Neighbors: Tanzania, Malawi, Mozambique, Zimbabwe, Namibia, Angola, Zaire
Official name: Republic of Zambia
Divisions: Nine provinces
Capital: Lusaka
Largest cities: Lusaka, Ndola, Kitwe, Mufulira, Chingola (in order of size)

Flag: The background field of green stands for the country's natural resources. An orange eagle, top right, flies over three vertical stripes of red, for freedom; black, for the people; and orange, for Zambia's great mineral wealth

□ Green □ Orange ■ Red ■ Black

National anthem: "Stand and sing of Zambia, proud and free"
Major languages: English (official), eight major African languages
Currency: Kwacha = 100 ngwee

1967 stamp marking the inauguration of the National Assembly Building

GEOGRAPHY

With an area of 290,587 square miles (752,617 sq. km), Zambia is Africa's seventeenth largest country. It is nearly 1.1 times as large as Texas in the United States (US).

Zambia consists mainly of gently rolling plateaus from 3,000 to 5,000 ft (900–1,500 m) above sea level. The Muchinga Mountains, in the northeast along the Malawi border, have peaks topping 7,000 ft (2,100 m).

Southern Zambia is part of the Zambezi River basin. The Zambezi River has been dammed to create the artificial Lake Kariba along the border with Zimbabwe. There are several natural lakes in the north. Lake Bangweulu is fed by the Chambeshi River. Its outlet, the Luapula River, feeds Lake Mweru, which in turn is drained by the Luvua, a headwater of the Congo (Zaire) River.

Zambia lies within the tropics, but its altitude moderates temperatures. The rainy season extends from November until March, and the rainfall is highest in the north. Wooded tropical savanna covers much of Zambia, and there are large swamps in some areas. The southwest has some evergreen forest.

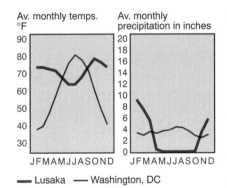

Av. monthly temps. °F
Av. monthly precipitation in inches

JFMAMJJASOND JFMAMJJASOND

— Lusaka — Washington, DC

ECONOMY

Chief farm products: Cassava, corn, cotton, fruits, livestock, millet, peanuts, sorghum, soybeans, sugar cane, tobacco, vegetables, wheat
Chief mineral resources: Copper, zinc, cobalt, lead, silver, gold
Chief industrial products: Cement, processed food, refined metals, sulfuric acid
Employment:

Services 17% — Agriculture 75%
Industry 8% —

In the US, agriculture employs 3% of the work force, industry 25%, and services 72%
Exports: Copper, cobalt, zinc, tobacco, lead
Per capita income: $350 (as compared with $25,860 in the US)

PEOPLE

Population: 9,200,000 (as compared with the US population of 260,529,000)
Major ethnic groups: Bemba, Maravi, Tonga
Religions: Christianity (72%), African religions (27%)

SOCIAL FACTS

- The average life expectancy at birth is 47 years, as compared with 76 years in the US
- Only 43% of the people live in urban areas, as compared with about 76% in the US
- Zambia is one of the world's top ten copper producers

- From 1911 until 1964, Zambia was called Northern Rhodesia, after the British imperialist Cecil Rhodes
- Zambia was named after the Zambezi, Africa's fourth longest river after the Nile, Congo (Zaire), and Niger rivers
- Woodcarving, basketry, and pottery are important art forms

KEY POINTS IN RECENT HISTORY

1924 Northern Rhodesia becomes a British territory
1953 The territory becomes part of the Central African Federation (CAF) with Southern Rhodesia and Nyasaland; many Africans oppose this step

1963 The CAF is dissolved
1964 The country becomes independent as Zambia (October 24); Kenneth Kaunda, leader of the United National Independent Party (UNIP), becomes president
1972 UNIP becomes sole legal party

1990 Opposition parties are legalized
1991 The Movement for Multiparty Democracy (MMD) defeats UNIP in parliamentary elections, and Frederick Chiluba defeats Kaunda in presidential elections

*See **Peoples of Central Africa** on the Bemba, Lozi, Lunda, and Tonga*

Zimbabwe

Location: Landlocked nation in Southern Africa

Neighbors: Botswana, Zambia, Mozambique, South Africa

Official name: Republic of Zimbabwe

Divisions: Eight provinces and two cities with provincial status

Capital: Harare

Largest cities: Harare, Bulawayo, Chitungwiza, Mutare, Gweru (in order of size)

Flag: The flag of Zimbabwe has horizontal stripes of green, yellow, red, black, red, yellow, and green. The triangle on the left contains a star and a depiction of the Great Zimbabwe soapstone bird

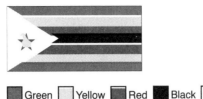

☐ Green ☐ Yellow ☐ Red ☐ Black ☐ White

National anthem: "Ishe komborarei Africa" ("God bless Africa")

Major languages: English (official), Shona, Ndebele

Currency: Zimbabwe dollar = 100 cents

1989 Stamp depicting the black rhinoceros, an endangered species

GEOGRAPHY

With an area of 150,873 square miles (390,760 sq. km), Zimbabwe is Africa's twenty-fifth largest country. It is about the same size as Montana in the United States (US).

A plateau region, at a height of about 3,000 to 5,000 ft (900–1,500 m) above sea level, makes up most of Zimbabwe. The central High Veld contains a mineral-rich ridge called the Great Dyke. On either side of the High Veld is a large but lower region called the Middle Veld. The smaller Low Veld consists of plains in the Limpopo, Sabi, and Zambezi river basins.

The Eastern Highlands, along the Mozambique border, contain the highest peak, Mount Inyangani, at 8,514 ft (2,595 m). Lake Kariba, an artificial lake that Zimbabwe shares with Zambia, was created by a dam on the Zambezi and is the country's largest lake.

Zimbabwe has a tropical climate, but temperatures are moderated by the altitude. Summers (from October until March) are generally hot and wet, and winters are cool and dry. Forests grow in the wet areas, including the Eastern Highlands, with grasslands at the highest levels. Woodland savanna covers most of the country.

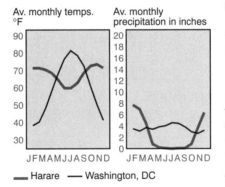

Av. monthly temps. °F / Av. monthly precipitation in inches

— Harare —— Washington, DC

ECONOMY

Chief farm products: barley, beef, coffee, cotton, maize, millet, peanuts, sorghum, soybeans, sugar, sunflower seeds, tea, tobacco, wheat

Chief mineral resources: Gold, asbestos, nickel, chromium

Chief industrial products: metal and wood products, processed food, textiles

Employment:

Services 24%
Industry 8%
Agriculture 68%

In the US, agriculture employs 3% of the work force, industry 25%, and services 72%

Chief exports: Metals and metal products, tobacco

Per capita income: $500 (as compared with $25,860 in the US)

PEOPLE

Population: 10,800,000 (as compared with the US population of 260,529,000)

Major ethnic groups: Shona, Matabele, Tonga, Venda, Sotho

Religions: Christianity (45%), African religions (40%)

SOCIAL FACTS

● The average life expectancy at birth is 58 years, as compared with 76 years in the US

● Only 31% of the people live in urban areas, as compared with about 76% in the US

● Zimbabwe literally means "house of stone." Dry-wall (without mortar)

structures, such as those at Great Zimbabwe, are unique in Southern Africa. They were built by a historic Shona civilization

● Zimbabwe has one of the world's highest rates of HIV infection

● Zimbabwe was once called Southern Rhodesia and then Rhodesia, after the British imperialist Cecil Rhodes

KEY POINTS IN RECENT HISTORY

1923 The country becomes a British colony called Southern Rhodesia

1953 The country becomes part of the Central African Federation (CAF) with Southern Rhodesia and Nyasaland

1963 CAF is dissolved; Ian Smith becomes prime minister of Rhodesia

(as the country is named when Northern Rhodesia becomes Zambia and Nyasaland becomes Malawi)

1965 The white government declares Rhodesia independent (November 11), an action which is widely condemned as illegal

1970 Rhodesia becomes a republic

1970s Black African guerrillas fight for majority rule and independence

1980 The country becomes legally independent as Zimbabwe (April 18)

1996 Robert Mugabe wins a fourth successive term as president

*See **Peoples of Southern Africa** on the Afrikaners, Khoisan, Matabele, Ndebele, and Shona*

Biographies

Abacha, General Sanni (born 1943)
Sanni Abacha became head of Nigeria's military government in November 1993. His postponement of the return to civilian rule, together with alleged abuses of human rights, provoked international criticism. In 1995, Nigeria's membership of the Commonwealth was suspended after the execution of nine political dissidents, including KEN SARO-WIWA.

Abbas, Ferhat (1899–1985)
One of the leaders of Algeria's fight for independence, Ferhat Abbas was the first president of the Algerian provisional government in exile (1958–61). He also served as president of Algeria's National Assembly (1962–4), until differences with AHMED BEN BELLA led to his resignation and house arrest (1964–5). Abbas was rehabilitated shortly before he died.

Abd al Kadir (1807–83)
Abd al Kadir, Emir (ruler) of Oran, led the resistance to the French conquest of Algeria. He fought the French from 1832, scoring several victories, but was eventually defeated and surrendered in 1847. Imprisoned in France, he was freed by Emperor Napoleon III in 1852 and died in Damascus, Syria.

Abd al Krim (1882–1963)
A Berber chief and a great Moroccan resistance fighter, Abd al Krim – "the Wolf of the Rif Mountains" – was founder and president of the Republic of the Rif (1921–6). He was defeated by a combined French and Spanish army of 250,000 troops in May 1926, and exiled to the island of Réunion in the Indian Ocean. He was freed in 1947 and went to Egypt.

Abd al Mumin (c. 1094–1163)
Abd al Mumin was a Berber chief who founded the Almohad dynasty in North Africa. He succeeded IBN TUMART, founder of the Almohad sect, and proclaimed himself caliph (ruler) of the dynasty. He overthrew the Almoravid dynasty, conquered Morocco, Tunis, and Tripoli, and paved the way for the Almohad conquest of Islamic Spain.

Sanni Abacha

Abdullah, Ahmad (1919–89)
Ahmad Abdullah became the first head of state of the Comoros in 1975, but later that year he was deposed in a coup. He was elected president after another coup in 1978, made the Comoros into an Islamic one-party state, and was reelected in 1984. In 1989, he was assassinated by his presidential guard and succeeded by SAID MUHAMMAD DJOHAR.

Abeni, Queen Salawo (born 1965)
Queen Salawo Abeni is a Nigerian singing prodigy who recorded her first album, *The Late Murtala Mohammed*, at the age of twelve. She specializes in Waka, a singing style featuring a female vocalist and drums. She sings mostly in the Yoruba language.

Abd al Kadir

Abiodan, Dele (born 1955)
A Nigerian singer and composer, Dele Abiodan created the style called Adawa, a mixture of Afro-Beat and juju, a Yoruba music style based on guitars. It includes talking drums and the Hawaiian steel guitar.

Abiola, Chief Moshood (born 1938)
Chief Abiola, a Yoruba Muslim, led the Social Democratic Party to victory in elections in Nigeria in 1993, but the military government suspended the results and, in 1994, he was arrested and charged with treason. He was replaced by the dictator General SANNI ABACHA. Abiola's wife Kudirat – a campaigner for the restoration of democracy in Nigeria – was murdered in 1996.

Abrahams, Peter (born 1919)
Peter Abrahams is a major South African novelist who wrote about the political struggles of black people, notably in *A Wreath for Udomo* (1956), *The View from Coyaba* (1985), and *Tell Freedom* (1954), his autobiography. He left South Africa at the age of twenty and wrote most of his works in exile.

Achebe, Chinua (born 1930)
A Nigerian poet and novelist, Chinua Achebe won the Commonwealth Prize for his book *Beware, Soul Brother* (1971). He is probably the most widely-read African writer, and his *Things Fall Apart* (1958) has been translated into over forty languages.

Ade, King Sunny Adeniyi (born 1947)
Now a world-famous musician, King Sunny Ade came from a Yoruba royal family and was one of the leaders of the Nigerian juju music craze of the 1980s. He was greatly influenced by IK DAIRO, one of the founders of juju (which came from an amalgamation of a kind of African blues with traditional Yoruba music).

Africanus, Leo *see* **Leo Africanus**

King Sunny Ade

Ahidjo, Ahmadou (1924–89)
As prime minister of Cameroon (1958–60), Ahmadou Ahidjo led his country to independence and was its first president (1960–82). He achieved the complex task of uniting the French- and English-speaking parts of the country. In November 1982, he resigned the presidency and handed over his responsibilities to the prime minister, PAUL BIYA. In 1983, he went into exile in France.

Aideed, Muhammad Farrah (1934–96)
A soldier and former diplomat, Muhammad Farrah Aideed was the best-known of the clan leaders who struggled for power in Somalia in the 1990s. He became internationally famous when his militia killed members of the United Nations peacekeeping mission, forcing it to withdraw. Aideed declared himself president of Somalia in 1995 but died as a result of fighting in 1996.

Aidoo, Ama Ata (born 1942)
Ama Ata Aidoo is a Ghanaian writer noted for her novels, plays, and poems about women in modern Africa. A chief's daughter, for twelve years she was a university professor of English. She lived in Zimbabwe for some time, but moved to the United States in the 1990s.

Akendengue, Pierre (born 1944)
Pierre Akendengue, a Gabonese musician, was forced into exile in 1972 after criticizing his country's government. He studied literature and psychology at French universities, but then lost his sight. *Nandipo*, the first major recording by his band, blended

music, poetry, and politics, with both traditional and modern instruments providing the backing. He received a presidential pardon in 1977.

Al Hajj Umar (1794–1864)

Al Hajj Umar, born Umar Said Tall in Futa Toro, northern Senegal, was the Fulani Muslim leader who founded the Tukolor Empire. In the 1840s, he established a fortress in the the town of Dinguiray (in present-day Guinea), where he trained and armed a powerful army. From there, in 1852, he began a jihad (Islamic holy war) during which he conquered the West African states of Kaarta, Segu, and Macina, but was driven out of Futa Toro by the French. In 1864, he was killed during a battle with Fulani, Bambara, and Tuareg forces who had rebelled against his rule and besieged the Macina town of Hamdullahi.

Alkali, Zaynab (born 1950)

Zaynab Alkali was the first woman novelist from northern Nigeria. She was born in Borno State to an Islamic family, but was brought up in a Christian community in eastern Nigeria. Her first novel, *The Stillborn* (1984), dealt with the ambitions of women in a male-dominated world.

Amin Dada, Idi (born 1925)

Commander of Uganda's army from 1968, Idi Amin seized power in January 1971. On becoming president of the country, he declared himself champion for life. His regime was harsh and brutal, and he murdered thousands of his opponents and expelled Uganda's Asian population. Amin was deposed by rebels led by YOWERI MUSEVENI and backed by the Tanzanian army in 1979 and fled into exile, finally settling in Saudi Arabia. Amin was once the heavyweight boxing champion of Uganda, a title he held from 1951 to 1969.

Ampadu, Kwame (born c. 1946)

A leader of Ghanaian popular music (1965–75), Kwame Ampadu dominated the guitar-based highlife style. This style relies on traditional African sources and jazz influences. "Nana" ("King") Ampadu, as he became known, formed the African Brother International band, which became the premier band in Ghana.

Anthony of Egypt (or Thebes or Memphis), Saint (c. 250–356)

Saint Anthony was an Egyptian Copt who founded the first Christian monastery. From the age of twenty, he lived as a hermit near the Red Sea, and in 305, he organized his fellow hermits into a monastery. At the age of one hundred he preached against false beliefs in Alexandria.

Aouita, Said (born 1959)

Said Aouita, a Moroccan runner, won gold in the 5,000 meters finals in the 1984 Los Angeles Olympics. Over the next four years, he broke the world records for 2,000 meters, 1,500 meters, and 5,000 meters.

Arabi, Ahmad (Arabi Pasha) (1839–1911)

Ahmad Arabi, an Egyptian soldier and revolutionary popularly known as Arabi Pasha, led a rebellion to overthrow the Egyptian rulers Ismail Pasha in 1879 and Tewfik Pasha in 1881. Britain invaded Egypt in 1882

Idi Amin

to maintain control of the Suez Canal, and defeated him at the Battle of Tell al Kebir. The British captured him and tried him for sedition, exiling him to Ceylon (now Sri Lanka) until 1901.

Armatto, Raphael Ernest Grail Glikpo (1913–53)

Raphael Armatto was born in Togoland, now part of Ghana, and was one of Ghana's leading poets. His work describes the African experience in colonial times. He studied medicine in Scotland and Germany, anthropology and French literature in France, and worked as a doctor in Northern Ireland.

Asabia (born 1957)

Asabia (Eugenia Asabia Cropper) is a Ghanaian singer and saxophonist. She turned professional after a successful tour of Togo as an amateur singer and has performed with several bands, preferring to work in her homeland.

Askia Muhammad (c. 1450–1528)

In 1493, Muhammad Toure seized the throne of the Songhay Empire (in present-day Mali) and took the title of Askia ("Usurper"). A devout Muslim, he overthrew the non-Muslim Sunni Baru, the son of SUNNI ALI, who rebuilt Songhay after its domination by the Empire of Mali. Muhammad greatly extended the empire and made it prosperous, but was deposed and exiled by his eldest son in 1528.

Awolowo, Obafemi (1909–87)

A major Yoruba leader, Nigerian statesman, and influential writer, Obafemi Awolowo was premier of Nigeria's Western Region (1954–9) and leader of the opposition in the federal parliament (1960–2) after independence. In 1962, Awolowo and other opposition leaders were arrested on charges of treasonable felony. Awolowo was eventually jailed.

Awoonor, Kofi Niydevu (born 1935)

Kofi Awoonor is a leading West African writer in Ewe and English. His poems and novels reflect African cultural traditions, especially those of the Ewe people. He was a university professor both in the United States (1967–75) and in Ghana, and has won prizes for his poetry and written histories of Ghana and studies of African literature.

Azikiwe, Nnamdi (1904–96)

Nnamdi Azikiwe was Nigeria's first president, from 1963 until 1966. In 1937, he took a leading part in the Nigerian nationalist movement, becoming president of the National Council of Nigeria and the Cameroons. He became prime minister of the eastern region (1954–9) and Governor-General of Nigeria (1960–3). During the Biafran (Nigerian Civil) War (1967–70), he first acted as spokesman for his fellow Igbo people, but he later supported the federal government.

Ba, Mariama (1929–81)

A Senegalese teacher and champion of women's rights, Mariama Ba sprang to fame with her prizewinning first novel *Une Si Longue Lettre* (1979). She died just as her second novel, *Le Chante Ecarlate*, was about to be published. Separated from her politician husband, Obeye Diop, she raised her nine children singlehanded.

Mariama Ba

Babangida, Ibrahim Badanosi (born 1941)

In 1985, as commander-in-chief of the army, Ibrahim Babangida led a coup against President Buhari and assumed the presidency himself. He held office until 1993, when, after declaring void the results of a general election won by Chief MOSHOOD ABIOLA, he stood down in favor of a nonelected interim government.

Balewa, Sir Abubakar Tafawa (1912–66)

Abubakar Tafawa Balewa was elected first federal prime minister of Nigeria in 1959. A Muslim northerner, he was spokesman for the Northern People's Congress (NPC). The NPC was determined that a federal Nigeria would not be dominated by Western-educated southerners, and argued for official recognition of Islam and for at least half of federal representatives to be northerners. He was knighted when Nigeria became independent in 1960, and assassinated in January 1966 during a military coup.

Ballinger, Margaret Hodgson (1894–1980)

Ballinger was a Scottish-born South African lecturer and a campaigner against apartheid. She also did pioneering historical research at the University of Witwatersrand. She and ALAN PATON formed the Liberal Party in 1953, and for many years she was one of four whites elected to represent black South Africans in parliament. She had retired from politics by 1960 and devoted herself to campaigning for African women's rights.

Banda, Dr Hastings Kamuzu (born 1905)

Hastings Banda was appointed prime minister of Malawi in 1963 and president in 1966. His policies contrasted strongly with the socialist aims of some of his neighbors, and he encouraged officials to follow his example in buying farms and investing in businesses. He was voted "president-for-life" in July 1971, but that title was withdrawn when multiparty government was restored in l993. He lost the 1994 elections and Bakili Muluzi became president. In 1995, he was cleared of murdering four of his former ministers.

Hastings Banda

Barnard, Dr Christiaan Neethling (born 1922)

Christiaan Barnard, a South African surgeon, performed the world's first human heart transplant, in 1967. The patient, Louis Washkansky, died of pneumonia eighteen days later, but other patients lived much longer. Barnard studied in South Africa and at the University of Minnesota. His books include an autobiography and works on medicine.

Sir Abubakar Balewa

Bekederemo, John Pepper Clark (born 1936)

John Bekederemo is one of Nigeria's leading writers and was professor of English at the University of Lagos until 1980. The son of an Ijaw chief, he wrote under the name "John Pepper Clark" for some years, reverting to his full name in 1985. His most important work is *The Ozidi Saga* (1976), a series of plays based on Ijaw epic drama.

Ben Ali, Zine al Abidine (born 1936)
In a peaceful takeover in November 1987, Zine al Abidine Ben Ali, prime minister of Tunisia since early October, replaced former President HABIB BOURGUIBA as head of state. He was reelected in 1989 and 1994. His government has been criticized for abuses of human rights, but praised for its economic reforms.

Ben Bella, Muhammad Ahmad (born 1916)
The first prime minister of Algeria (1962–3), Ahmad Ben Bella became the first elected president, in 1963. His dictatorial style of government aroused opposition, and he was deposed and arrested in a bloodless military coup in 1965, led by HOUARI BOUMEDIENNE. He was detained until 1979. One of the leaders of the struggle for Algerian independence, Ben Bella was twice imprisoned by the French (1950–2 and 1956–62).

Beti, Mongo (born 1932)
Mongo Beti (real name Alexandre Biyidi) is one of Cameroon's leading writers, and his novels reflect the adverse effects of colonialism on African ways of life. He uses the French language, having studied at the Sorbonne in Paris, where he obtained a doctorate in literature. His best-known novel is *Poor Christ of Bomba* (1965), about a missionary's failure to understand African culture.

Bikila, Abebe (1932–73)
Abebe Bikila, the great Ethiopian marathon runner, then virtually unknown and running barefoot, won the gold medal in the marathon at the 1960 Rome Olympics. He was the first Black African to do so and also set a new world record time of 2 hrs 15 mins 16.2 secs. He went on to take gold at the 1964 Tokyo Olympics, where he again set a new world record, of 2 hrs 12 mins 11.2 secs. He was paralyzed in an automobile accident in 1969, but became a paraplegic athlete (archery and javelin) and founded the Ethiopian Paraplegic Sports Association.

Biko, Steve (Stephan Bantu) (1946–77)
A founder of South Africa's Black Consciousness movement, Steve Biko was the first president of the all-black South African Students' Organization. He was also an organizer of the Black Community Program, which encouraged black pride and opposition to apartheid, and the government banned him from political activity in 1973. He died of head injuries while in police custody.

Biya, Paul (born 1933)
Paul Biya, prime minister of Cameroon (1975–82), became the country's second president when AHMADOU AHIDJO resigned in 1982. He survived a coup attempt in 1984, which caused considerable loss of life, and after widespread protest, he legalized opposition parties in 1991. Biya was reelected president in an uncontested election in 1988 and in multiparty elections in 1992.

Blondy, Alpha (born 1953)
An Ivory Coast singer and composer, Alpha Blondy was greatly influenced by the reggae music of the West Indies. He studied trade and English

Steve Biko

Jean-Bédel Bokassa

at Columbia University in the United States, but was sent to a psychiatric hospital for two years by his parents when he returned home a Rastafarian. He sings in English, French, and the Dyula language of his mother.

Blyden, Edward Wilmot (1832–1912)
Edward Blyden was born in the Virgin Islands, but became a professor and major political leader in Liberia, where he settled in 1853. He served as secretary of state there (1864–6), but had to flee to Sierra Leone when his enemies tried to lynch him. He campaigned for African unity and opposed the idea of white superiority.

Bokassa, Jean-Bédel (1921–96)
As the Central African Republic's supreme military commander, Bokassa seized power from DAVID DACKO in 1966 and served as president until 1976, when he made himself "Emperor" of the "Central African Empire." His rule was harsh and dictatorial and he was responsible for many deaths, including those of children. The republic was restored by a coup in 1979, led by Dacko, and Bokassa went into exile. He returned in 1986 and served six years in prison for murder and fraud before dying from a heart attack in 1996.

Bongo, Omar (born 1935)
Omar (formerly Albert-Bernard) Bongo has been president of Gabon since 1967. He also served as prime minister from 1968 until 1976. He made Gabon a one-party state in 1968, and despite some discontent, the country retained its political stability until the late 1980s, when increasing unrest forced a switch to multiparty politics in 1990.

Botha, P. W. (Pieter Willem) (born 1916)
Botha was prime minister (1978–84) and then president (1984–9) of South Africa. His attempts to modify apartheid while maintaining white supremacy alienated the right wing of his National Party, while failing to satisfy black or international opposition to apartheid. He resigned, unwillingly, in 1989 and was replaced by F. W. DE KLERK.

P. W. Botha

Boulmerka, Hassiba (born 1968)
After becoming the first Algerian to win a world running championship in 1991, Hassiba Boulmerka was denounced by Muslim clerics for "running with naked legs in front of men." Despite this criticism, she went on to take gold in the 1,500 meters at the 1992 Barcelona Olympics.

Boumedienne, Houari (1925–78)
Boumedienne replaced BEN BELLA as president of Algeria after a coup in 1965. He established an Islamic socialist government and served as president until 1978. Before independence, he had led guerrilla operations against the French.

Hassiba Boulmerka

Bourguiba, Habib ibn Ali (born 1903)
A radical nationalist, Habib Bourguiba was Tunisia's first prime minister (1956–7) and its first president (1957–87). He attempted to curb Islamic fundamentalists during his years as president and maintained moderate, pro-Western foreign policies. He was declared president-for-life in 1975, but was deposed by

Houari Boumedienne

his prime minister, BEN ALI, in 1987 on the grounds that he was unfit to continue due to senility and ill-health.

Boutros-Ghali, Boutros (born 1922)

Boutros Boutros-Ghali

In 1992, Boutros-Ghali, an Egyptian, became the first African Secretary-General of the United Nations. Egypt regarded his appointment as recognition of its moderating influence in the region. He had earlier served in the Egyptian government as deputy prime minister and, as foreign minister, he helped to win Arab support for the 1991 Gulf War.

Brink, André (born 1935)

André Brink is a dissident South African writer who caused a sensation in the 1960s with his politically inspired novels in Afrikaans, which won widespread acclaim in English translation. *Kennis van die aand* (1973), which he translated as *Looking on Darkness*, was banned by the South African government. He won the Martin Luther King Memorial Prize in 1980.

Brutus, Dennis (born 1924)

Dennis Brutus, a South African poet of mixed parentage, had his works banned by the government in the 1960s because of his antiapartheid views. He was arrested, shot in the back while trying to escape, and then jailed. He went into exile in 1966, settling first in England and then the United States. His *Letters to Martha* are poems written while in prison.

Buthelezi, Chief Mangosuthu Gatsha (born 1928)

Chief Buthelezi

A member of Zulu nobility, Chief Buthelezi became chief executive in the KwaZulu "homeland" in South Africa in the early 1970s. At first a supporter of the African National Congress (ANC), he later formed the Zulu Inkatha movement, which developed into the Inkatha Freedom Party (IFP). This party, which favors maximum autonomy for KwaZulu/Natal (formerly KwaZulu) province, won the provincial elections in 1994, but it finished third in the national elections. Buthelezi then became Minister for Home Affairs in the new South African government.

Buyoya, Pierre (born 1949)

A Tutsi army officer, Pierre Buyoya became president in Burundi in 1987, displacing Jean-Baptiste Bagaza. In 1993, Buyoya was defeated in multiparty elections, but his successor, a Hutu named Melchior Ndadaye, was assassinated later that year, sparking off widespread ethnic conflict. Buyoya again became president in 1996 displacing the Hutu president Sylvestre Ntibantunganyu.

Cabral, Amílcar (1931–73)

Leader of the independence struggle against Portuguese rule in Guinea-Bissau, Amílcar Cabral was assassinated in 1973. He was the founder of the independence movement Partido Africano da Independência do Guiné e Cabo Verde (PAIGC) in 1956.

Cabral, Luiz (born 1929)

Brother of AMILCAR CABRAL and a prominent leader in the independence struggle, Luiz Cabral became the first president of Guinea-Bissau in 1974. Cabral promoted the interests of Cape

Verdeans in Guinea-Bissau while allowing the economy to decline. He was overthrown in a coup led by the prime minister, JOÃO VIEIRA, in 1980.

Cetshwayo (c. 1826–84)

Cetshwayo, a nephew of the great Zulu leader SHAKA, ruled the Zulu kingdom from 1872 and resisted British and Boer colonialism. In 1879, he defeated the British at Isandhlwana but was later defeated and captured at Ulundi. Part of his kingdom was restored to him in 1883, but soon after he was driven out by an antiroyalist faction.

Cheops *see* **Khufu**

Chilembwe, John (c. 1860–1915)

John Chilembwe, a Baptist minister, studied theology in the United States and founded the Providence Industrial Mission at Mbombwe, Nyasaland in 1900, which set up seven schools. In 1915, he led an attack against British rule in Nyasaland (now Malawi). This attack was provoked by the cruelty of white plantation owners. It failed, and Chilembwe was captured and shot.

Chiluba, Frederick (born 1943)

Frederick Chiluba, a former labor leader, became the second president of Zambia by defeating KENNETH KAUNDA in multiparty presidential elections in 1991. His Movement for Multiparty Democracy (MMD) party also won the majority of seats in the National Assembly elections.

Chipenda, Daniel (1931–96)

From 1962, Daniel Chipenda was a prominent guerrilla leader of the Movimento Popular de Libertação de Angola (MPLA) in the independence struggle against the Portuguese. In 1975, the MPLA split and Chipenda became allied with the rival Frente Nacional de Libertação de Angola (FNLA). Following the defeat of the FNLA by the MPLA, Chipenda went into exile in Portugal. He returned to Angola in 1992 and tried to negotiate peace in the ongoing civil war. He managed to make peace with rebel leader JONAS SAVIMBI, and attempted to mediate between him and Angolan president JOSÉ EDUARDO DOS SANTOS.

Cetshwayo

Chissano, Joaquim Alberto (born 1939)

Joaquim Chissano became prime minister of Mozambique in 1974 and president in 1986. He took over as president after the death of SAMORA MACHEL, with whom he had worked closely in the Frente de Libertação de Moçambique (Frelimo) during its fight against Portuguese colonial rule. In 1992, he signed a peace treaty with AFONSO DHLAKAMA, leader of the rebel Resistência Nacional Moçambicana (Renamo). Chissano was reelected president in multiparty elections in 1994.

Cleopatra VII (69–30 BCE)

Cleopatra VII was the last of the Ptolemy dynasty (who were of Macedonian (Greek) origin) to rule Egypt. She took a great interest in her subjects' welfare and won their affection. Cleopatra became queen in 51 BCE but was deposed by supporters of her husband (and younger brother), Ptolemy XIII. She was restored to the throne in 47 BCE by Julius Caesar, a Roman general. Later, she became the lover of another Roman general,

Cleopatra VII

Samuel Ajayi Crowther

Mark Antony. They set up an empire based on Egypt, but were defeated by the Romans at the naval Battle of Actium (31 BCE). In 30 BCE, Antony committed suicide after hearing a false report that Cleopatra had died. Later that year, Cleopatra – unable to save her dynasty – also committed suicide, supposedly by causing a poisonous snake to bite her breast.

Coetzee, J. M. (John Michael) (born 1940)

Coetzee, an Afrikaner, is a South African academic and novelist who has won many literary prizes for his vivid novels, which deal with social and political themes. Among them, *Life and Times of Michael K* (1983), which won the Booker Prize in Britain, is outstanding. Coetzee also won the Jerusalem Prize in 1987 for his opposition to apartheid.

Compaoré, Captain Blaise (born 1951)

Blaise Compaoré became president of Burkina Faso after a coup in 1987 and was reelected in 1991. In 1983, he had helped to organize the coup that brought his predecessor, THOMAS SANKARA, to power. Sankara was killed in the 1987 coup, a fact that made Compaoré widely unpopular.

Conté, Lansana (born 1945)

Lansana Conté took power in Guinea in 1984, when he led a bloodless coup a few days after the death of the first president, SEKOU TOURÉ. At first, he introduced liberal policies, but after a failed coup in 1985, he adopted a more repressive approach. After the introduction of a multiparty system in 1991, he was elected president in

Lansana Conté

1993. In 1996, he survived a crisis when the army mutinied over pay.

Crowther, Bishop Samuel Ajayi (c. 1809–91)

Samuel Crowther was a pioneer of Yoruba language studies and the first West African to become a bishop. A Creole born in Yorubaland, in what is now Nigeria, he was captured by slave traders in 1819 but rescued and freed by the British in 1822. He was ordained as a priest in London in 1825 and returned to Yorubaland as a missionary. Crowther became Bishop of Niger in 1864 and translated the Bible into Yoruba. He also wrote *Grammar and Vocabulary of the Yoruba Language*.

Dacko, David (born 1930)

In 1960, David Dacko became the first president of the Central African Republic. He was deposed in a coup led by his nephew JEAN-BÉDEL BOKASSA in 1966 and placed under house arrest, but he returned to office when he overthrew Bokassa, with French assistance, in a popular bloodless coup in 1979. Although committed to political liberalization, Dacko attempted to curb opposition parties. After reports of ill-health, he was persuaded to hand over power to a military government, led by ANDRÉ KOLINGBA, in 1981.

Dadié, Bernard Binlin (born 1916)

Bernard Dadié is a militant Ivory Coast nationalist who combined a career as a politician with a huge volume of writing. His output included essays, novels, plays (often satirical), poetry, and short stories, greatly influenced by folk tales. He served as Ivory Coast's Minister of Cultural Affairs from 1977 to 1986.

Dairo, IK (Isaiah Kehinde) (1931–96)

IK Dairo was one of the founders of modern Nigerian juju music. In 1956, he formed the Morning Star Band (later the Blue Spots Band), in which he played guitar, talking drum, and accordion. He often toured overseas, and was made a Member of the Order of the British Empire by Queen Elizabeth II. A devout Christian, he founded the Eternal Sacred Order Church in Lagos. For a year, he was visiting professor of African music at Washington State University, Seattle.

Darko, George (born 1951)

George Darko is a Ghanaian guitarist who scored a hit when he blended two styles: highlife (a mixture of African dance music with Western music) and funk (a form of modern jazz). He won international fame when he toured the United States and Europe with his band, Bus Stop.

de Klerk, F. W. (Frederik Willem) (born 1936)

F. W. de Klerk succeeded P. W. BOTHA as president of South Africa in 1989. Under his leadership, the racial policies of apartheid were swiftly dismantled. The release of NELSON MANDELA in 1990 led to multiracial negotiations and elections in 1994, when a multiparty government was set up. Mandela became president and THABO MBEKI and de Klerk became deputy presidents. De Klerk shared the 1993 Nobel Peace Prize with Nelson Mandela.

Dempster, Roland Tombekai (1910–65)

Roland Dempster was Liberia's first poet laureate. His poetry, published in several books, echoes the forms and manners of the English classics. Dempster was successively a civil servant, a journalist, and finally a professor at the University of Liberia.

Dhlakama, Afonso (born 1953)

In 1982, Afonso Dhlakama became president of the Resistência Nacional Moçambicana (Renamo), a guerrilla force founded in 1976, with Rhodesian and later South African support, to destabilize Mozambique. A former member of the Frente de Libertação de Moçambique (Frelimo), which had fought for Mozambique's independence from Portuguese colonial rule, he joined Renamo shortly after it was formed.

Dhlomo, Herbert Isaac Ernest (1903–56)

Herbert Dhlomo was a Zulu novelist, playwright, and poet who wrote in both Zulu and English. His poetry reflects his anger at the plight of the Zulu people under white rule. Dhlomo was successively a school teacher and a journalist, and was a great influence on other Zulu writers in English. He was the younger brother of ROLFUS DHLOMO.

Dhlomo, Rolfus Reginald Raymond (1901–71)

Rolfus Dhlomo wrote what is believed to be the first novel in English by a Zulu writer, *An African Tragedy* (1928). Most of his other novels were historical stories written in the Zulu language. Dhlomo, the

F. W. de Klerk

Manu Dibango

elder brother of HERBERT DHLOMO, spent most of his life as a journalist.

Dibango, Manu (born 1933)

Manu Dibango, a Cameroonian saxophonist, pianist, and composer, dominated African music for more than fifty years. He studied classical music in Paris, then switched to jazz, playing in Belgium, Zaire, and New York City, NY.

Dingane (died c. 1840)

In 1828, after he and his brother Mhlangane assassinated their half-brother SHAKA, Dingane killed Mhlangane and proclaimed himself king of the Zulu. In 1838 he made a pact with PIET RETIEF, one of the Boer leaders of the Great Trek, then treacherously killed the Boers. A few months later, the Boers routed the Zulus at the Battle of Blood River and Dingane fled to Swaziland, where his half-brother Mpande killed him.

Dingiswayo (c. 1770–1818)

Dingiswayo was ruler of Mthethwa, a kingdom that dominated present-day KwaZulu/Natal in the late 1700s and early 1800s. He became overlord of thirty chiefdoms, including the Zulu chiefdom ruled by SHAKA, one of his generals and military advisors. He was killed when his army was defeated by that of a neighboring kingdom, Ndwandwe, in 1818. This defeat led to the breakup of the Mthethwa kingdom and the rapid expansion of Zulu power.

Diop, Alioune (1910–80)

Alioune Diop was a Senegalese writer who founded the journal *Présence Africaine*. Many African political leaders wrote for it, and it was published in Paris, where Diop was senator for Senegal and worked as a professor of classical literature.

Diop, Bigaro Ismail (1906–89)

Bigaro Diop was a Senegalese poet who popularized the traditional folk tales of the Wolof people. He qualified as a veterinarian in France, then set up in practice in what was then French West Africa. He worked in Paris, France from 1942 until 1944.

Diori, Hamani (1916–89)

Hamani Diori became the first president of Niger when the country gained independence from France in 1960. After an assassination attempt in 1965, Diori harshly repressed criticism of his regime, but when Niger was badly hit by drought in 1973, some of his ministers were found with stocks of food and accused of hoarding food aid and selling it at inflated prices. In 1974, amid accusations of high-level corruption, Diori was overthrown by Seyni Kountché in a military coup and imprisoned (his wife died during the fighting). He was released from prison in 1980, but stayed under house arrest until 1984.

Diouf, Abdou (born 1935)

Abdou Diouf became Senegal's first prime minister from 1970 until 1981, when he succeeded LÉOPOLD SÉDAR SENGHOR as president. Diouf set about reorganizing Senegal's political system and allowed opposition parties to proliferate. In 1981, he used Senegalese troops to reinstate the Gambian president, Alhaji Sir DAWDA

JAWARA, who had been ousted by a military coup. In 1982, Diouf and Jawara united their countries to form the confederation of Senegambia, with Diouf as president. He was elected president of Senegal in his own right in l983 and reelected in 1988 and 1993. The Senegambia confederation dissolved in 1989.

Djohar, Said Muhammad (born 1918)

Said Djohar, head of the Comoros Supreme Court, became interim president of the country in 1989, following the assassination of AHMAD ABDULLAH. Elected in 1990, Djohar sought to balance the ethnic and political factions in his country. In 1995, he fled after a failed coup and returned in 1996 to be given a symbolic position, but only after he agreed not to contest the elections.

Doe, Samuel Kenyon (1951–90)

A former army sergeant, Samuel Doe became president of Liberia in 1980, following a military coup in which President WILLIAM TOLBERT was killed. Doe was elected president in 1985, despite allegations of vote rigging, and he was accused of human rights abuses. A civil war broke out in 1989. In 1990, Doe, a member of the Krahn people, was captured, tortured, and killed by a rival group. His death led to the escalation of Liberia's civil war.

Dollar Brand *see* Ibrahim, Abdullah

dos Santos, José Eduardo (born 1942)

Dos Santos became president of Angola on the death of ANTONIO AGOSTINHO NETO in 1979. He was reelected in 1985 and 1992, and in 1994–5 negotiated the end of the war with South African-backed rebels.

Ekwensi, Cyprian Odiatu Duaka (born 1921)

Cyprian Ekwensi is a Nigerian novelist who took as his main theme immoral lives of some African city-dwellers. This was the theme of his first major novel, *People of the City* (1954). He also wrote children's books. He studied pharmacy in England and taught it in Nigeria. After supporting the Biafran rebellion of 1967–70, he returned to pharmacy as a career, while continuing to write.

El Anatsu (born 1944)

El Anatsu is a Ghanaian-born sculptor who has won wide acclaim for his innovative approach to woods and styles. He studied at the University of Science and Technology at Kumasi, Ghana, served as artist-in-residence at the Community of Arts in Cummington, Massachusetts, in 1987, and then became sculpture professor at the University of Nigeria.

Emecheta, Buchi Florence Onye (born 1944)

Buchi Emecheta is an Igbo Nigerian novelist who uses the position of women in Africa today as her central theme. She married at sixteen and moved to London, England in 1962, but her marriage broke up and she raised her five children on her own. Among her best books is *The Bride Price* (1976), whose theme is Nigerian marriage taboos. In *The Family* (1990), she deals with the problems black people and single mothers face in Western society.

Samuel Doe

Buchi Emecheta

71

Emin Pasha, Mehmed (1840–92)

Emin Pasha was born in Germany and originally named Eduard Schnitzer. He adopted the name Mehmed Emin in Albania in 1865, when he became a Muslim, and later became Pasha (administrator) of Equatorial Province in Sudan. An explorer and physician, Emin Pasha was also a skilled linguist and his studies added enormously to the knowledge of African languages. He also wrote valuable geographical papers and collected many specimens of African flora and fauna. He fought against slavery and was murdered by Arab slave traders at Stanley Falls (now Boyoma Falls, Zaire).

Eyadéma, Gnassingbe (formerly Etienne) (born 1937)

Following a bloodless coup in 1967, Gnassingbe Eyadéma – who had served in the French army – became president of Togo, ousting NICOLAS GRUNITZKY. In 1969, he set up the Rassemblement du Peuple Togolais (RPT), which later became the sole political party. He was reelected president under a new constitution in 1993. An unpopular leader, he has begun to make Togo's political system more democratic but there have been many attempts to overthrow him.

Farah, Nuruddin (born 1945)

Nuruddin Farah is Somalia's leading modern writer. After studying in Somalia and India, he worked in Somalia, but emigrated to Europe when his writings were censored. He is best known for his novels in English, such as *A Naked Needle* (1976), and for his plays for the British Broadcasting Corporation (BBC). Unable to return to Somalia, he has settled in Nigeria.

Farouk I (1920–65)

Farouk I, a descendent of MEHEMET ALI, was the last king of Egypt. He reigned from 1937 until 1952, when he was deposed by army officers led by General MUHAMMAD NEGUIB. He was known for his extravagance, which, together with the defeat of Egyptian forces by Israel in 1948–9 and his failure to end the British military occupation of Egypt, made him unpopular. In 1959, he became a citizen of Monaco.

First, Ruth (1925–82)

Born in Johannesburg, South Africa, Ruth First was a leading campaigner against South Africa's apartheid policies. She joined the Communist Party as a student and married JOE SLOVO, a South African lawyer, in 1949. She was charged with treason in 1956 and, in 1964, she left South Africa. She was assassinated in Maputo, Mozambique by a parcel bomb sent to her office there.

Fodio, Usman dan *see* Usman dan Fodio

Franco (1939–89)

Franco (original name L'Okanga La Ndju Pene Luambo Makaidi) was a virtuoso Zairean guitarist and a leader of African popular music for more than thirty years. He headed TPKO Jazz, Africa's most famous band. The initials stand for Tout Puissant Orchestre Kinois, "All-Powerful

Kinshasa Band." His use of the Swahili and Lingala languages has led to Lingala becoming a cult language among young people in East Africa. Franco had several wives and eighteen children.

Fugard, Athol (born 1932)

Athol Fugard is a South African playwright and actor of mixed Afrikaner and English parentage. He attacked apartheid in his plays and frequently tangled with the authorities, notably over his greatest play – *"Master Harold". . . and the Boys* (1982) – which was banned in South Africa because it dealt with the friendship between a white boy and a black waiter.

Garang de Mabior, John (born 1945)

In 1983, John Garang, a Dinka from southern Sudan, became leader of the rebel Sudanese People's Liberation Movement (SPLM) and its military wing, the Sudanese People's Liberation Army (SPLA). His movement opposes such government policies as the use of Arabic in schools and the imposition of Sharia (Islamic holy) law.

Gebrselassie, Haile (born 1973)

Ethiopian Gebrselassie is one of the world's top runners in 5,000 meters and 10,000 meters events. Having set the 5,000 meters world record in June 1994, he went on to slice 8.5 seconds off the 10,000 meters record a year later. In 1995, he also set a new world record in the 5,000 meters, removing nearly 11 seconds from the record he had lost to Kenyan MOSES KIPTANUI earlier in the summer. He is a current

Olympic champion after taking gold in the 10,000 meters at the 1996 Atlanta Olympics.

Glover, Emmanuel Ablade (born 1934)

Emmanuel Glover is a Ghanaian painter, sculptor, and textile designer, who combines African art styles with modern European styles. He studied art in Ghana, England, Kent State University (Ohio), and Ohio State University. He became professor of art education at the University of Science and Technology at Kumasi, Ghana, and was elected a fellow of the Royal Society of Arts in London, England.

Gordimer, Nadine (born 1923)

Nadine Gordimer is an outspoken white critic of apartheid who won South Africa's first Nobel Prize for Literature, in 1991. Before apartheid was abolished, the government had banned four of her novels, including *The Late Bourgeois World* (1966) and *Burger's Daughter* (1979), dealing with the Soweto riots of 1976, because of their political views.

Nadine Gordimer

Gouled Aptidon, Hassan (born 1916)

Hassan Gouled, who was born into a nomadic Somali family, became the first president of Djibouti when it gained independence in 1977. He was reelected in 1981, 1987, and 1993.

Gowon, Yakubu (born 1934)

Yakubu Gowon became Nigeria's head of state and commander-in-chief of its armed forces in 1966, and led the country during the Biafran (Nigerian Civil) War (1967–70). He was deposed in 1975 and went into exile first in Britain and then in Togo.

Grunitzky, Nicolas (1937–94)

Nicolas Grunitzky served as prime minister of Togo (1956–8) and became president of Togo in 1963 after the overthrow of SYLVANUS OLYMPIO. Dependence on France increased under him and, in 1967, he was ousted in a bloodless coup by GNASSINGBE EYADÉMA and exiled.

Habyarimana, Juvénal (1937–94)

Juvénal Habyarimana, an army officer, took power in Rwanda in a bloodless coup that ousted President GRÉGOIRE KAYIBANDA in 1973. He ruled the country until he was killed, together with President Cyprien Ntaryamira of Burundi, when their plane was shot down in April 1994. Both presidents were Hutu and their deaths provoked terrible conflict between the Hutu and Tutsi in Rwanda, Burundi, and Zaire.

Haile Selassie I (1892–1975)

Emperor Haile Selassie I

Originally Ras (Prince) Tafari, Haile Selassie was Emperor of Ethiopia from 1930 until the army deposed him in 1974. He was exiled to Britain during the Italian occupation of Ethiopia (1936–41), and after his return he sought to introduce reforms, but his critics considered that the rate of change was too slow. He was a prominent figure in African affairs, especially in the Organization of African Unity (OAU). He also came to be revered as a divine being by the Rastafarian religious group, which is named after him.

Hamilcar (c. 270–228 BCE)

Hamilcar, father of HANNIBAL, was a Carthaginian general who resisted Roman attempts to capture the city-state of Carthage, in modern Tunisia. His full name, Hamilcar Barca, means "Hamilcar Lightning."

Hannibal (247–182 BCE)

Hannibal was Carthage's greatest general, and is best known today for taking an army, equipped with elephants, through Spain and France and across the Alps to attack the Romans. The son of HAMILCAR, he fought the Romans in Spain and Italy from 221 to 203 BCE, when he was recalled to defend Carthage. He was defeated by the invading Romans at the Battle of Zama. For a time, he ruled Carthage, but was driven into exile and later committed suicide.

Hassan II (born 1929)

King of Morocco since 1961, Hassan II became commander of the armed forces in 1956 and prime minister in 1960. He became chairman of the Organization of African Unity (OAU) in 1972, but Morocco suspended its participation in the OAU in 1985 when representatives of the rebel Polisario group – the Sahrawi Arab Democratic Republic – were admitted.

Hatshepsut (c. 1540 – c. 1481 BCE)

Hatshepsut was one of the few women to rule Ancient Egypt in her own right. She became queen in about 1505 BCE, probably jointly with Tuthmosis III, who was her nephew and stepson. She was devoted to religion, and built a magnificent temple at Deir al Bahri and two obelisks at the Karnak temple complex. She also sent an expedition to the Land of Punt (probably in modern Somalia), an exploit depicted in the Punt Hall at Deir al Bahri.

Head, Bessie (1937–86)

Bessie Head, daughter of a white woman and a black stablehand, was a South African novelist who wrote powerful novels drawing on her own experiences in a racist society. In *A Question of Power* (1974) she coupled that with the problems of mental breakdown. From the mid 1960s, she lived as a refugee in Botswana with her son.

Houphouët-Boigny, Félix (1905–93)

Félix Houphouët-Boigny became the first president of Ivory Coast, in 1960, and he continued in this office, exercising a paternal style of government, until his death in 1993. He was born in Yamoussoukro, which in 1983 became the new political and administrative capital of Ivory Coast; Abidjan, the former capital, remains the economic and financial capital. During a visit in 1990, Pope John Paul II consecrated a basilica in Yamoussoukro; it is the largest Christian church in the world, and cost over US$800 million to build.

Ibn Battuta (1304–68)

Ibn Battuta, born in Morocco, was probably the greatest Arab explorer and geographer. From 1325 to 1349, he traveled through East Africa and the basin of the Niger, as well as large parts of Asia including India and China. In the 1350s, he crossed the Sahara Desert and visited the medieval Songhay and Mali empires, of which he left graphic descriptions.

Ibn Khaldun (1332–1406)

Ibn Khaldun was a leading Arab philosopher and historian and has been called the "father" of sociology. Born in Tunis, he held posts in Morocco and Spain before settling in Egypt, where he was chief judge five times. His writings include histories of the Arabs and the Berbers.

Ibn Tumart, abu Abdullah Muhammad (c. 1078–1130)

Ibn Tumart was a Berber religious leader who founded the Almohad religious sect in Morocco. He proclaimed himself Mahdi (one who is guided) and gathered a following of Berbers from the Atlas Mountains, paving the way for the Almohad dynasty that ruled North Africa and Spain from 1150 to 1269. He was succeeded by ABD AL MUMIN.

Ibrahim, Abdullah (born 1934)

Abdullah Ibrahim is a jazz pianist, cellist, saxophonist, and flautist who recorded South Africa's first black jazz album with his band, Jazz Epistles, in 1960. He combines jazz techniques with the melodies and rhythms of African music. He went to the United States in 1962 to play with Duke Ellington, and has since toured in the US and in Europe. His name was originally Adolph Johannes Brand, and he changed it to Abdullah Ibrahim after becoming a Muslim in 1968. Many of his earlier performances and recordings were under the name of Dollar Brand.

Idris Aloma (c. 1575–1617)

Idris Aloma was the greatest ruler of the Muslim empire of Kanem-Borno

Bessie Head

Félix Houphouët-Boigny

in what is now northern Nigeria, southeast Niger, and western Chad. He equipped his soldiers with firearms and conquered Borno's neighbors, and the empire he built lasted fifty years.

Idris I (1890–1983)

Idris I was king of Libya from 1951, when the country became independent, until 1969, when he was deposed in a coup led by MUAMMAR AL QADDAFI and the monarchy was abolished. He had earlier led Libyan resistance to Italian rule.

Imhotep (2900s BCE)

Imhotep was an Ancient Egyptian sage and architect. He was adviser to Pharaoh Zoser, for whom he designed the Step Pyramid at Saqqara – the first true (smooth-sided) pyramid ever built. He was also the only physician to have been venerated as a god after he died. In around 500 BCE, he was worshipped as the son of Ptah, the god of Memphis (once the capital of Egypt), and the Greeks identified him with Asclepius, their god of medicine.

Ishola, Haruna (1918–83)

Nigerian composer and singer Haruna Ishola popularized the Apala style, originally a music of Yoruba Muslims, in which talking drums and other drums accompanied singers.

Jabavu, John Tengo (1859–1921)

John Tengo Jabavu was a South African journalist and lay preacher who founded *Imvo Zabantsundu* ("Native Opinion"), the first newspaper edited by a black South African. Jabavu, a Xhosa, fought for higher education for black people,

King Idris I

and established the "Native College" at Fort Hare, South Africa, which is now Fort Hare University.

Jawara, Alhaji Sir Dawda Kairaba (born 1924)

Sir Dawda Jawara was the longest-serving Gambian head of state. He was prime minister from 1963 to 1970, and president from 1970 until 1994. He survived several attempted coups, but was finally deposed by a military junta in 1994.

Jonathan, Chief (Joseph) Leabua (1914–87)

Chief Leabua Jonathan was the first prime minister of Lesotho when it became independent in 1966, and he ruled the country for the next twenty years. A great-grandson of Lesotho's founder, MOSHOESHOE I, Jonathan was a leading nationalist politician before independence. After independence, he forced King MOSHOESHOE II to become mainly a figurehead and, in 1970, suspended the constitution and ruled by decree. He was overthrown by a military coup in 1986.

Jordan, Archibald Campbell (1906–68)

Archibald Jordan was a Xhosa novelist, poet, and teacher who made a study of Xhosa language and literature. The only one of his three novels to be published, *Iggoumbo yeminyanya* ("The Wrath of the Ancestral Spirits"), contrasted Xhosa and Western customs. He lectured at the University of Cape Town, then traveled to the United States, where he became a professor of African languages and literature at the University of Wisconsin.

Joseph, Helen Beatrice May (1905–92)
British-born Helen Joseph was one of the first whites in South Africa to take a prominent part in the struggle against apartheid. In 1955, she was a founding member of the Congress of Democrats, the white wing of the African National Congress (ANC).

Juba I (c. 85–44 BCE)
Juba I, a Berber king of Numidia (Algeria), considered himself ruler of all North Africa. He was defeated by the Romans, committed suicide, and was succeeded by his son, JUBA II.

Juba II (c. 50 BCE – c. 24 CE)
Juba II was made ruler of Numidia by the Romans after they defeated his father, JUBA I. He married a daughter of CLEOPATRA and Mark Antony.

Jugnauth, Sir Aneerood (born 1930)
Aneerood Jugnauth became prime minister of Mauritius in 1982 and introduced economic policies that increased the country's prosperity. However, in elections in December 1995, he was swept from power by an opposition alliance that favored a fairer distribution of the fruits of economic success.

Kagame, Alexis (1912–81)
A Rwandan Roman Catholic priest, Alexis Kagame was the historian and chief philosopher of the Tutsi people. He wrote most of his many historical and philosophical works in French, and his poetry and some other works in the Rwandan language. He advocated the Africanization of Christianity in Africa, rather than maintaining traditional European missionary ideas.

Kalle, le Grand (1930–82)
Le Grand Kalle (Joseph Kabaselle Tshamala) led the transition from traditional to modern in the music of his native Zaire. He influenced such musicians as FRANCO and TABU LEY, who issued an album of songs in his memory after his death. His band, African Jazz, played rumbas and sambas with an African flavor.

Kallé, Pepé (born 1951)
Pepé Kallé is a Zairean bandleader who became a star in the 1970s with his band Empire Bakuba. The band's music is characterized by a fast beat and fascinating cross rhythms. Among its most typical recordings is *Kwassa Kwassa* (1989). Kallé is called the "Elephant of Zaire" because of his height and fame.

Kalthum, Umm (1910–75)
Umm Kalthum was an Egyptian singer of classical Islamic music. When she was young, her father, embarrassed at seeing a girl publicly singing religious songs, dressed her as a boy. She never sang "pop" music, but her music was – and still is – extremely popular, and for over fifty years she dominated the classical music scene in Egypt and other parts of the Arab world.

Kanda Bongo Man (born 1955)
Kanda Bongo Man, a Zairean singer and composer, emigrated to France in 1979 because he saw no prospect of a successful recording career in his home country. He is now based in Paris and internationally famous.

Kante, Mory (born c. 1951)
Mory Kante, a member of a musical

family in Guinea, performs regularly in Europe and Africa. He uses the kora, a West African double harp, with brass and electric piano to create a sound combining funk, rock, and soul. He maintains that all modern dance rhythms originated in Africa.

Kasavubu, Joseph Ileo (1913–69)

In 1960, Joseph Kasavubu, who favored a federal system of government for the Congo Republic (now Zaire), became the country's first president. Faced with an army mutiny and the secession of Katanga (now Shaba) province, Kasavubu dismissed his prime minister PATRICE LUMUMBA, who favored the creation of a strong central government. Kasavubu was deposed in 1965 by General MOBUTU SESE SEKO.

Kaunda, Kenneth David (born 1924)

Kenneth Kaunda

The first president of Zambia, Kenneth Kaunda was born in Nyasaland (now Malawi). He became a major figure in the late 1950s for his opposition to the white-minority ruled Central African Federation. Kaunda served as president from 1964 until 1991, when he was defeated in multiparty elections. He gave help and support to many black nationalist groups in the white-minority ruled countries of Southern Africa.

Kayibanda, Grégoire (born 1924)

Grégoire Kayibanda, a Hutu, became the first president of Rwanda when the country became independent in 1962. He was reelected in 1965 and 1969, but he was overthrown by a military group in 1973 and replaced by JUVÉNAL HABYARIMANA.

Salif Keita

Keino, Kipchoge Hezekiah (born 1940)

Kipchoge Keino, a Kenyan athlete, was one of the world's greatest long-distance runners. He set world records in 1965 for the 3,000 meters and 5,000 meters, and won gold medals at the Olympic Games in Tokyo (1968) and Munich (1972). After retiring in 1980, he and his wife have devoted themselves to caring for homeless and abandoned children.

Keita, Modibo (1915–77)

In 1959, Modibo Keita became president of the Mali Federation, consisting of Senegal and French Soudan. This federation broke up in August 1960, and French Soudan became independent as Mali, with Keita as its first president. He was deposed by a military group led by MOUSSA TRAORÉ in 1968.

Keita, Salif (born 1949)

A Malian composer and singer, Salif Keita is descended from the kings of medieval Mali. His music with the band Les Ambassadeurs, later reformed as Super Ambassadeurs, combines Islamic vocals with solos on saxophones and guitars.

Kenyatta, Jomo (c. 1889–1978)

Jomo Kenyatta was prime minister of Kenya (1963–4) and president from 1964 until 1978. He studied anthropology at London University, England, in the 1930s, and wrote a major study of Kikuyu life, *Facing Mount Kenya* (1938). In 1952, he was arrested and imprisoned for his alleged role in managing the Mau Mau rebellion against British rule. Released from prison in 1959, he spent a further two years under house arrest. When he was eventually freed, in 1961, he assumed leadership of the Kenya African National Union (KANU), which won the preindependence elections in 1963. During his time as president, he used the slogan *Harambee* ("pull together") to encourage ethnic and racial harmony in Kenya.

Kenyatta, Margaret Wambui (born 1928)
The daughter of the Kenyan leader JOMO KENYATTA and his first wife, Margaret Kenyatta became an active campaigner on behalf of third-world women. During her father's jail term she helped him to keep in touch with his supporters. In 1960, she entered local politics and became mayor (1970–6) of Nairobi, the capital.

Kerekou, Mathieu Ahmed (born 1933)
Mathieu Kerekou became president and head of the government of Dahomey (now Benin) in 1972, following a coup. He proclaimed the country a Marxist-Leninist (socialist) state, but the government abandoned Marxism-Leninism in 1989. Kerekou was defeated by Nicéphore Soglo in multiparty elections in l991, but regained power in l996.

Khama, Sir Seretse (1921–80)
Seretse Khama became the first prime minister of Botswana (formerly Bechuanaland) in 1965, and the country's first president from its independence in 1966 to his death in 1980. He was exiled from Bechuanaland from 1950 to 1956 because of his marriage to a white British woman in 1948. As president,

he helped to make his country one of Africa's most stable democracies.

Khufu (Cheops) (2500s BCE)
Khufu – also known as Cheops, the Greek name for him – was ruler of the kingdom of Memphis in Ancient Egypt. He ordered the building of the Great Pyramid at Giza, which is the largest of the Egyptian pyramids, plus smaller pyramids for three of his wives. One of his successors was his son Khafre (Chephren), who built the second-largest of the Giza pyramids.

Kimathi, Dedan (1931–57)
Dedan Kimathi was the leader of the Mau Mau rebellion that opposed British rule in Kenya in the 1950s. He was captured in 1956 and executed.

Kiptanui, Moses (born 1971)
One of the world's top runners, Kenyan Kiptanui has broken an unprecedented seven world records, including the 3,000 meters (indoor and outdoor), the 3,000 meters steeplechase, and the 5,000 meters. In 1995, he became the first man to run the 3,000 meters steeplechase in under eight minutes; an event for which he won a silver medal at the 1996 Atlanta Olympics.

Kolingba, André Dieudonné (born 1936)
André Kolingba became head of state of Central African Republic in 1981, when he seized power from DAVID DACKO in a peaceful coup, but he was defeated by ANGE-FÉLIX PATASSÉ in multiparty elections in 1993. Kolingba had earlier served in the army, reaching the rank of general in 1973. During the years of JEAN-BÉDEL

BOKASSA's dictatorship, Kolingba was abroad, in the diplomatic service.

Kutako, Chief Hosea (1870–1970)

Paramount chief of the Herero people of South West Africa (now Namibia), Chief Kutako opposed German colonization and the subsequent rule of the territory by South Africa. He was wounded in the Herero revolt in 1904–5, when around three-quarters of his people were either killed or driven from the country. From the 1950s, he regularly petitioned the United Nations for independence.

Kuti, Fela Anikulapo- (born 1938)

Fela Kuti is a Yoruba musician who became a major musical influence in Nigeria. His musical style, known as Afro-Beat, combines African rhythms and styles with American jazz and blues. His outspoken political views have earned him several terms of imprisonment and house arrest. He married twenty-seven women in 1978, as a protest against Western ways, and openly opposes feminism.

Lamizana, Sangoulé (born 1916)

Sangoulé Lamizana, who became army chief of staff of Upper Volta (now Burkina Faso) in 1961, led a military coup to overthrow MAURICE YAMEOGO and became head of state in 1966. He served as president until 1980, when he was ousted by a military coup led by Colonel Zerbo.

Leakey, Louis Seymour Bazett (1903–72)

Louis Leakey was one of Africa's greatest archeologists and anthropologists, and he proved that the first human beings appeared in that continent. Leakey was a Kenyan, the son of British missionaries. With his wife MARY LEAKEY, and later with their son RICHARD LEAKEY, he found important fossil remains in East Africa, especially in Olduvai Gorge, Tanzania. These fossils included the 2-million-year-old remains of an early hominid (humanlike) species, *Homo habilis* ("Handy Man"). Leakey also discovered evidence that human beings were living in California over 50,000 years ago. His work, and that of his family, suggests that Africa is one of the first homes of humankind.

Leakey, Mary Douglas (1913–1996)

Mary Leakey is an English-born archeologist who moved to Kenya after marrying LOUIS LEAKEY in 1936. In 1948, she discovered the fossil remains of a primitive ape thought to have lived twenty-five to forty million years ago. Together with her husband she made many other important discoveries and she has written several books including *Africa's Vanishing Art: The Rock Paintings of Tanzania* (1983).

Leakey, Richard Erskine Frere (born 1944)

Richard Leakey is a Kenyan who has a double career as an anthropologist and a politician. He is the son of LOUIS LEAKEY and MARY LEAKEY, and with them found many important fossils of early apes and humans. From 1968 to 1989, he was a director of the National Museum of Kenya, later becoming head of the Kenya Wildlife Service. His political views led the Kenyan government to remove him from his wildlife post, but in 1995 he founded a new political party, Safina ("Noah's Ark").

Leo Africanus (c. 1494–c. 1552)
Leo Africanus (real name Al Hassan ibn Muhammad al Wazzan) was a Spanish-born Arab traveler and geographer. He traveled extensively in Africa and Asia Minor, and documented his African experiences in his book *Africa Descriptio* (1526). He was captured by Venetian pirates and taken to Rome, where he lived for twenty years and became a Christian. He then returned to Africa and died in Tunis.

Letsie III (born 1964)
The son of King MOSHOESHOE II of Lesotho, Crown Prince David Mohato Bereng Seeisa was made king, with the title Letsie III, by the country's military government in 1990. In 1995, he voluntarily abdicated to let his father, who had been deposed by the military, return. When his father was killed in a car crash in 1996, however, Letsie III once again became king.

Ley, Tabu (born 1940)
Tabu Ley led the development of "Congo" music and is ranked second only to FRANCO as a performer of African popular music. He was born in Zaire, and is also known as Rochereau. He has written more than 2,000 songs and produced over 150 albums. He moved to exile in Paris when the political situation in Zaire deteriorated in the late 1980s, and in 1993 he produced an album, *Exil-Ley*, commenting on his exile.

Louw, Nicholaas Petrus van Wyck (1906–70)
Nicholaas Louw was one of South Africa's leading Afrikaans academics and writers. His three volumes of poetry all won literary prizes, and he also wrote essays and radio plays. In 1950 he became professor of Afrikaans language and literature at the University of Amsterdam, in the Netherlands. He returned to South Africa, to teach at the University of the Witwatersrand, in 1958.

Lumumba, Patrice Emergy (1925–61)
Patrice Lumumba was the first prime minister of the Congo Republic (now Zaire) from June to September 1960, when he was dismissed by President JOSEPH KASAVUBU. Lumumba was shot dead in 1961, allegedly by rebels from Katanga (now Shaba) province. His death caused a strong reaction throughout Africa, where he was widely regarded as a hero.

Luthuli, Chief Albert John (1898–1967)
Chief Luthuli, a leading Zulu figure in the struggle against apartheid in South Africa, was awarded the 1960 Nobel Peace Prize. President-general of the African National Congress (ANC) from 1952 until it was banned in 1960, he was arrested in 1956 and charged with treason, but released in 1957. His autobiography, *Let My People Go*, appeared in 1962.

Chief Albert Luthuli

Maathi, Wangari Muta (born 1940)
Wangari Maathi, a Kenyan scholar and feminist, founded the Greenbelt Movement in 1977. This is a reforestation program whose fifty thousand women members plant trees

to replace those felled for lumber. When she started the movement, she was a professor in biology at the University of Nairobi; she resigned to stand for parliament, was disqualified, and was not allowed back into the university. Her husband, a member of parliament, was pressured into divorcing her.

Machel, Samora Moises (1933–86)
Samora Machel became the first president of Mozambique when the country gained its independence in 1975, and remained in office until he was killed in a plane crash in 1986. Machel had been active in the independence war against the Portuguese (1964–74) and was president of the ruling Frente de Libertação de Moçambique (Frelimo) party, which followed Marxist-Leninist (socialist) policies.

Macías Nguema, Francisco (1922–79)
The first president of Equatorial Guinea (1968–79), Francisco Macías Nguema was a brutal dictator whose reign of terror led to the flight of up to two-thirds of the population. He was deposed in a military coup in 1979, led by his nephew OBIANG NGUEMA MBASOGO, and was executed.

Mahdi *see* **Muhammad Ahmad al Mahdi**

Mahfouz, Naguib (born 1911)
Naguib Mahfouz, an Egyptian novelist, won the 1988 Nobel Prize for Literature, the first writer in Arabic to do so. Among his forty novels are the three books of *The Cairo Trilogy* (1956–7), in which he portrays the city where he was born and has lived all his life. He also

Miriam Makeba

Daniel François Malan

wrote movie scripts for Egyptian director SALAH SEIF. Some of his work has aroused fierce criticism in the Arab world, and in 1995 two men were sentenced to death for trying to murder him.

Makeba, Miriam Zensi (born 1932)
Miriam Makeba is a leading South African singer who was forced to leave the country in 1963 because of her opposition to apartheid. She settled in the United States, where she won fame as "the empress of African song" and became an international star. Forced to leave the United States because of her marriage to Black Panther leader Stokely Carmichael, she settled in Guinea for some years and represented that country at the United Nations. (She was married twice, her first husband being the trumpeter HUGH MASEKELA.) She returned to South Africa in 1990.

Malan, Daniel François (1874–1959)
Daniel Malan became prime minister of South Africa after defeating JAN SMUTS in the 1948 elections. He is best known for the official introduction of apartheid. He retired from office in 1954.

Mambety, Djibril Diop (born 1945)
Djibril Mambety, a Wolof from Senegal, is an actor turned film producer who emphasizes the clashes between African and Western culture in his films. In *Badou Boy* (1972), he did this through the story of a street urchin in Dakar, the capital.

Mancham, James Richard (born 1929)
James Mancham became the first president of the Seychelles when the

country became independent in 1976, but he was deposed by his prime minister FRANCE-ALBERT RENÉ in 1977. He had earlier served as chief minister, from 1970 until 1974.

Mandela, Nelson Rolihlahla (born 1918)
Nelson Mandela, leader of the African National Congress (ANC), was elected president of South Africa in the country's first multiracial elections in 1994. Mandela qualified as a lawyer and worked with OLIVER TAMBO. He became a leader of the ANC before it was banned in 1960 and founded Umkonto we Sizwe (the military wing of the ANC) in 1961. He was one of the defendants in the so-called Treason Trial (1956–61) of 156 antiapartheid activists, every one of whom was acquitted. After this, Mandela continued his antiapartheid activities and in 1962, along with WALTER SISULU and seven others, he was arrested and charged with sabotage and terrorism. All except one were sentenced to life imprisonment. Mandela was released in 1990, having become an international symbol of the struggle against apartheid. During his imprisonment, his wife WINNIE MANDELA did much to ensure that his plight was not forgotten by the outside world. After his release, he successfully led negotiations for a new, nonracial constitution for South Africa. He shared the 1993 Nobel Peace Prize with F. W. DE KLERK.

Mandela, Winnie (born 1934)
Winnie (Nomzano Zaniewe Winnifred) Mandela emerged as a major opponent of apartheid and a controversial figure in her own right during her husband NELSON MANDELA's twenty-eight-year imprisonment. After qualifying as a social worker, she married him in 1958. Her first arrest took place three months later, and in 1962 she was banned from political activity for the first time. For the next twenty years she was banned, restricted, detained, and jailed a number of times. In 1990, after her husband's release from prison, she took a prominent role in the African National Congress (ANC) until her 1991 conviction for assault and kidnapping. She was divorced from Nelson Mandela in 1996.

Manga, Bebe (born 1948)
Bebe Manga (full name Elizabeth Prudence Manga Bessem), is a Cameroonian singer-songwriter and pianist. She won fame in 1982 with *Amie*, a song recorded in Paris, France, which sold more than a million copies.

Mansa Musa (c. 1264–1337)
Musa became mansa (king) of the medieval Empire of Mali in 1307, and set about reorganizing trade (especially the exporting of copper and gold) and spreading Islam. In 1324, he set off on pilgrimage to Mecca with a large retinue and about twenty tons of gold. On the way, he stopped off in Cairo, where his lavish spending caused severe inflation.

Mapfumo, Thomas (born 1945)
Thomas Mapfumo is a pioneer of popular African music in Zimbabwe. He devised the chimurenga music

Nelson Mandela

Thomas Mapfumo

style, which combines the rhythms of the thumb piano (mbira) with more modern instruments. His first recording in Shona, *Hoyoka* ("Watch Out"), made with the Acid Band in 1977, was banned by the then white-minority government.

Margai, Sir Milton Augustus Stiery (1895–1964)

Milton Margai was chief minister of Sierra Leone from 1954 to 1958, and the country's first prime minister from 1958 until his death in 1964. He was succeeded as prime minister by his half-brother Albert Margai.

Masekela, Hugh Ramopolo (born 1939)

Hugh Masekela, a trumpeter, became South Africa's leading jazz artist but spent thirty-four years in self-imposed exile because of apartheid. For some years he was married to the singer and fellow South African exile MIRIAM MAKEBA. In 1960, he went to the United States to study at the Manhattan School of Music, New York, and his record *Grazin' in the Grass* topped the charts in the United States in 1968. He left the United States and settled in West Africa, then returned to South Africa in 1994.

Masire, Sir (Quett) Ketumile Joni (born 1925)

A founder of the ruling Botswana Democratic Party (BDP), Ketumile Masire became Botswana's vice-president in 1966. He became president in 1980, following the death of SERETSE KHAMA, and he was reelected in 1984, 1989, and 1994.

M'Ba, Léon (1902–67)

Léon M'Ba became president of Gabon in 1960 when the country became independent. He had earlier served as head of the government from 1957 until 1960. In 1964, with the help of French troops, he survived an attempted coup. He was reelected in 1967, but died later that year and was succeeded by OMAR BONGO.

Mbarga, Prince Nico (born 1950)

West African singer Prince Nico Mbarga (real name Nicholas Mbarga) had a major hit with his song *Sweet Mother* in 1976. Sung in pidgin English, it was a bestseller for two years. Mbarga's father was a Cameroonian and his mother was Nigerian. He worked in Nigeria with his band, Rockafil Jazz, but the government expelled four of the band's members who were Cameroonians, and he had to recruit Nigerians to replace them.

Mbeki, Thabo (born 1942)

Thabo Mbeki became First Deputy President of South Africa in 1994 and, by 1996, he was rated the most likely successor to NELSON MANDELA as leader of the African National Congress (ANC) and president of South Africa. Born in Transkei, Mbeki studied economics in Britain and became active in the ANC. In 1975, he became the youngest member of the ANC executive, and in 1993, he became ANC chairperson.

Mboya, Thomas Joseph (1930–69)

Tom Mboya, a Luo, was general secretary of the Kenya Federation of Labour from 1953 until 1962. He was prominent in opposing British colonial rule in the late 1950s when

Sir Milton Margai

Hugh Masekela

JOMO KENYATTA and other older leaders were in prison. He helped to found the Kenya African National Union (KANU) in 1960 and became its general secretary, and was later a member of the Kenyan government. He was assassinated in 1969.

Mehemet Ali (1769–1849)

Mehemet Ali, also known as Muhammad Ali, was an Albanian-born Ottoman (Turkish) soldier who became viceroy (ruler) of Egypt in 1805, ruling on behalf of the Ottoman Empire. He massacred his main enemies, the Mamluks, who were the remnants of a Turkish dynasty that had been defeated by the Ottomans in 1517. He also reformed the Egyptian administration, army, and navy, and conquered large parts of Sudan, and when he fell out with his Turkish masters, his army defeated them. As a result, the Ottomans made him hereditary ruler of Egypt, and his descendants ruled until a republic was declared in 1953. The last of them to rule was FAROUK I, deposed in 1952.

Menelik II (1844–1913)

Menelik II was the king of Shoa, the central province of Ethiopia, and he became Emperor of Ethiopia in 1889. He modernized Ethiopia and kept it from Italian invasion, defeating an Italian army at the Battle of Adowa (modern Adwa) in 1896 and thus preserving Ethiopian independence.

Mengistu, Haile Mariam (born 1937)

Haile Mariam Mengistu seized power in Ethiopia in 1974 after a revolution that removed the emperor, HAILE SELASSIE I. In 1977, he became Ethiopia's first president. Mengistu pursued socialist policies and received aid from the former Soviet Union, but his period in office was marked by famine and civil war. He was overthrown by rebel forces in 1991 and took refuge in Zimbabwe.

Mensah, E. T. (1919–91)

E. T. Mensah, a Ghanaian composer, saxophonist, trumpeter, and bandleader, became the leader of the highlife style of playing in West Africa in the 1950s. When the West African big-band era ended in 1969, Mensah retired, becoming a government pharmacist. He made a comeback in the 1970s and was known as "The King of Highlife."

Mensah, Kwaa (1920–91)

Kwaa Mensah was a Ghanaian guitarist who became known as the "Grandfather" of the palm-wine style of popular music, which evolved into the highlife style. He rose to fame in the 1950s with his guitar band, but then his popularity waned. His work was revived for a time in the 1970s.

Micombero, Michel (1940–83)

In 1966, while the mwama (king) of Burundi was abroad, Micombero, the prime minister, declared the country a republic and made himself president. Micombero, a Tutsi, consolidated Tutsi supremacy in Burundi and purged the army and government of Hutus. After an abortive coup attempt in 1972, between one hundred thousand and two hundred thousand Hutu were brutally massacred. He was deposed in 1976 by Colonel Jean-Baptiste Bagaza and arrested.

Mehemet Ali

Emperor Menelik II

Mobutu Sese Seko

Mobutu Sese Seko (born 1930)

Mobutu Sese Seko, originally named Joseph-Désiré Mobutu, has been Zaire's head of state since 1965. He became an army commander in 1960, and briefly led a provisional government in Congo (Léopoldville), which is now Zaire. In 1965, he again took power and became president, restoring the power of the central government and making Zaire a one-party state. He promised a multiparty system in 1990, but he has set no election dates. Mobutu has been accused of corruption and widely criticized for his autocratic rule.

Moi, Daniel arap (born 1924)

Daniel arap Moi was Kenya's vice-president from 1967 until 1978, when he succeeded JOMO KENYATTA as president. His party, the Kenya African National Union (KANU) was the sole legal party from 1982 until 1991 – when opposition parties were legalized. In elections in 1992, Moi, who has been criticized for human rights abuses, was reelected president.

Mokhehle, Ntsu (born 1918)

A nationalist leader, Ntsu Mokhehle won Lesotho's 1970 elections but the results were declared void and Mokhehle was imprisoned until 1972. After a failed coup attempt in 1974 – allegedly by Mokhehle's supporters – he was forced to flee the country. Following the introduction of a democratic constitution, Mokhehle's Basotho Congress Party (BCP) won elections in 1993 and he became prime minister. He survived two attempted coups in 1994.

Moshoeshoe I

Momoh, Joseph Saidu (born 1937)

Joseph Momoh became commander of the Sierra Leone army in 1983, and in 1985, he was the sole presidential candidate of Sierra Leone's only political party, the All-People's Congress (APC). Initially popular, Momoh used tough measures to crack down on the corruption that had flourished under his predecessor, Siaka Stevens. He refused to consider adopting multiparty politics, however, and was removed from office in l992 by a military coup led by Valentine Strasser.

Mondlane, Eduardo (1920–69)

A prominent Mozambican nationalist, Eduardo Mondlane became president of the liberation movement Frente Nacional de Libertação de Angola (Frelimo) in 1962. He led a guerrilla war against the Portuguese rulers of Mozambique from 1964, and was assassinated in Tanzania in 1969.

Morceli, Noureddine (born 1970)

Morceli, an Algerian, is one of the greatest runners ever. He has broken world records in the 1,000, 1,500, 2,000, and 3,000 meters and the mile. At the 1996 Atlanta Olympics, he took gold in the 1,500 meters.

Moshoeshoe I (1786–1870)

Moshoeshoe I, sometimes known as Moshesh, was a Sotho chief who created the kingdom of Basuto (now Lesotho). He united the various clans of the Sotho people, fought off numerous attacks by neighboring peoples, and fought the British and the Boers. In 1868, at his request, the British annexed his land (as the

Basutoland protectorate) to prevent it being taken over by the Boers.

Moshoeshoe II (1938–96)

Born Constantine Bereng Seeiso, Moshoeshoe II was the grandson of MOSHOESHOE I. He became king of Lesotho in 1960, but went into exile for eight months in 1970 after a clash with the country's first prime minister, Chief LEABUA JONATHAN. He continued as king, with reduced powers, until 1990, when he was deposed and exiled after refusing to sanction changes proposed by the then military government. He was restored to the throne in January 1995, but was killed in a car accident the following year and succeeded by his son, LETSIE III.

Moutawakel, Nawal al (born 1962)

Nawal al Moutawakel, a Moroccan runner, won the first-ever Olympic 400 meters hurdles for women when the event was introduced in the 1984 Los Angeles Olympics. She was the first woman from an Islamic nation and the first African woman, other than a white South African, to win a solo Olympic medal. She was also the first Moroccan to win an Olympic gold medal.

Mphalele, Es'kia (born 1919)

South African writer Es'kia (formerly Ezekiel) Mphalele was exiled for twenty years from his homeland because he protested against apartheid. His novels and short stories reflect the struggles of black people in a racist society. He spent part of his exile in teaching in Nigeria and Kenya, then went to the United States where he obtained a doctorate in literature at the University of Denver. He subsequently became a professor at the University of the Witwatersrand, South Africa. His books include the autobiography *Down Second Avenue* (1959).

Mpiosso, Matima Kinuani (1951–96)

Matima Mpiosso, a Zairean guitarist, was leader of the group Zaïko Langa Langa, which he founded while still at school. He combined Zairean folk tunes and rhythms with rock to produce an individual sound that was popular in Europe and Japan. Arthritis stopped him playing guitar some time before his early death.

Mqhayi, Samuel Edward Krune Loliwe (1875–1945)

Samuel Mqhayi was a leading Xhosa-language poet and novelist, and also a teacher and scholar who helped to standardize Xhosa spelling and grammar. His first novel was *Ityala lama-wele*, the story of twins quarreling over which of them was the heir to their father's inheritance. He published several volumes of verse and three biographies.

Mswati I (c 1820–65)

Mswati I founded the Swazi nation, which was named after him. He was the king of the Ngwane kingdom that had been united by his father, Sobhuza I. Mswati, who ruled from 1845 until 1865, was a great general and made his kingdom one of the most powerful in the region.

Mswati III (born 1968)

Mswati III, son of SOBHUZA II, is the king of Swaziland. Educated in

Nawal al Moutawakel

Mswati I

Britain, he was formerly named Prince Makhosetive. He was chosen as heir to the throne following the death of his father in 1982, and was officially installed as king when he reached the age of eighteen in 1986. He reorganized the government, but there has been growing public dissatisfaction with the political system, with many opposition groups demanding change.

Muana, Tshala (born 1950s)

Tshala Muana is a Zairean singer who made her name first as a dancer, especially as a modern interpreter of traditional dances. In the 1970s, she moved to Ivory Coast as a singer, and she was voted Best African Female Singer in 1984 for her album *Tshala Muana*, which was recorded in Paris.

Mubarak, Muhammad Hosni (born 1928)

Hosni Mubarak

A former air force officer, Hosni Mubarak became president of Egypt in 1981 following the assassination of ANWAR SADAT, having served as vice-president from 1975. Mubarak has pledged to deal firmly with Muslim extremists in Egypt and to continue the peace process with Israel. In 1990, he sent Egyptian troops to help defend Saudi Arabia after Iraq's invasion of Kuwait, and in 1995, he survived an assassination attempt during a visit to Ethiopia.

Mugabe, Robert Gabriel (born 1924)

Robert Mugabe, president of Zimbabwe, was a largely self-educated teacher who founded the anticolonialist Zimbabwe African National Union (ZANU) with

Al Mahdi

NDABANINGI SITHOLE in 1963. He was detained by the then ruling British authorities in Southern Rhodesia (now Zimbabwe) in 1964, and imprisoned until 1974 for his nationalist, anticolonial activities. From 1976 until 1979, Mugabe was joint leader – with JOSHUA NKOMO – of the Patriotic Front guerrilla movement, which fought IAN SMITH's illegal white-minority regime in Rhodesia. As leader of ZANU, Mugabe was elected prime minister of Zimbabwe (defeating Bishop ABEL MUZOREWA) when it became fully independent in 1980. In 1988, ZANU merged with the main opposition party – Joshua Nkomo's Zimbabwe African People's Union (ZAPU) – and Zimbabwe became a one-party state. Mugabe became executive president in 1987 and was reelected in 1990 and 1996.

Muhammad Ahmad al Mahdi (1848–85)

Muhammad Ahmad, who assumed the title of Mahdi (Muslim Messiah) in 1881, was a former civil servant turned slave trader who went on to lead the Sudanese rebellion against Anglo-Egyptian rule in 1882. He captured eastern Sudan in 1883, made Al Obeid his capital, and annihilated an Egyptian army that had been sent to retake it. In 1885, he captured Khartoum after a five-month siege and moved his capital to Omdurman, where he died later that year. The Islamic state he had established lasted until 1898, when the Mahdist forces were defeated by General Kitchener's Anglo-Egyptian army at the Battle of

Omdurman. His great-grandson, Sadiq al Mahdi, has been prime minister of Sudan two times.

Muhammad Ali *see* **Mehemet Ali**

Muhammad Toure *see* **Askia Muhammad**

Musa *see* **Mansa Musa**

Museveni, Yoweri Kaguta (born 1945)

Yoweri Museveni took part in the overthrow of Uganda's dictator IDI AMIN DADA in 1979. Museveni became president of Uganda in 1986 after his National Resistance Army had defeated government forces, ending a five-year conflict. He has been criticized for his ban on political parties which, he claims, encourage tribal divisions.

Muzorewa, Bishop Abel Tendekayi (born 1925)

Abel Muzorewa became the first black bishop of the United Methodist Church, in 1968. He was a prominent opponent of IAN SMITH's illegal white-minority government in Zimbabwe in the 1970s. In elections in 1979, Muzorewa became the country's first black prime minister, but he was heavily defeated by ROBERT MUGABE in 1980. Muzorewa returned to politics in 1994, but he withdrew his candidacy in the 1995 presidential elections, criticizing the way in which they had been conducted.

Mveng, Engelbert (born 1930)

Engelbert Mveng, a Jesuit scholar from Cameroon, is a historian, artist, and theologian. For some years he was head of cultural affairs for the Cameroon Ministry of Education and Culture, and in 1980 became secretary-general of the Ecumenical Association of Third-World Theologians. He painted a huge mural for the Afro-American Catholic Church of Holy Angels in Chicago.

Mwinyi, Ali Hassan (born 1925)

Ali Hassan Mwinyi became president of Tanzania in 1985, after President JULIUS NYERERE retired. He was reelected in 1990 and served until 1995, when, having completed the maximum of two terms in office, he was replaced by Benjamin Mkapa. Mwinyi pursued liberal economic policies and introduced a multiparty constitution in 1993.

Mzilikazi (c. 1790–1868)

Mzilikazi established the Ndebele/Matabele kingdom around Bulawayo, in what is now Zimbabwe. His territory became known as Matabeleland. Mzilikazi led a number of Ndebele north from Natal to Transvaal to escape from the Zulu under DINGANE, and then farther north still to escape from the Boer settlers.

Naidoo, Jay (Jayaseelan) (born 1954)

A leading trade unionist and opponent of apartheid, Jay Naidoo was elected general secretary of the Congress of South African Trade Unions (COSATU) in 1985. He played a major role in organizing the mass protests against apartheid policies during the 1980s. After the democratic elections in 1994, he was appointed as Minister for Reconstruction and Development.

Nasser, Gamal Abd an- (1918–70)

Nasser was prime minister of Egypt (1954–6) and president from 1956

Yoweri Museveni

Gamal Abd an-Nasser

Nefertiti

until 1970. He was one of the leaders of a military coup that overthrew King FAROUK I in 1952, and took power after ousting General MUHAMMAD NEGUIB in 1954. Nasser pursued socialist policies aimed at raising living standards and was widely respected by the Arab world. To finance the building of the Aswan High Dam, he nationalized the Suez Canal, provoking an invasion by British, French, and Israeli troops – a conflict that was ended by the United Nations. Nasser offered to resign after military failures in the 1967 Six-Day War with Israel, but the Egyptian people refused to accept his offer.

Ncube, Sister Bernard Nekie Zellie (born 1935)

A member of the Companions of Angela religious order in South Africa, Sister Bernard is a leading women's activist. She is also a member of the African National Congress (ANC) national executive committee, and a member of the South African parliament. She was an active opponent of apartheid and has been imprisoned six times.

N'Dour, Youssou (born 1959)

Youssou N'Dour is a Wolof musician and singer from Senegal. He created the mbalax style of African music by adding African elements to the Cuban and American soul music then common in Senegal, and later experimented by adding rock and jazz. Internationally famous, he has made two tours of the United States and took part in the 1988 Amnesty International Human Rights Tour.

Youssou N'Dour

Nefertiti (c. 1385–c. 1350 BCE)

Nefertiti helped her husband, the Egyptian pharaoh (king) Amenhotep IV (Akhnaton), in his attempt to change the religion of Ancient Egypt from worship of its numerous traditional gods to worship of just one – Aton, the Sun. Nefertiti, who was famed for her beauty, had six daughters. One, Ankhesenpaaten, married Tutankhamen, who became pharaoh of Egypt at the age of twelve, restored the worship of the old gods, and died at eighteen.

Neguib, Muhammad (1901–84)

An Egyptian general, Muhammad Neguib became prime minister and president of Egypt after the overthrow of King FAROUK I in 1952. Popular for his condemnation of British policies in Egypt, Neguib was a conservative Muslim. He was removed from office in 1954 and replaced by the more radical GAMAL ABD AN-NASSER.

Neogy, Rajat (1938–95)

Rajat Neogy, a Ugandan journalist was the founder-editor of *Transition*, an influential literary magazine. He criticized the government for many years and was jailed for sedition. After his release, he edited the magazine in Ghana, then emigrated to the United States, where he died.

Neto, Dr Antoniu Agostinho (1922–79)

A poet and Marxist politician, Agostinho Neto became the first president of Angola (1974–9). He had led the Movimento Popular de Libertação de Angola (MPLA) forces in the guerrilla war against the Portuguese colonial regime from

1961 until 1974. Neto presided over the beginning, in 1975, of Angola's civil war between the government and rebel forces (principally those of JONAS SAVIMBI), which continued for sixteen years after his death.

Ngouabi, Marien (1938–77)

Marien Ngouabi seized power in Congo in 1968 in a coup that deposed Alphonse Massamba-Débat. He adopted Marxist-Leninist policies and became president in 1970. Power struggles and ethnic tensions during Ngouabi's presidency led to political instability in the country and he was assassinated in 1977.

Ngugi, John (born c. 1963)

A Kikuyu athlete from Kenya, John Ngugi won the 5,000 meters gold medal at the 1988 Seoul Olympics. He has won the World Cross Country Championships a record five times, winning in four consecutive years from 1986 onward.

Ngugi wa Thiong'o (born 1938)

Ngugi wa Thiong'o (formerly known as James Ngugi) is a Kenyan novelist and playwright who wrote the first novel in English by an East African, *Weep Not, Child* (1964). He later switched to writing in Kikuyu, and in 1977 he co-wrote a play with Ngugi wa Marii that offended the government. This led to his detention without trial for a year, and he later went into exile.

Nico, Dr (1939–85)

Dr Nico (real name Kasanda wa Mikalay Nicholas), a Zairean guitarist and composer, was a leading exponent of "Congo" music, which combines jazz and African styles. He was a dominant figure on the music scene for ten years and made many records, but very little money.

Nimeri, Gaafar Muhammad (born 1930)

Gaafar Nimeri was president of Sudan from 1969 until 1985. A professional soldier, he seized power in a coup in 1969. He was elected president in 1971 and worked to raise food production throughout the country, but his attempts to introduce Sharia (Islamic holy) law alienated many people in the non-Muslim, largely Christian south. He was deposed by a coup in 1985.

Gaafar Nimeri

Nkomo, Joshua Mqabuko Nyongolo (born 1917)

Joshua Nkomo was the leader of the nationalist Zimbabwe African People's Union (ZAPU) from the 1960s. Nkomo and ROBERT MUGABE were joint leaders of the Patriotic Front guerrilla movement which campaigned against IAN SMITH's illegal white-minority government of Rhodesia from 1976 until 1979. In the 1980 elections, however, Nkomo's ZAPU was defeated by Mugabe's Zimbabwe African National Union (ZANU). Nkomo was given a cabinet position in Mugabe's government but was dismissed in 1982 after conflicts between ZAPU and ZANU. In the 1980s, Nkomo's native Matabeleland harbored dissidents from Mugabe's rule and this led to further tensions between ZAPU and ZANU. In 1988, however, the two parties merged and Nkomo became one of Zimbabwe's two vice-presidents.

Kwame Nkrumah

Sam Nujoma

Julius Nyerere

Nkrumah, Dr Kwame (1909–72)
Kwame Nkrumah became prime minister of Gold Coast (later Ghana) in 1951, and then the first president of Ghana, in 1960. He was overthrown in a military coup in 1966. A campaigner against white domination, Nkrumah was widely respected throughout Africa. He became increasingly autocratic, however, and economic crises dogged his final years in office.

Nujoma, Sam Daniel (born 1929)
Sam Nujoma founded the South West African People's Organization (SWAPO) in 1958, and from 1966 led it in a guerrilla war against the illegal occupation of South West Africa (present-day Namibia) by South Africa. Nujoma became president of Namibia on its independence in 1990 and was reelected in 1994.

Nyame, E. K. (1927–77)
E. K. Nyame was Ghana's most popular guitar band leader. With his Akan Trio he played at state functions when President Kwame Nkrumah visited Liberia. His early songs were written in English, but later songs were all in the Twi language. His popularity was such that he was given a state funeral when he died, in 1977.

Nyerere, Julius Kambarage (born 1922)
Julius Nyerere, leader of the Tanganyika African National Union (TANU) – later named Chama Cha Mapinduzi (CCM) – became Tanganyika's first prime minister in 1961 and its first president in 1962. In 1964, he became president of the united Tanzania (Tanganyika and Zanzibar). He retired in 1985, but remained chairman of the CCM until 1990. A pioneer of ujamaa (self-help) policies and African socialism, Nyerere was successful in introducing social reforms, but his economic policies were less successful. In the mid 1990s, he acted as mediator in Burundi peace talks.

Nzinga Nbandi, (Anna) (1582–1663)
Nzinga was a queen of Ndongo and later queen of Matamba (both in what is now Angola). As queen of Ndongo, she tried to keep her country free from Portuguese control and fought the slave trade. In 1623, she went to the Portuguese colony of Angola to negotiate with the governor, and while there, she was baptized a Christian as Dona Aña de Souza. The negotiations failed, however, and the Portuguese drove her out of Ndongo in 1624. She then conquered the kingdom of Matamba, which allied itself with the Dutch and became prosperous by collaborating with the Portuguese slave trade.

Obey, Ebenezer (born 1942)
Ebenezer Obey, a Nigerian bandleader, pioneered modern juju, a guitar-based musical style that originated in Yoruba-speaking western Nigeria. Obey called his version of juju the Miliki System. Many of his songs reflect his strong Christian beliefs. He has made several tours of the United States.

Obiang Nguema Mbasogo, Teodoro (born 1942)
Obiang Nguema became president of Equatorial Guinea in 1979 after

leading a coup against his uncle, President MACIAS NGUEMA. Under Obiang, power remained highly centralized and, despite the introduction of a multiparty system, Obiang was elected in 1996 with more than ninety-nine percent of the vote. His opponents had withdrawn, objecting to voting irregularities.

Obote, Apollo Milton (born 1924)
Milton Obote led Uganda to independence in l962, serving as its first prime minister. In 1966, he deposed the head of state, King Mutesa II of Buganda, and made himself executive president. In 1971, he was himself deposed, by IDI AMIN DADA. Obote returned from exile in Tanzania to regain the presidency in 1980 but was again deposed in 1985.

Ogot, Grace Emily Akinyi (born 1930)
Grace Ogot is a Kenyan who won fame as a novelist and short story writer and worked to preserve the folk tales of the Luo people. She combined her writing with politics, serving as a member of parliament and as a delegate to the United Nations. Her earlier career was as a midwife in Uganda and England.

Ojukwu, Chukwuemeka Odumegwu (born 1933)
Chukwuemeka Ojukwu was president of the breakaway state of Biafra during the Biafran (Nigerian Civil) War (1967–70). He went into exile after the rebellion collapsed.

Okigbo, Christopher (1932–67)
Christopher Okigbo was one of Nigeria's finest poets, and has been an inspiration to other Nigerian writers. Most of his poetry, all written in English, survives in the collection *Collected Poems* (1986). Many of his poems have a mystical element. He worked as a teacher and librarian, but in 1967, he joined the army of Biafra, which tried to break away from Nigeria, and was made a major. He was killed in action within a month.

Okosun, Sonny (born 1947)
Sonny Okosun, a Nigerian guitarist and composer, is a former actor who created a mixture of reggae and rock styles that he named ozzidi. This name was derived from the Igbo words "ozi di," meaning "there is a message," and his songs contain much social and political comment.

Okri, Ben (born 1959)
Ben Okri is a Nigerian broadcaster, poet, fiction writer, and journalist. He moved to Britain at the age of nineteen to study at the University of Essex, and later settled in London. His novel *The Famished Road* won the 1991 Booker Prize in Britain.

Olajuwon, Hakeem (Born 1963)
Hakeem Olajuwon is a Nigerian basketball player who made his name in the United States with the Houston Rockets, whom he joined in 1984. He became an American citizen in 1993, and in 1994 was voted Most Valuable Player in the National Basketball Association. A devout Muslim, he converted a disused building in Houston, Texas, into a mosque.

Olympio, Sylvanus (1902–63)
Sylvanus Olympio was prime minister of Togo (1958–60) and became the country's first president

Chukwuemeka Ojukwu

when it gained independence in 1960. Olympio was a prominent campaigner for reunification of the Ewe people, who are divided between Togo and Ghana. He was killed in a military coup in 1963 and replaced by NICOLAS GRUNITZKY.

Ongala, Remmy (born 1947)

Remmy Ongala, born in Zaire, is Tanzania's most popular musician. In 1980, he formed the band Super Matimila, of which he is lead singer and guitarist, and later recorded with it in England. His lyrics attack the evils of racism and poverty.

Opoku Ware II (born 1919)

A Ghanaian lawyer, Opoku Ware succeeded his uncle Sir Osei Agyeman-Prempe II as asantehene (king) of the Asante people in 1970.

Opoku Ware, Lady Victoria (1929–96)

The senior wife of OPOKU WARE II, Lady Victoria was an influential figure at court and accompanied the king on foreign trips. In 1981, she helped to arrange the Asante exhibitions that were staged in London and New York. A powerful personality, she used her influence to defend the Asante kingdom's interests while maintaining an allegiance to the Ghanaian state.

Osei Bonsu (1779–1824)

Lady Victoria Opoku Ware

Osei Bonsu expanded the Asante Empire to its greatest size, covering modern-day Ghana and parts of Togo, Burkina Faso, and Ivory Coast. The seventh Asante king, his name means "Osei the Whale." He encouraged Asante arts and crafts and made the nation rich from their goldmines.

Osei Tutu (died 1717)

Osei Tutu united the separate Asante chiefdoms in the 1670s to create the Asante Empire, now part of Ghana as the Asante Kingdom. To join the empire, the chiefdoms had to acknowledge the authority of the Golden Stool. This was a wooden stool, covered in gold and said to have been conjured from the sky, that symbolized the spirit of the Asante. Osei Tutu embarked on a series of wars of expansion in 1701, and was killed in battle in 1717.

Ould Daddah, Moktar (born 1924)

The first president of Mauritania (1960–78), Moktar Ould Daddah worked to unify his ethnically divided people. Dissatisfaction with Mauritania's unsuccessful and costly attempt to take over the southern part of Spanish (now Western) Sahara, however, led to his overthrow.

Ousmane Sembene (born 1923)

Sembene Ousmane was the first major African moviemaker. Born in Senegal, he wrote several novels before directing *La Noire de... (Black Girl)*. His other movies include *Mandabi* (1968) and *Ceddo* (1977), considered to be his masterpiece.

Oyono, Ferdinand Leopold (born 1929)

Leopold Oyono is a Cameroonian writer and diplomat who wrote several novels in the 1950s and 1960s critical of colonial rule. Brought up as a Roman Catholic, Oyono completed his education in Paris, France, where he obtained a law degree. Following Cameroon's independence, he served as an ambassador to the United States and other countries, and in the 1990s was minister of external relations.

Patassé, Ange-Félix (born 1937)

Ange-Félix Patassé, a former prime minister, was elected president of Central African Republic in 1993, ending twelve years of absolute rule by ANDRÉ KOLINGBA. In 1996, French troops helped Patassé to put down an army mutiny.

Paton, Alan Stewart (1903–88)

Alan Paton was a white South African writer whose best-selling novel *Cry, the Beloved Country* (1948) helped to alert the world to the problems of apartheid. He had seen many of those problems in his years as principal of a reformatory. His second novel, *Too Late the Phalarope* (1953) dealt with the relationship between a white man and a black woman, and was banned by the government. He founded the South Africa Liberal Party with MARGARET BALLINGER in 1953, and was its president until 1960.

P'Bitek, Okot (1931–82)

Okot P'Bitek, a Ugandan poet and anthropologist, did much to promote African culture and values. He wrote in both English and in Luo, and his first novel, *Lar tar miyo kinyero wi lobo*, was in Luo. He studied law and anthropology at British universities, and had an academic career in Uganda and later in exile in Kenya. For a time he was writer-in-residence at the University of Iowa.

Piankhy (died c. 712 BCE)

From 751 to 712 BCE, Piankhy was the Nubian king of Kush (part of modern Sudan). He was a brilliant general, and he conquered Egypt and became its pharaoh (king). When he invaded Egypt, his forces were moving down the Nile while a Libyan chief, Tefnakht, was advancing upriver. Piankhy defeated Tefnakht and some Egyptian forces, seized the throne, then sailed back up the Nile to Kush with a great haul of loot.

Plaatje, Solomon Tshekiso (1876–1932)

In 1912, Sol Plaatje was a cofounder of the South African Native National Congress, which became the African National Congress (ANC) in 1923. His book *Native Life in South Africa* (1916) was an indictment of the misery caused by the Natives Land Act of 1913, while his novel *Mhundi* celebrates the importance of African culture and African history. Largely self educated, Plaatje also translated several of Shakespeare's plays into the Setswana language.

Player, Gary (born 1936)

Gary Player was one of the world's leading golfers of the 1960s and 1970s. In 1959, he won the British Open championship, at twenty-four the youngest player to do so. He has won all the major international golf championships, including the US Open, the US Masters, and the US PGA title. He spends part of his time in Florida and part on a farm near Johannesburg, South Africa, where he breeds horses and supports a school for 430 poor black children.

Pukwana, Dudu Mtutuzel (born 1938)

Dudu Pukwana is a South African musician who had to move to Europe

Ange-Félix Patassé

in 1964 because the band he was in, the Blue Notes, contained both white and black musicians, which was illegal under apartheid laws. He settled in London, playing and recording with numerous bands.

Qaddafi, Muammar al (born 1942)

Muammar al Qaddafi

Muammar al Qaddafi became leader of Libya and commander-in-chief of the armed forces in 1969 after the overthrow of King IDRIS I. At home, Qaddafi sought to reorganize Libyan society along socialist, nationalist lines. Abroad, his support for radical movements, such as the Black Panthers in the United States and the Irish Republican Army (IRA) in Northern Ireland, made him a controversial figure. In 1986, US planes bombed several sites in Libya, missing Qaddafi but killing thirty-seven people, many of them civilians.

Rabéarivelo, Jean-Joseph (1901–37)

Jean-Joseph Rabéarivelo was Madagascar's leading poet. Most of his poems were written in French, on themes including death and catastrophe, but he also wrote in his mother tongue, Hova. Unable to find what he considered a worthwhile job, he became depressed, took to drugs, and committed suicide.

Rabeh Zobeir *see* **Rabih bin Fadl Allah**

Rabemananjara, Jean-Jacques (born 1913)

A Madagascan politician and poet, Jean-Jacques Rabemananjara played an important role in the liberation struggle against French colonial rule. As a deputy of the Mouvement Démocratique pour la Rénovation Malagache (MDRM), he was imprisoned and exiled to France from 1947 until 1950 after extremist MDRM members organized a violent revolt in which about eighty thousand people were killed. From 1960, he served in the government of PHILIBERT TSIRANANA as foreign minister.

Rabih b. (bin) Fadl Allah (c. 1840–1900)

Rabih b. Fadl Allah was a Sudanese adventurer who carved out a huge empire in west-central Africa, south of Lake Chad. A former slave, he became an Egyptian soldier, then took to slave trading himself. He raised a large army, based himself in what is now Chad, and began twenty years of conquest. He was eventually killed by a French army at the Battle of Lakhta.

Ramanantsoa, Gabriel (1906–79)

Gabriel Ramanantsoa, Madagascar's armed forces commander, became president in 1972, when PHILIBERT TSIRANANA relinquished power to him in the face of widespread strikes and riots. He was initially popular for his maintenance of order and prosecution of corrupt officials, but in 1975, after several coup attempts, he handed over power to a military government and was succeeded by DIDIER RATSIRAKA.

Ramgoolam, Sir Seewoosagur (1900–85)

Seewoosagur Ramgoolam served as chief minister of Mauritius from 1961 and became the country's first prime minister in 1964. He was prime minister when Mauritius became independent in 1968, but was defeated in the 1982 elections by ANEEROOD JUGNAUTH.

Ramses II (reigned 1304–1237 BCE)

It has been suggested, but never proved, that Ramses II was the Egyptian pharaoh (king) who oppressed and enslaved the Israelites, as described in the Bible. Known as Ramses the Great, he was one of the most successful pharaohs and left many fine buildings, including the huge temple at Abu Simbel. His mummified body was discovered at Queen HATSHEPSUT's temple at Deir al Bahri in 1881.

Ransome-Kuti, Funmilayo (1900–78)

Funmilayo Ransome-Kuti was a Nigerian feminist leader who helped to save market women from exploitation. She formed working women into the Nigerian Women's Union, which founded clinics for mothers and children and helped to teach people to read and write. She died from injuries received when troops, who were raiding her son's house to punish him for criticizing the authorities, threw her from a second floor window.

Ratsiraka, Didier (born 1936)

Didier Ratsiraka, a former naval officer, became head of state in Madagascar in 1975, after the downfall of GABRIEL RAMANANTSOA. He was popular with both students and the bourgeoisie for his nationalist sentiments, and pledged to carry out administrative and rural reforms. He was elected president in 1976 and, despite several coup attempts, remained in office until he was defeated by Albert Zafy in the 1993 presidential elections.

Rawlings, Jerry John (J. J.) (born 1947)

Jerry Rawlings

Son of a Scottish father and a Ghanaian mother, Jerry John Rawlings seized power in Ghana in a peaceful coup in 1979, but ruled for only 112 days before restoring civilian government. Rawlings, an air force officer, was immensely popular for his anticorruption policies. He again seized power in 1981, but his reluctance to return power to a civilian government after this second coup lost him some support. In 1992, however, he was elected president in democratic multiparty elections.

René, France-Albert (born 1935)

France-Albert René, prime minister of Seychelles, seized power in 1977 to become the country's second president, replacing JAMES MANCHAM. René created a one-party state and followed policies of nonalignment. He was reelected in multiparty elections in 1993.

Retief, Piet (1780–1838)

Piet Retief

Piet Retief was a leader of the Voortrekkers, the South African Boer farmers who migrated north on the Great Trek to escape British rule in the Cape. In 1837, he published a declaration listing the grievances of the Boers against the British, and led a party into Natal, stronghold of the Zulu. The Zulu king, DINGANE, refused to grant him land and in 1838 killed Retief and his followers.

Ribas, Oscar Bento (born 1909)

Oscar Ribas, an Angolan of mixed African and European parentage, was the leading novelist and ethnologist of Portuguese colonial Africa. He

Fatuma Roba

Anwar al Sadat

Samori Toure

became totally blind at the age of twenty-one, but continues to research and write. He made an influential study of the Kimbundu people, but his most important work is a study of Angolan literature.

Roba, Fatuma (born 1973)

Fatuma Roba, an Ethiopian runner, was the women's marathon gold medalist in the 1996 Atlanta Olympics. Roba, a policewoman who had won marathons in Marrakech and Rome in 1996, is the first African woman to take a gold medal in the Olympic marathon.

Robert, Shaaban (1909–62)

Shaaban Robert was a Tanzanian poet and novelist who wrote a number of verse novels with anticolonial themes and turned Swahili from a classical tongue into a modern language. He also began the practice of writing it in Roman script instead of Arabic.

Rochereau *see* Ley, Tabu

Saadawi, Nawal al (born 1931)

An Egyptian doctor and novelist, Saadawi became Egypt's Director of Public Health but her books, which focus on the lives of women in the Arab world, antagonized the authorities and she was dismissed. She went on to work as an advisor on women's programs for the United Nations. Her long campaign for women's rights in Egypt led to her imprisonment under ANWAR SADAT. She has since devoted her time to writing, journalism, and speaking on women's issues. Saadawi's books, which have won many literary awards, include *The Hidden Face of Eve: Women in the Arab World* (1980), *Woman at Point Zero* (1983), and *God Dies by the Nile* (1985).

Sadat, Muhammad Anwar al (1918–81)

Anwar Sadat, vice-president of Egypt, became president on the death of GAMAL ABD AN-NASSER in 1970. He is remembered for his dramatic peace initiative that led to the Camp David peace treaty, signed in 1979, ending the conflict between Egypt and Israel. He shared the 1978 Nobel Peace Prize with Israel's Menachem Begin. Sadat was assassinated in 1981 by Muslim extremists.

Samori Toure (c. 1830–1904)

Samori Toure led West African resistance to French colonialism. At first a trader, he served in the army of the Sise people for several years, then formed his own army and built up the Second Mandinka Empire, which by 1881 stretched from Guinea to Ivory Coast. He fought of French advances for seven years, but, after years of fighting he was captured and imprisoned in 1898, then exiled.

Sangare, Oumou (born 1968)

Oumou Sangare, a Malian singer, is the most popular female vocalist in West Africa and has been called the "Madonna of Mali." She has been singing in public since she was six, and her music is based on the hunting and harvest dances of her native land. The songs on her 1996 album *Worotan* deal with love, jealousy, and the position of women in society.

Sankara, Thomas (1949–87)

Sankara became prime minister of Burkina Faso in 1982, after a military coup led by Colonel Ouédraogo, who became president. Frustrated by Ouédraogo's failure to tackle the country's dire economic problems, Sankara staged another coup in 1983 and took over as president. A popular leader, he embarked on a series of ambitious development programs intended to restructure the economy and make the rural areas self-reliant. To do so, Sankara had to cut government spending in other areas. This brought him into conflict with the country's powerful trade unions, and the subsequent discontent led one of his closest advisors, BLAISE COMPAORÉ, to mount a coup in 1987 in which he was killed.

Saro-Wiwa, Kenule Beeson (1941–95)

Ken Saro-Wiwa, A Nigerian writer, campaigned for his fellow Ogoni people, whose region had been polluted by the oil industry. In 1994, he was charged with the murder of four moderate Ogoni leaders. Despite international pleas for leniency, he was executed in 1995.

Sassou-Nguesso, Denis (born 1943)

Sassou-Nguesso became president of Congo in 1979, promising to continue the government's Marxist policies, though his policies were, in practice, more liberal than those of his predecessors. In 1990, bowing to public pressure, the government renounced Marxist ideology, and in 1991, it legalized opposition parties and stripped Sassou-Nguesso of all his powers. In the 1992 multiparty elections, Sassou-Nguesso was defeated by Pascal Lissouba.

Savimbi, Jonas (born 1934)

Jonas Savimbi led the forces of the União Nacional para a Independência Total de Angola (UNITA), formed in 1966 to fight in the Angolan war of independence from Portuguese rule (1961–74). After independence (in 1975), UNITA fought a twenty-year war against AGOSTINHO NETO's government forces, which finally ended in 1994–5.

Schreiner, Olive (Emilie Albertina) (1855–1920)

Olive Schreiner was a South African writer who sprang to fame with her novel *The Story of an African Farm* (1883), originally published under the pen-name "Ralph Iron." She was a pioneer of feminist writing and a campaigner for women's rights.

Seif, Salah Abou (1915–96)

Salah Seif, formerly a civil servant and then a journalist, was one of Egypt's most important film directors. He made eight films with the Nobel prizewinner NAGUIB NAHFOUZ as scriptwriter, and his 1977 production *The Death of the Waterbearer* was chosen as the Egyptian Film Association's film of the year.

Senghor, Léopold Sédar (born 1906)

A distinguished poet, Léopold Senghor became the first president of Senegal in 1960. He favored moderate "African socialism" and restricted political activity – by 1966, Senegal was a one-party state. He worked to modernize agriculture, prevent corruption, and establish close ties with neighboring countries. He also developed a philosophy

Oumou Sangare

Ken Saro-Wiwa

called "negritude" that celebrated African culture and values. A declining economic situation and pressure for political reforms led to Senghor's resignation in late 1980. He was succeeded by ABDOU DIOUF.

Shabalala, Joseph (born c. 1940)

Joseph Shabalala is a Zulu singer who created the South African vocal group Ladysmith Black Mambazo. The ten-man group, singing mainly gospel songs, perfected a distinctive Zulu harmonic style. In 1981, Shabalala became a priest in the Church of God of the Prophets.

Shaka (1787–1828)

Shaka

A brilliant military strategist, Shaka became a general in the army of DINGISWAYO, king of Mthethwa, and founded the Zulu kingdom in 1818. He won many victories in what is now KwaZulu/Natal, practicing the strategy of total warfare – complete annihilation of the enemy. In 1828, he was murdered by his half-brothers Mhlangane and DINGANE.

Siad Barre, Muhammad (born 1919)

Muhammad Siad Barre became president of Somalia in 1969, following a military coup. His rule was marked by civil war and war with Ethiopia, and he was overthrown by rebel forces in January 1991.

Sisulu, Nontsikelelo Albertina (born 1918)

Albertina Sisulu and her husband WALTER SISULU were leading figures in the struggle against apartheid in South Africa and were imprisoned or placed under house arrest for long periods. She was a leader of the African National Congress (ANC) Women's League, became president of the Federation of African Women in 1984, and was elected a member of parliament in 1994.

Sisulu, Walter Max Ulyate (born 1912)

Walter Sisulu, like his wife ALBERTINA SISULU, was a prominent South African antiapartheid campaigner. Together with NELSON MANDELA, he was one of the 156 black activists tried and acquitted in the so-called Treason Trial (1956–61). In 1962, Sisulu and Mandela were arrested again, along with seven others, and charged with sabotage and terrorism. All except one were sentenced to life imprisonment in 1964. Sisulu was released in 1989, and in 1991 he became deputy president of the African National Congress (ANC).

Sithole, Rev. Ndabaningi (born 1920)

Ndabaningi Sithole, a clergyman, politician, and influential writer, was a major figure in the nationalist struggle in Rhodesia (now Zimbabwe) in the 1960s and 1970s. He founded the anticolonialist Zimbabwe African National Union (ZANU) with ROBERT MUGABE in 1963. He was imprisoned from 1965 until 1974, but in 1978 he helped to achieve an agreement with IAN SMITH's white-minority government for constitutional change. This agreement was considered inadequate by the other leading nationalists, Robert Mugabe and JOSHUA NKOMO, and Sithole's political influence declined when a new agreement was negotiated in 1979. In November

1996, he was taken to court charged with planning to assassinate Mugabe and overthrow the government.

Skunder Boghassian (born 1937)

Skunder Boghassian is an Ethiopian painter who has achieved worldwide fame as an abstract and surrealist artist. His style reflects elements of Coptic, European, and West African art. He taught at the Fine Arts School at Addis Ababa, Ethiopia's capital, but after the 1974 revolution he took up a teaching post at Howard University in Washington, DC.

Slovo, (Yossel) Joe Mashel (1926–95)

Born in Lithuania, Joe Slovo became a leading South African opponent of apartheid. A member of the Communist Party of South Africa (CPSA), he was barred from political activity in 1954. He later helped to found the military wing of the African National Congress (ANC), but he spent many years in exile before returning to South Africa in 1990. He was appointed minister for housing in South Africa's first multiracial government in 1994.

Smith, Ian Douglas (born 1919)

Ian Smith became prime minister of the white-dominated Rhodesia (now Zimbabwe) in 1964 and in 1965 he made an illegal Unilateral Declaration of Independence (UDI) from Britain in order to maintain white domination of the government. This eventually led to civil war between Smith's government forces and those of ROBERT MUGABE and JOSHUA NKOMO. Smith continued to serve as prime minister until 1979, when an interim

multiracial government led by Bishop ABEL MUZOREWA was established.

Smuts, Jan Christiaan (1870–1950)

A South African politician and prime minister, Jan Smuts fought against the British in the Anglo-Boer War (1899–1902), becoming a general. Later, he worked to reconcile the Boer and British populations. He served as South Africa's prime minister from 1919 until 1924, and again from 1939 until 1948.

Sobhuza II (1899–1982)

Sobhuza II was king of Swaziland from 1921 and made his country strong and prosperous. As head of state from 1968, when Swaziland became independent from Britain, he regained large areas of land that had been taken by European settlers. He abolished the country's democratic constitution in 1973 and ruled the country with a council of ministers, but introduced a new constitution in 1979, allowing for a partly elected parliament and a "traditional" Swazi National Council. After his death, he was succeeded by his son MSWATI III.

Sobukwe, Robert Mangaliso (1924–78)

A founder of the antiapartheid Pan-Africanist Congress (PAC) in South Africa, and its president from 1959, Robert Sobukwe helped to organize demonstrations against the Pass Laws in 1960. During one of these, at Sharpeville, the police opened fire on demonstrators and 69 people were killed and 180 wounded. This event, which became known as the Sharpeville massacre, focused world attention on the antiapartheid

Ian Smith

struggle. Sobukwe was banned from political activity and imprisoned – under a law used only against him and nicknamed the "Sobukwe clause" – from 1960 until 1969.

Sofola, Zulu (born 1935)

Zulu Sofala

Zulu Sofala, Nigeria's first woman playwright, writes on a variety of themes. She was educated in the United States, and became professor of performing arts at the University of Ilorin, Nigeria.

Sonni Ali *see* Sunni Ali

Soyinka, Wole (born 1934)

The first Black African to win a Nobel Prize in literature (1986), Wole Soyinka is an outstanding and prolific Nigerian playwright, novelist, critic, editor, and poet. His first play (*Invention*, 1955) was staged in London, England, as were *Brother Jero, Kongi's Harvest* (both 1965), and *The Swamp Dwellers* (1958), which he has adapted for a 1967 film. His first novel, *The Interpreters* (1965), has been called the first truly modern African novel. In 1984, he directed his first feature film, *Blues for a Prodigal*. Much of Soyinka's work dwells on the interplay of African and Western cultures in African society. He has been harshly critical of both the colonial and independent regimes in Africa, which has earned him periods of house arrest, exile, and imprisonment. Since 1988, Soyinka has been the professor of African studies and theater at Cornell University, NY.

Sundiata Keita (died 1255)

Sundiata, who founded the medieval

Efua Sutherland

Empire of Mali, was a member of the royal family of Kangaba, a kingdom close to historic Ghana. Because he was disabled from birth, when the Susu people murdered his brothers in 1224 they spared him as they thought he would be no threat. But despite his lameness, he became a great soldier and defeated the Susu in 1235. By 1240, he had conquered all of the Empire of Ghana. Sundiata was known as the "Lion of Mali."

Sunni Ali (died 1492)

Sunni Ali built the Songhay Empire of West Africa in the fifteenth century, after his people's domination by the Empire of Mali. He was at first ruler of the kingdom of Gao, which was controlled by Mali, and in about 1464, he began to free Gao from Mali and unite the Songhay people. He conquered large areas of Mali, and captured the important cities of Timbuktu and Djenné. His son and successor, Sunni Baru, was overthrown by ASKIA MUHAMMAD.

Sutherland, Efua Theodora (1924–96)

Efua Sutherland was a major Ghanaian poet and dramatist. She founded the Ghana Drama Studio in Accra, and in 1963 began a research program into African literature at the University of Ghana. She wrote several books for children, and her plays *Foriwa* and *Edufa* (both 1967) focused on women's roles.

Suzman, Dame Helen (born 1917)

Between 1953 and her retirement in 1989, Helen Suzman was the chief voice of liberalism in South Africa's parliament. Daughter of a Lithuanian

Jewish immigrant, she was first elected to parliament in 1953 as a member of the United Party. After the United Party split in 1959, she became a member of the antiapartheid Progressive Party, and from 1961 until 1974, she was its sole representative in parliament. She was awarded the United Nations Human Rights Award in 1978.

Tala, André-Marie (born 1950)

André-Marie Tala is a Cameroonian guitarist who lost his sight as a teenager. He gave his first major concert in 1971, in Yaoundé, the capital of Cameroon. In 1972, he went to Paris to record his first singles, and he settled there in 1979. He has written film scores, and in 1994 produced his first CD, *Bend Skin*, based on Cameroonian folklore.

Tambo, Oliver Reginald (1917–93)

Oliver Tambo directed the activities of the African National Congress (ANC) while in exile from South Africa from 1960 until his return in 1990. He had joined the ANC in 1944 and, like his friend and former law partner NELSON MANDELA, was one of the defendants in the so-called Treason Trial (1956–61). He became acting president of the ANC in 1967 and was president from 1977 until 1991, when Mandela succeeded him. In July 1991, he was named ANC vice-president.

Tekle, Afewerk (born 1923)

Afewerk Tekle, Ethiopia's leading artist, was effectively court painter to Emperor HAILE SELASSIE. He had planned to be a mining engineer, but trained in art in London, England. He combined both African and European styles in his work, and is famous for his stained glass windows.

Tewodros (or Theodore) II (c. 1816–68)

Tewodros II, born Theodore Kassai, reunified Ethiopia, then called Abyssinia, by conquering rival chiefs who had split the country between them. He was crowned king in 1855 as Tewodros II. After failing to form alliances with Britain and France against Ethiopia's Muslim neighbors, he developed a hatred of Europeans and imprisoned a number of them at the fort of Magdala. A British army sent to free them defeated him, and he then shot himself.

Tlali, Miriam (born 1933)

Miriam Tlali, a South African novelist and journalist, had her first two novels banned under the apartheid regime because they criticized its policies. Much of her work is concerned with the troubled black township of Soweto. She studied at universities in South Africa and Lesotho, but had to give up through lack of funds.

Todd, Sir Reginald Stephen Garfield (born 1908)

Garfield Todd was prime minister of the Federation of Rhodesia and Nyasaland from its formation in 1953 until 1958, when his party's policies were rejected as too liberal by the white-dominated electorate. Born in New Zealand, Todd went to Southern Rhodesia (now Zimbabwe) as a missionary in 1934. An opponent of the illegal regime of IAN SMITH, he

Oliver Tambo

was detained from 1965 until 1966 and again from 1972 until 1976.

Tolbert, William Richard Jr. (1913–80)
William Tolbert was vice-president of Liberia from 1951 to 1971, and succeeded WILLIAM TUBMAN as president in 1971. During his time in office, Liberia's economy suffered because of falls in the prices of iron ore and rubber, and a rise in rice prices in 1979 led to rioting. He was assassinated during an army coup, led by SAMUEL DOE, in 1980.

Tombalbaye, Ngarta (1918–75)
Ngarta Tombalbaye (formerly François Tombalbaye) was the first president of Chad, serving from 1962 until he was assassinated during an army coup, led by Félix Malloum, in 1975. He had earlier served as prime minister (1959–62).

Moïse Tshombe

Touré, Ahmad Sekou (1922–84)
A major figure in the struggle for independence from colonial rule, Sekou Touré became president of Guinea in 1958. From 1971, following an unsuccessful invasion by opposition forces based in Guinea-Bissau, Touré imposed restrictions on the opposition, but improved his human rights record before his death in 1984. He was succeeded as president by LANSANA CONTÉ.

Toure, Ali Farka (born 1939)
Ali Farka Toure is a Malian musician who took up the guitar when he was eighteen. He soon became well known in Mali, and international success came in the late 1980s, when recordings and concerts made him popular in Britain.

Traoré, Moussa (born 1936)
Moussa Traoré, an army officer, became head of state of Mali in 1968 after leading a military coup that deposed MODIBO KEITA. He was himself deposed by another coup in 1991, led by Amadou Toure. During his period in office, droughts in the semidesert Sahel region caused widespread famine in Mali.

Tshombe, Moïse Kapenda (1919–69)
Moïse Tshombe led the mineral-rich "Republic of Katanga" (now the province of Shaba) that declared itself independent from the Congo Republic (now Zaire) in 1960. Following the occupation of Katanga by United Nations troops in 1963, Tshombe went into exile. In 1964 he returned to become head of the central government of the Congo Republic, but he was dismissed in 1965. He again went into exile, in Spain, after MOBUTU SESE SEKO took power, and a Congolese court sentenced him to death in his absence. In 1967, he was kidnapped and taken to Algeria, where he remained under house arrest until his death.

Tsiranana, Philibert (born 1912)
Philibert Tsiranana became the first president of Madagascar in 1959. He was reelected in 1972, but his poor health, accompanied by demonstrations against his regime, led him to appoint GABRIEL RAMANANTSOA in his place and he resigned as president.

Tubman, William V. S. (Vacanarat Shadrach) (1895–1971)
William Tubman was president of

Liberia from 1944 until his death in 1971, when he was succeeded by WILLIAM TOLBERT. Through his "open-door" policies, he attracted foreign investment and reduced the country's dependence on the United States.

Tutu, Desmond Mpilo (born 1931)
Desmond Tutu was a powerful and eloquent antiapartheid campaigner. His emphasis on nonviolent resistance to the apartheid regime earned him the 1984 Nobel Peace Prize. His appointment as Archbishop of Cape Town, in 1986, made him head of the Anglican Church in South Africa, Lesotho, Mozambique, Namibia, and Swaziland; he retired in 1996. After the downfall of the apartheid regime, he set up the Truth and Reconciliation Commission to give the enforcers of apartheid the opportunity to confess their crimes and seek forgiveness. This has been opposed by many of apartheid's victims and their families, who feel that the guilty should be tried for their crimes. His demand that the African National Congress (ANC) also seek amnesty for its past human rights abuses has sparked controversy.

Ulasi, Adaora Lily (born c. 1932)
Adaora Ulasi is a Nigerian journalist and author who used pidgin English in her first novel, *Many Thing You No Understand* (1970), to highlight the relationship between colonial administrators and local people before independence. The daughter of an Igbo chief, she studied in the United States and later divided her time between Nigeria and England.

Usman dan Fodio (1754–1817)
In 1804, Usman dan Fodio, a Fulani ruler and Islamic scholar, proclaimed a jihad (Islamic holy war) that led to the creation of a Fulani-Hausa empire – the Sokoto Caliphate – in present-day Benin, Cameroon, Niger, and northern Nigeria. He later handed over power to his son Muhammad Bello, and retired to teach and write.

Uwaifor, "Sir" Victor (born 1941)
"Sir" Victor Uwaifor is a Nigerian musician who began his career as an amateur wrestler. As a bandleader and playing many instruments himself, he created fresh rhythms and dances. His recording *Joromi* was a major hit in West Africa, and financial success enabled him to open a hotel and set up his own television studio.

van Riebeeck, Jan (1618–77)
Jan van Riebeeck, an official in the service of the Dutch East India Company, headed the first Dutch settlement at the Cape of Good Hope, in 1652. In 1657, he allowed some of the soldiers under his command to set up farms on Khoikhoi grazing lands. These soldiers became the first of South Africa's Boers – "boer" is the Dutch word for "farmer" and the historical name of the Afrikaners.

Verwoerd, Dr Hendrik Frensch (1901–66)
Hendrik Verwoerd was prime minister of South Africa from 1958 until his assassination in 1966; he was succeeded by JOHN VORSTER. He favored the breaking of his country's ties with the Commonwealth, which it left in 1961. He had earlier served as

Adaora Ulasi

Hendrik Verwoerd

minister of "native affairs," when he developed strict apartheid policies with the support of the premier, Johannes Strijdom, whom he succeeded. His administration was marked by further development and ruthless application of the highly controversial apartheid policy. In fact, he has been called the architect of apartheid for his efforts to enforce it.

Vieira, João Bernardo (born 1939)
In 1980, João Vieira, prime minister of Guinea-Bissau, led a military coup against LUIZ CABRAL and became head of state. He was made executive president in 1984, then reelected in 1989 and again in 1994 in the country's first multiparty elections.

Vorster, John (1915–83)
John (formerly Balthazar Johannes) Vorster was the prime minister of South Africa following the assassination of HENDRIK VERWOERD in 1966 until 1978. He was elected president in 1978, but resigned in 1979 following a political scandal. He enforced apartheid policies, but sought to make contacts with other African governments.

Weah, George (born 1966)
George Weah, a Liberian soccer player, became in one year (1996) African Player of the Year, European Player of the Year, and World Footballer of the Year. He has played in more than fifty international games and also for the French league teams AC Monaco and Paris St. Germain, and scored seventy-five goals in six seasons. In 1996, the Italian team AC Milan paid US$10 million for him.

He supports his national team financially, paying for their uniforms and fares to overseas games.

Welensky, Sir Roland (Roy) (1907–91)
Roy Welensky was prime minister of the Central African Federation (CAF) from 1956 until 1963, when it was broken up to form Malawi, Zambia, and Rhodesia (now Zimbabwe). A former trade unionist and heavyweight boxing champion, Welensky entered politics in 1938 and worked for the creation of the white-minority ruled CAF. When it collapsed, he retired from politics.

Yameogo, Maurice (1921–93)
Maurice Yameogo was the first president of Upper Volta (now Burkina Faso) from 1958 until 1966, when he was deposed by a military coup led by SANGOULÉ LAMIZANA. He was imprisoned from 1966 until 1970, when he went into exile.

Youlou, Abbé Fulbert (1917–72)
A Roman Catholic priest, Abbé Youlou became the first president of Congo in 1959. In 1963, he was forced to resign and went into exile after widespread unrest and a general strike. He was succeeded as president by Alphonse Massamba-Débat.

Zenawi, Meles (born 1955)
Meles Zenawi, an opponent of the military regime of HAILE MARIAM MENGISTU, became head of state of Ethiopia in 1991, at the end of the civil war. He was elected by the Council of Representatives set up by the ruling coalition, the Ethiopian People's Revolutionary Democratic Front. He was reelected in 1994.

Further reading

Africa South of the Sahara 1996, London: Europa Publications, 25th edn (1995).

Ajayi, J. F. A. and Crowder, M., *Historical Atlas of Africa,* Cambridge (UK): Cambridge University Press (1985).

Amadiume, I., *Male Daughters, Female Husbands: Gender and Sex in an African Society,* London: Zed Books (1987).

Baines, J. and Málek J., *Atlas of Ancient Egypt,* Oxford (UK): Phaidon Press (1980).

Barnard, A., *Hunters and Herders of Southern Africa: A Comparative Ethnography of the Khoisan Peoples,* Cambridge (UK): Cambridge University Press (1992).

Beach, D., *The Shona and their Neighbors,* Cambridge, MA: Blackwell Publishers (1994).

Beauclerk, J., *Hunters and Gatherers in Central Africa,* Oxford (UK): Oxfam (1994).

Beckwith, C. and Saitoti, T., *Maasai,* London: Elm Tree Books (1980).

Beckwith, C. and van Offellen, M., *Nomads of Niger,* New York: Harry N. Abrams Inc. (1983).

Blier, S., *African Vodun: Art, Psychology, and Power,* Chicago, IL: University of Chicago Press (1995).

Boone, S. A., *Radiance From the Waters: Ideals of Feminine Beauty in Mende Art,* New Haven, CT: Yale University Press (1986).

Brockman, N. C, *An African Biographical Dictionary,* Santa Barbara, CA: ABC-Clio (1994).

Brown, M., *A History of Madagascar,* London: Damien Tunnacliffe (1995).

Catchpole, B. and Akinjogbin, I. A., *A History of West Africa in Maps and Diagrams,* London: Collins (1992).

Chatty, D., *From Camel to Truck: the Bedouin in the Modern World,* New York: Vantage Press (1986).

Clark, J. D., *Cambridge History of Africa,* Cambridge (UK): Cambridge University Press (1982).

Connah, G., *African Civilisations,* Cambridge (UK): Cambridge University Press (1987).

Crowder, M., *West Africa: an Introduction to its History,* Harlow (UK): Longman Group (1977).

Diagram Group, *African History On File,* NY: Facts On File (1994).

Encyclopedia Africana Project, *Dictionary of African Biography,* vol 3, Algonac, MI: Reference Publishers Inc. (1995).

Fagg, W., *African Majesty,* Ontario, Canada: Art Gallery of Ontario (1981).

February, V., *The Afrikaners of South Africa,* London: Paul Kegan (1991).

Fisher, A., *Africa Adorned,* London: W. Collins & Co. Ltd (1984).

Gibbs Jr., J. (ed), *Peoples of Africa,* New York: Holt, Rinehart, & Winston (1965)

Graham, R., *The Da Capo Guide to Contemporary African Music,* New York: Da Capo Press (1988).

Haskins, J. and Biondi, J., *From the Afar to the Zulu,* New York: Walker Publishing Co. (1995).

Henze, P. B., *The Horn of Africa: from War to Peace,* London: Macmillan (1991).

Kamil, J., *Coptic Egypt,* Cairo (Egypt): American University in Cairo Press (1987).

Kaplan, S., *The Beta Israel (Falasha) in Ethiopia,* New York: New York University Press (1992).

Katz, R., *Boiling Energy: Community Healing Among the Kalahari Kung,* Cambridge, MA: Harvard University Press (1982).

Kennedy, J., *New Currents, Ancient Rivers: Contemporary Artists in a Generation of Change,* Washington, DC: Smithsonian Institution (1992).

Knappert, J., *African Mythology,* London: Diamond Books (1995).

Koloss, H. J., *Art of Central Africa,* New York: Metropolitan Museum of Art (1990).

Lipschutz, M. and Rasmussen, R., *Dictionary of African Historical Biography,* Oxford (UK): Heinemann (1978).

Mack, J., *Emil Torday and the Art of the Congo,* London: British Museum.

Mack, J., *Ethnic Jewellery,* London: British Museum (1988).

Mazrui, A., *The African Condition,* Oxford (UK): Heinemann (1986).

Mbiti, J. S., *African Religions and Philosophy,* Oxford (UK): Heinemann (1969).

Meyer, L., *Black Africa: Masks, Sculptures, and Jewelry,* Paris (France): Terrail (1992).

Middle East and North Africa 1996, London: Europa Publications, 42nd edn (1995).

Middleton, J. and Rassam, A. (eds), *Encyclopedia of World Cultures: Africa and the Middle East,* Boston, MA: G. K. Hall & Co. (1995).

Minority Rights Group (ed), *World Directory of Minorities,* Chicago, IL: St. James Press (1990).

Morrison D., Mitchell, R., and Paden, J., *Black Africa: A Comparative Handbook,* New York: Innington Publishers Inc. (1984).

Moss, J. and Wilson, G., *Peoples of the World: Africans South of the Sahara,* Detroit, IL: Gale Research (1991).

Murray, J., *Cultural Atlas of Africa,* Oxford (UK): Phaidon Press (1981).

Needham, D. E., Mashingaidze, E. K., & Bhebe, N., *From Iron Age To Independence. A History of Central Africa,* Harlow (UK): Longman Group (1984).

Nyaka Tura, J., *An Anatomy of an African Kingdom: History of Bunyoro-Kitara,* New York: Anchor Press (1973).

Odhiambo, A., Ouso, T., and Williams, J., *A History of East Africa,* Harlow (UK): Longman Group (1977).

Oliver, R. and Crowder, M., *Encyclopedia of Africa,* Cambridge (UK): Cambridge University Press (1981).

Olson, J. S., *The Peoples of Africa: An Ethnohistorical Dictionary,* Westport, CT: Greenwood Press (1996).

Oshomha, I., *The Ibo of East Central Nigeria,* (Nigeria): New Era Publishers (1990).

Peoples of Africa, New York: Arco (1978).

Phillips, T. (ed), *Africa: The Art of a Continent,* New York: Royal Academy of Arts (London) and Prestel Verlag (NY) (1995).

Powell, I., *Ndebele: A People and their Art,* London: New Holland Ltd (1995).

Rake, A., *100 Great Africans,* Metuchen, NJ: Scarecrow Press (1994).

Ray, B. C., *Myth, Ritual, and Kingship in Buganda,* New York: Oxford University Press (1991).

Rogge, J., *Too Many, Too Long: Sudan's Twenty-year Refugee Problem,* Totowa, NJ: Rowman & Allenheld (1985).

Roy, C. D., *Art and Life in Africa,* Iowa, IA: University of Iowa Museum of Art (1992).

Sagay, E., *African Hairstyles,* Oxford (UK): Heinemann (1983).

Sertima, I. van (ed), *Golden Age of the Moor,* New Brunswick (Canada): Transaction Publishers (1992).

Shelemay, K., *Music, Ritual, and Falasha History,* East Lansing, MI: Michigan State University (1986).

Shillington, K., *History of Southern Africa,* Harlow (UK): Longman Group (1987).

Soyinka, W., *Myth, Literature and the African World,* Cambridge (UK): Cambridge University Press (1990).

Spring, C., *African Textiles,* London: Bracken Books (1989).

Trimingham, J. S., *The Influence of Islam Upon Africa,* Harlow (UK): Longman Group (1980).

Turle, G., *The Art of the Maasai,* New York: Alfred A. Knopf (1992).

Turnbull, C., *The Mbuti Pygmies: Change and Adaption,* New York: Holt, Rinehart, & Winston (1983).

Vansina, J., *Art History in Africa,* Harlow (UK): Longman Group (1984).

Vogel, S., *African Masterpieces,* New York: Center for African Art and Musée de l'homme (1985).

Weekes, R. V. (ed), *Muslim Peoples: A World Ethnographic Survey,* 2nd edn, Westport, CT: Greenwood Press (1984).

Wiseman, J. A., *Political Leaders in Black Africa,* Brookfield, VT: Edward Elgar Publishing Co. (1991).

Six-volume combined index

Peoples pages and national profiles are printed in **bold**; *italic* page numbers refer to illustrations, captions, or maps.

Volume codes
N   North Africa
W   West Africa
E   East Africa
C   Central Africa
S   Southern Africa
NoA Nations of Africa

A
Ababda Beja people N46
Abacha, Sanni NoA59, *59*
Abatembuzi people E84
Abbas, Ferhat NoA59
Abd al Kadir NoA59, *59*
Abd al Krim N53; NoA59
Abd al Mumin NoA59
Abdullah, Ahmad NoA59
Abdullah ibn Muhammad *see* Khalifa
Abeni, Queen Salawo NoA59
Abiodan, Dele NoA59
Abiola, Chief Moshood NoA60
Abu Bakr W84
Achebe, Chinua NoA60
Ade, King Sunny W*92*; NoA60, *60*
Afar language E33, *105*
Afar people E24, **32–35**
Affonso I C*16*
Africanus, Leo *see* Leo Africanus
Afrikaans language S33–34, *36*, 42, 50, 104
Afrikaners S24, 28, 29, **30–35**, 36, *36*, 37, 79, 87, 99, 103
  see also Boers
Afroasiatic languages N103, *103*; W101, *101*; E105, *105*; C103, *103*; S105, *105*
Agaja W57
Agaw language E50, *105*
Agyeman Prempe I W31
Ahidjo, Ahmadou NoA60
Ahmadu, Caliph W*17*
Aideed, Muhammad Farrah NoA60
Aidoo, Ama Ata NoA60
Aïr, Sultanate of N93
Ait Haddidou Berber people N87
Ajemic (Hausa) script W69
Aka Mbenga people C72
Akan languages W32, *100*
Akan peoples W30, 54
Akendengue, Pierre NoA60–61
Al Bakri W38
Al Hajj Umar W*62*; NoA61
Algeria N5, 6, *6*, 21, *24*; NoA**6**
Ali, Ras E89
Alkali, Zanyab NoA61
Almohads N53
Almoravids N*17*, 53; W84
Alodia N67
Alwa N67
Amanitore, Queen N*66*
Amarar Beja people N46
Ambo *see* Ovambo language
Ambomou Azande people C30
Americo-Liberians W**82–83**
Amhara people E24, **38–41**, 89, 91, 92
Amharic language N30; E39, 50, *105*
Amharic script E39, *40*
Amin Dada, Idi E*19*, 46, 63, 86; NoA61, *61*
Ampadu, Kwame NoA61
Amr ibn al As N30
Angola C5, 6, *7*, 21, *24–25*, 93; NoA**7**
Anlo Ewe language W51
Anlo Ewe people W50
Antaifasy people S*56*
Antaimoro people S*56*
Antaisaka people S*56*
Antambahoaka people S*56*
Antandroy people S*56*

Antankarana people S*56*
Antanosy people S*56*, *59*
Anthony of Egypt, Saint N*60*; NoA61
Aouita, Said NoA61
Arab people N24–25, 26, 28, **30–33**, 34, 36, 37, 39, 48–50, 60, 61, 62, 92, 97; W27, 41, 63, 71, 84, 85; E*17*, 27, 29, 38, 94, 98, 99, *99*, 100, 102; C*23*; S42, 59, 61, 77
Arabi, Ahmad NoA61–62
Arabic language N26, 28, 30–31, 42, 46, 54, 61, 89, 102, *103*; W27, 63, 69, 85, 100, *101*; E29, 96, *96*, 100, 104, *105*; S59, 104, *105*
Arabic script N*32*, 53
Armatto, Raphael E.G.G. NoA62
Arusha Maasai people E70, 71
Arusi Oromo people E88
Asabia NoA62
Asante Empire W*17*, 30–31
Asante Kingdom W31, 32
Asante language W32, 101
Asante people W25, **30–33**, 77
Ashanti *see* Asante people
Asians, East African E25, 29, **44–47**
Askia Muhammad W40, *40*; NoA62
Asua people C74
Australopithecines E36, *36*, 37, *37*
Awolowo, Obafemi NoA62
Awoonor, Kofi NoA62
Axumite Kingdom N66; E*23*, 27, 38, 39, 49
Azande language C30–31, *102*
Azande people C24–25, **30–33**, 58
Azikiwe, Ndami NoA62

B
Ba, Mariama NoA62, *62*
Babangida, Ibrahim NoA63
Babban Gwani Mikaila W*23*, 69
Babito dynasty E84, 85
Babito people E85, 87
Bachwezi dynasty E84, 87, *87*
Baganda *see* Ganda people
Baggara people N25, **40–43**, 45, 50, 76, 77
Bahima people E78, 87
Bahutu *see* Hutu people
Bairu people E87
Baka Mbenga people C72
Bakongo *see* Kongo people
Bakuba *see* Kuba people
Balewa, Sir Abubakar Tafawa NoA63, *63*
Ballinger, Margaret NoA63
Bamana *see* Bambara people
Bambara people W24, **34–37**
Banda, Dr Hastings NoA63, *63*
Bantu languages C74, *102*; S*104*, 105
Bantu-speaking peoples N28; E26, 52, 98; S26, 28, 31, 53, 64, 70, 72, 78, 82, 86, 90, 94, 98
Banyoro *see* Nyoro people
Bapedi Empire S79
Baqqara *see* Baggara people
Bara people S*56*
Bararetta Oromo people E88
Barotse *see* Lozi people
Basese Ganda people E52, 53
Basotho *see* Sotho people
Basuto Kingdom S79, *79*
Bateke *see* Teke people
Batswana *see* Tswana people
Baya language C34, *102*
Baya people C24–25, **34–35**
Bedouin Arab people N31, 33, 40
Begemder, Kingdom of E89
Behanzin W58, *59*
Beja language N46, 103, *103*
Beja people N25, **46–47**, 87
Bekerderemo, John Pepper Clark NoA63
Bemba language C36, 102
Bemba people C24–25, **36–37**
Ben Ali, Zine al Abidine NoA64
Ben Bella, Muhammad Ahmad NoA64
Bena Yanda clan C36

Beni Amer Beja people N46
Benin W5, 6, *7*, 21, *24*; NoA**8**
Benin City W*23*, 98, 99, *99*
Benin, Kingdom of W**98–99**
Berber Jews N36, 38
Berber languages N49, 53, 54, 94, *103*; W69, 85, *101*
Berber people N24, 26, 28, 30, 48–49, 49, **52–55**, 58, 59, *80*, 87, *87*, 92; W27, 37, 38 84, 85
Beta Israel *see* Falasha people
Beti, Mongo NoA64
Betsileo people S56, *56*, 57, *59*
Betsimisaraka kingdom S57
Betsimisaraka people S*56*, 57, *60*
Bezanozano people S*56*
Bikila, Abede NoA64
Biko, Steve S*40*; NoA64, *64*
Bilé, Moni C59
Bini language W98, 99, *100*
Bini people W98, 99
Bisharin Beja people N47
Biya, Paul NoA64
Blondy, Alpha NoA64–65
Blyden, Edward NoA65
Bobangi people C95
Boers S*17*, 27, 31, *34*, 53, 65, 83, *83*, 91, 95
  see also Afrikaners
Bokassa, Jean-Bédel C*19*, 34, 92; NoA65
Bokora Karamojong people E62
Bokwe, John Knox S97
Bongo Mbenga people C72
Bongo, Omar NoA65
Borana Oromo people E88, *93*
Borno *see* Kanem-Borno
Bororo Fulani people W60, 63–64, *63*, 65, *66*, 67
Botha, Louis S36
Botha, P. W. NoA65, *65*
Botswana S5, 6, *7*, 21, *24*; NoA**9**
Boulmerka, Hassiba NoA65, *65*
Boumedienne, Houari NoA65, *65*
Bourgiba, Habib Ibn Ali NoA65–66
Boutros-Ghali, Boutros NoA66, *66*
Breytenbach, Breyten S35
Brilliant, Ekambi C59
Brink, André S35; NoA66
Brutus, Dennis NoA66
Buganda Kingdom E27, 53, 54, 55, 85
Bunyoro Kingdom E27, 53, 86
Bunyoro-Kitara Empire E84, 85, 87
Burkina Faso W5, 6, *7*, 21, *24*; NoA**10**
Burundi E5, 6, *7*, 20, 21, *24*, 59, *61*; NoA**11**
Bushmen S52
Bushongo group C54, 56
Buthelezi, Chief S*21*, 38, 41, 99; NoA66, *66*
Butonga C98, 99
Buyoya, Pierre NoA66

C
Cabral, Amílcar NoA66
Cabral, Luiz NoA66–67
Camara Laye W77
Cameroon W5, 6, *7*, 21, *25*; NoA**12**
Candomblé religion W*55*
Cape Colored people S24, **42–43**, 53
Cape Malay people S24, **42–43**
Cape Verde W5, 6, *6*, 21; NoA**13**
Carthaginians N52, **58–59**, 58–59, *59*, 75
Central African Republic C5, 6, *7*, 21, *24–25*, 92–93; NoA**14**
Cetshwayo S99; NoA67, *67*
Chad W5, 6, *7*, 21, *25*; NoA**15**
Cheb Khaled N*50*
Cheops *see* Khufu (Cheops)
Chilembwe, John NoA67
Chiluba, Frederick C36, *62*; NoA67
Chinese people S42, 56, 59, 60
Chipenda, Daniel NoA67
Chissano, Joaquim NoA67
Chiti C36
Chitimukulu C36
Chiweshe, Stella C63

Six-volume combined index

Six-volume combined index